The Synthesis

THE SYNTHESIS

N. Popovic

PWBC, London

Published in 2008 by PWBC, London

Personal Well-Being Centre
books@personalwellbeingcentre.org

ISBN 978-0-9548387-7-5

Proofreading and editing: Julia Kantic

Printed in the UK, by Stephen Austin, Hertford

Cover image: Ring of Hot Blue Stars Pinwheels Around Yellow Nucleus of Hoag's Object Galaxy
Image credit: NASA and The Hubble Heritage Team (STScI/AURA)
Acknowledgement: Ray A. Lucas (STScI/AURA)

CONTENTS

THE MEANING

THE BEING

THE MIND

THE PROCESS

PREFACE

Three social forces seem to be gaining momentum at present: religious fundamentalism among the affluent (who believe that it can help them preserve their status), religious fundamentalism among the deprived (who believe that it can help them change theirs) and secular relativism (predominantly among those occupying the middle ground). What all of them have in common is self-centredness and self-interest, which is not conducive to developing a global society. This book offers an alternative outlook, based on a shared purpose that could have a unifying power. Our choice at the moment is to live either in a rational but meaningless world, or in a meaningful but irrational world. The Synthesis is an attempt to see the world as both, rational and meaningful. Common sense, science, spirituality and philosophy are combined in a unique way to achieve this aim.

There are several instances in the text of an unconventional use of language:

S/he (pronounced /s-hi:/) is used instead of 'he or she'.
Shim (pronounced /ʃim/)is used instead of 'her or him'.
Shis (pronounced /ʃiz/) is used instead of 'his or her(s)'.
Shimself (pronounced /ʃimself/ is used instead of 'himself or herself'.

B.C.E. (before common era) is used instead of B.C.
C.E. (common era) is used instead of A.D.

THE METHOD

This book will discuss some fundamental issues, such as the nature and meaning of life, the nature of the mind, and biological, individual and social development. Before these subjects are considered though, the method used in the process needs to be clarified first.

Knowledge of the world, as the philosopher Aristotle argued many centuries ago, comes through experience interpreted by reason[1]. However, throughout history, experience as a source of knowledge has acquired different faces. For example, scientific observation is considered empirical (based on experience), but this is very different from ordinary experience - it is even assumed that to reach objectivity, scientists have to detach from any personal involvement. In fact, three qualitatively distinct types of experience can be recognised overall: personal experience, impersonal experience (observation), and transpersonal experience (experience that transcends common perception). These have led to three corresponding approaches to knowledge acquisition: common sense, science and spirituality. On the other hand, it is generally accepted that reasoning (the other component mentioned above besides experience) has given rise to philosophy[2].

What all these four approaches share is that they are dynamic processes. Due to language and other limitations, we can never grasp truth fully, but we can keep moving closer and closer. So, in principle, knowledge acquisition can go on endlessly. However, each of these approaches has been situated within social frameworks and practices that have an organising and restraining function. Common sense is rooted in various cultural settings, science is normally associated with materialism, spirituality is traditionally linked to various religions, and philosophy is frequently embedded in certain ideologies or '-isms' (such as Marxism, existentialism, post-modernism).

In this part, common misconceptions about these four approaches, their relevance, the relationship to their respective social frameworks, and their limitations are examined first. On this basis two claims are made. One is that each of them is incomplete on its own. The other is that remaining strictly within their respective frameworks is not helpful any longer. It is suggested that more comprehensive and coherent understanding than we have at present requires rising above the existing frameworks and the synthesis of essential elements imbedded in these approaches. A model that attempts to do so (and is implemented throughout the book) is described at the end.

---

[1] The concern here is only with unmediated knowledge. Indirect sources, such as verbal communications or written materials, may well be the main ones nowadays. They are not included as a distinct category though, because of their derivative nature (in principle, they can be traced back to the above sources).

[2] In practice, of course, none of these approaches relies strictly on one source, and they all use reason to some degree.

THE COMMON SENSE APPROACH

Common sense is based on ordinary personal experiences (that are then shared). Although often neglected in scholarly writings, it is the most widely spread way of acquiring knowledge, skills and understanding. Common sense essentially uses heuristic methods that enable drawing intuitive insights or tacit knowledge from our experience. Because of such a nature, common sense is best expressed through narratives (myths, stories, articles, movies), although its vocal supporters sometimes come from other fields (e.g. mathematician Thomas Reid and philosopher George E. Moore).

SOME MISCONCEPTIONS ABOUT COMMON SENSE

Common sense is less valid than other approaches - the success of science in particular has often led to a derogatory attitude towards common sense (sometimes labelled 'folk psychology'). To show its apparent inferiority, the examples of people believing in the past that the Sun goes around the Earth or that the Earth is flat are often brought up. Common sense, indeed, can sometimes be wrong, but this cannot justify diminishing its value and importance. Most of the knowledge gained in such a way has at least a pragmatic validity. Other approaches, when they go against common sense, more often than not eventually appear to be mistaken. For example, during the reign of behavioural psychology many parents were indoctrinated to bring up children in the 'scientific' manner, which appeared to be, at least in some instances, damaging for children and parents alike. Eventually, such ways of upbringing were abandoned and common sense prevailed again (even the wife of John Watson, who founded behaviourism, admitted that she was not a good behaviourist in this respect).

Common sense is simplistic - in fact, common sense is probably the most intricate approach of all. This is because it deals with non-linear, complex systems. Linear systems may be more precise, but they are inevitably simplifications and therefore not fully adequate in many situations.

Common sense is relativistic - common sense may, indeed, vary from individual to individual or from culture to culture to some extent, but it is often forgotten that what people share is much greater than what they do not. Common sense, stripped of its cultural idiosyncrasies, can be surprisingly universal. The differences are often the result of an adaptation to diverse (historical or present) circumstances.

THE RELEVANCE OF COMMON SENSE

Common sense is the basis for the other approaches. Science, philosophy and spirituality may try to move away from personal experiences but they all have roots in, and must start from common sense. As Reid pointed out, those who ignore the common-sense principles in building their metaphysics find their reductive constructions built upon sand, which makes reaching the conclusions that their own positions require impossible (Honderich 1995, p.142). Although science sometimes corrects the errors of common sense, even scientific theories ultimately depend on its support.

The other value of common sense is that it can deal with complex systems that are difficult to address adequately by using other approaches. Even with all the help of modern technology, science sometimes needs years to prove what is self-evident from the common sense perspective, and some phenomena may be so intricate that science or philosophy may never hope to achieve fully independent results and have to invoke a commonsensical evidential basis. Futurist Alvin Toffler (of 'Future Shock' fame) writes:

> Where 'hard data' are available, of course, they ought to be taken into account. But where they are lacking, the responsible writer – even the scientist – has both a right and an obligation to rely on other kinds of evidence, including impressionistic or anecdotal data and the opinions of well-informed people (1970, p.15).

One simple example is that most of us have few difficulties accurately reading even subtle emotional states of others. After many years of research science is making some progress in this direction, but it is still far from being able to match the subtlety taken for granted in personal experiences.

Common sense has a huge practical value. Everyday life and human reactions are to a large extent based on personal experiences rather than scientific, spiritual or philosophical insights. Common sense does not rely on verbal interpretations, so it can be more direct and quicker. Such an intuitive grasp of a situation is often essential.

This approach can also guard against the extremes of the other ones. For instance, although reductionist science denies phenomena such as free will, the self and sometimes even the uniqueness of experience, ordinary life and language go on regardless, fully acknowledging them (e.g. every legal system is based on personal responsibility and hence, assumes the notion of free will[1]). There is a sort of 'bad faith' among scientists, philosophers and those with spiritual inclinations who take for granted certain beliefs in day-to-day life, but deny the same in their practices.

---

[1] Judge David Hodgson has written extensively on this topic (see, for example, Hodgson, 1994).

COMMON SENSE AND CULTURE

As already mentioned, culture can be taken as a social framework of this approach. Any culture is, to a large extent, an external expression of common sense, its formalisation within a particular community. Such cultural frameworks have had an important role throughout history in the preservation and homogenisation of societies. However, culture can also be restrictive and distorting. Common sense tends to be solidified and transmitted inertly by the culture it is embedded in. This solidification is often the reason why common sense in some cases appears to be in conflict with rationality and gives rise to superstitions.

Superstitions are often associated with spirituality, mysticism and the like, but this is mistaken. Even atheists can be superstitious (and, of course, spiritual people may not be). It is more likely that superstitions and other cultural idiosyncrasies originate in individual or group interpretations of personal experiences that in some instances become collective beliefs. This is why there are many superficial differences among cultures. For example, a black cat crossing one's path is interpreted as good luck in one culture and bad luck in another. Both interpretations might have had local historical bases that were lost, while only the form (in this case an association between the colour of a cat and luck) has remained. In other words, something that perhaps made sense in certain circumstances may be perpetuated by culture even after it ceases to make sense.

Hostility towards homosexuality in many cultures, for instance, could have been, to some extent, justified in the past by fear of annihilation, when a culture was preserved in relatively small communities that needed to reproduce in order to secure their survival. After all, the Spartans (who won the war against the Athenians) seemed to disappear partly due to practically constitutionalised homosexuality that led to a decrease in their population. However, nowadays, when there is no danger that a national entity or culture may be extinguished because of lack of off-spring, there is no reason for such hostility. Yet, many cultures still harbour an antagonistic attitude towards homosexuality. Other sinister attitudes such as chauvinism, racism, xenophobia, sexism and so on, may also have been cultural distortions of certain social processes (e.g. the division of labour) that may have made sense at a particular historical moment. The same, of course, applies to epistemological issues: how reality is perceived and interpreted. It is not surprising then, that many misunderstandings and unnecessary frictions surface in a world with so many cultures. This is not to say that cultural differences should be disregarded but, especially in multicultural societies, a heavy reliance on culture can be divisive rather than unifying (leading, in some cases, to self-imposed ghettoisation).

THE LIMITATIONS OF COMMON SENSE APPROACH

The limitations of this (and other) approaches can be grouped in three categories: extrinsic ones (the result of factors extraneous to experience), limitations of common sense as a social practice (ensuing from the way knowledge is shared and communicated) and intrinsic limitations.

Extrinsic limitations

Bias - insights based on personal experiences are difficult to distinguish from one's preferences, desires or fears. They are often coloured by the character of the person and shis past. Also, there is a tendency to interpret these insights in such a way as to satisfy one's needs and confirm existing beliefs, which may give rise to superstition and other unproductive ways of explaining reality. Even if this subjectivity is avoided, such insights are shaped by specific circumstances and may lack universality.

Dogmatism - when beliefs based on common sense become embedded in a particular cultural framework, they are very difficult to change and often become dogmatic.

Limitations of common sense as a social practice

Elusiveness - common sense is based on clues often too complex and subtle to be rationally explained and systematically described. This is why common sense, more than any other approach, finds its expression in narrative art (from myths and dramatisations to stories and films). However, such a way of knowledge transmission may be sometimes vague and not easily understood.

Intrinsic limitations

Limited scope - common sense is limited in scope. Not all aspects of reality are accessible to personal (even if collective) experiences. The far corners of the universe, the world of subatomic particles, or the processes in the living cell, are not within the reach of common sense. By the same token, an exploration of reality beyond the ordinary perception require a transcendence of typical personal experiences. Furthermore, some understandings can only be achieved by using logic and reasoning in a more systematic and strict way than common sense usually does.

Imprecision - common sense relies on 'rule of thumb' methods and, therefore, is not very precise. This often does not matter, but sometimes more exact methods are needed.

The above indicates that common sense is a valuable approach but not sufficient on its own, so it needs to be combined with other ones.

THE SCIENTIFIC APPROACH

This is the dominant approach at the moment. At its best, it combines inductive method (observation and experiment) and deductive method (e.g. theories, mathematical findings) and produces reliable explanations of natural phenomena.

SOME COMMON MISCONCEPTIONS ABOUT SCIENCE

Science is a modern Western invention - there is a widespread belief that science was invented in Europe and did not exist before the 17th century. In fact, science has thrived in various parts of the world (e.g. in the Arabic, Indian and Chinese cultures) since ancient times. The science of the present day is influenced and partly based on their findings. Ancient and Middle Age Europe had science too (although, following St Augustine, the observation was rejected in favour of deduction). What modern science that started in the period of Enlightenment did, was to shift the emphasis to inductive method[1]. Its original aim was to dispose of speculations and place science on firmer foundations. However, over time, only the observation of natural phenomena and experiment have become a legitimate science.

Science and technology are the same - although they may contribute to each other, science and technology should not be equated. Science is about increasing human knowledge and understanding, while technology is about producing tools, more often on the basis of trial and error than scientific discoveries[2] (Edison, one of the greatest inventors, for example, was *not* a scientist). Technology existed before science and thrived even when science was suppressed (for example in Byzantium and occasionally in China).

---

[1] An inductive argument involves a generalisation based on a number of specific observations. A deductive argument, on the other hand, begins with particular premises, and then moves logically to a conclusion which follows from those premises. Therefore, deduction is more theoretical.

[2] The following observation may be illuminating in this respect: '... up to [the mid nineteenth century] natural science had made no major contribution to technology. The industrial revolution had been achieved without scientific aid. Except for the Morse telegraph, the great London Exhibition of 1851 contained no important industrial devices or products based on the scientific progress of the previous fifty years. The appreciation of science was still almost free from utilitarian motives' (Polanyi, 1958, p.182).

Science and technology have sometimes even been in conflict in the Western world. When the first commercial trains were produced, scientists warned that people could not tolerate travelling faster than 30mph. While the pioneers of air flights were struggling to make the first aircrafts, scientists (and journals such as the 'Scientific American') stubbornly resisted the possibility that a heavy solid object could fly, and refused to acknowledge the success of the Wright brothers even after many demonstrations. William Preece, one of Britain's most distinguished scientists at that time, declared Edison's attempt to produce the electric bulb 'a completely idiotic idea' and rejected Bell's telephone. There are many other examples of technology advancing not because of, but despite official science (and there are also examples of scientific discoveries that have much preceded their practical applications or technological devices that would support them). In practice, the difference between science and technology is clear. The patent law, for example, 'draws a sharp distinction between a *discovery*, which makes an addition to our knowledge of nature, and an *invention*, which establishes a new operational principle serving some acknowledged advantage' (Polanyi, 1958, p.177). The latter can be patented; the former is the property of all. In recent times, however, for whatever reasons, identifying science and technology has been encouraged.

Science is only compatible with materialist ideology - this is often taken for granted by many scientists and non-scientists alike. Yet a materialistic position is not innate to science. Science was linked to materialism in the 19th century Europe to secure the supremacy of a particular method[1]. Many of science's greatest names were not materialists: Copernicus was a priest, and Mendel, the founder of genetics, was a monk; Newton was deeply religious (occasionally using theological arguments in science, such as when he suggested that the world has an atomic structure because it is most conducive to God's purpose). Even Galileo never had a quarrel with God, only with the Church; astrophysicist Lemaître who first proposed the idea of the Big Bang in the 1920s, was also a priest. The inventor of the laser and Nobel prize laureate for physics, Chares Townes, had spiritual inclinations, as well as Faraday, Joule, Kelvin, Maxwell, Tesla and even Einstein. Science neither has proved nor can prove that reality is only material. There is nothing intrinsic to science that would preclude the possibility of non-material aspects of reality, although studying such phenomena would possibly require a different method. In fact, some branches of science (e.g.

---

[1] The claim that all reality is physical was explicitly expressed even later, in 1963 by philosopher J. J. Smart, who stated that 'there is nothing in the world over and above those entities which are postulated by physics' (1963, p.651).

quantum physics) have already moved away from assuming that matter and the laws that govern it make the basic fabric of the universe.

Science is about collecting data, classifying and describing observable phenomena - this is only one form of science. An attempt in the 19th century to reduce science to such endeavours did not succeed. In fact, there are three distinct aspects of science: theoretical insights based on rational principles and using methods such as mathematics, geometry and logic; empirical research based on observation and experiments; and the interpretation of data. These three aspects do not always go together. Some landmark theories were even based on incorrect data (e.g. Galileo's work, or the theory or relativity in relation to the Michelson-Morley experiment of 1887[1]). Einstein famously said that 'it is theory that teaches us what observations are and what they mean' (Honderich, 1995, p.807).

Science is fully objective – scientifically 'objective' means that a number of experts agree about the likelihood of certain claims. So, the objectivity of science is valid only within an already accepted framework (that itself cannot be objectively justified[2]). For example, what sort of experiments are carried out, what is looked for in an experiment, how the data is interpreted and so on, depend on the experimenters' pre-assumptions. Moreover, as historians and sociologists point out, 'scientists often depend on patronage and choose their problems and their methods accordingly' (Honderich, 1995, p.808). Even if this is put aside, an ambiguity remains: how do scientists know that an experiment has been done in the right way if they do not know the right outcome? Relying on stringent procedures may not be enough. For instance, experiments on gravitational radiation suppose to establish whether these tiny fluctuations exist or not, but there are so many factors that can effect such experiments that any conclusion can be questioned. Although science strives to be objective, in many cases scientific certainties are not so much the result of experimental method, but rather the way often ambiguous

---

[1] According to Einstein own account, the Michelson-Morley experiment had, in fact, a negligible effect on forming his theory. The philosopher of science, Polanyi, claims that 'its findings were, on the basis of pure speculation, rationally intuited by Einstein before he had ever heard about it' (1958, p.10).

[2] The following statement is still relevant: 'Ernest Nagel writes that we do not know whether the premises assumed in the explanation of the sciences are true; and that were the requirement that these premises must be known to be true adopted, most of the widely accepted explanations in current science would have to be rejected as unsatisfactory. In effect, Nagel implies that we must save our belief in the truth of scientific explanations by refraining from asking what they are based upon. Scientific truth is defined, then, as that which scientists affirm and believe to be true' (Polanyi, 1969, p.73).

results are interpreted. Perhaps not surprisingly, scientists tend to dismiss measurements or outcomes that do not fit with the established theories. The famous physicist Robert Oppenheimer allegedly commented: 'We can't find anything wrong with it, so we will just have to ignore it'.

Scientific knowledge is proven knowledge - science heavily relies on and is biased in favour of inductive method (observation and experimentation). However, in the 18th century, the philosopher Hume pointed out that inductive method, though attractive and useful, was logically invalid. It is not only that the predictions one can make on the basis of induction are not fully reliable, but also that they are not even the only predictions consistent with the accumulated evidence. This is not to say that induction is not valuable, but that relying on this method alone is not sufficient. In an attempt to get around this problem, the philosopher of science Karl Popper argued that science is not about proving that a conjecture is true, but proving that it is false. This is called falsificationism. Science progresses by attempting to falsify theories rather than by proving them to be true.

Science provides a coherent, unified perspective - no branch of science provides a complete picture of its field. There are still many fundamental questions that remain unanswered (how the physical forces relate to each other, the origin of the universe and life, how proteins unfold and how an embryo is formed, what is consciousness and how it relates to the brain etc.). Some accepted theories are not even mutually compatible (e.g. the theory of relativity and quantum physics). Even within the same field certain phenomena are interpreted in contradictory ways (light, for instance, is sometimes considered a wave and sometimes a particle, although their properties are irreconcilable). Scientists among themselves often disagree, as the existence of many competing theories shows. In fact, according to the philosopher of science David Chalmers, there is no single category 'science' (1980, p.166). Attempts to apply the same method to every branch of human knowledge have failed to produce the desired results.

The scientific worldview is timeless - despite the tendency to present scientific results and theories as timeless, they are in fact not. In the 1960s Thomas Kuhn famously proposed that science evolves through paradigm shifts - one dominant view is replaced with another, and this process does not depend only on scientific discoveries. An obvious example is a shift from the Maxwellian Electromagnetic view to the Einsteinian relativistic view, but there are many other albeit less grand cases in every branch of science. The concept of paradigm shifts in its original form may be open to some criticisms, but the validity of its basic tenet is hard to dispute.

THE RELEVANCE OF SCIENCE

Although some technological advances that profoundly affect human life have happened irrespective of and in some cases despite science, there is no doubt that science has drastically changed the world in one way or another. Its pragmatic value is well documented in every popular science book, but the contribution of science to knowledge and understanding should not be underestimated either. Not only has science in many cases stimulated inventions such as telescopes or microscopes, but it has also managed to utilise creatively the data produced by such instruments (e.g. using the 'Doppler effect' to determine the movements of distant stars). The attempts of some scholars (such as Paul Feyerabend) to relativise science are undue exaggerations.

There is another aspect of science that makes it so relevant. The scientific approach provides procedures rather than only end-results. The transparency of the way particular results are obtained is important because it means that most of the findings can be tested by repeating the process, which enables greater objectivity, minimises reliance on authority and stimulates change. Such a practice makes science more progressive than those approaches that demand the acceptance of certain claims without any way to verify or (even more importantly) to refute them independently. This has not only a profound effect on understanding the natural world but on the human psyche too, because it enables everybody (at least in theory) to make informed judgements.

Focusing on the procedures also prevents science from being attached to a particular tradition, culture or nationality, so it is in a better position to attain greater universality. Unprecedented cross-cultural recognition is one of its significant achievements. Science classes throughout the world are remarkably similar, which says much about the universality of scientific knowledge. This may not be surprising, considering that science deals with phenomena that are easier to verify than those that are traditionally associated with spirituality or philosophy. Nevertheless, science has managed to achieve that to which religions have aspired for centuries.

The scientific approach also has a quality of concreteness, an ability to resolve problems experimentally, in a way that philosophers for example cannot. In other words, although science goes through so-called paradigm shifts, they are often accumulative rather than completely different changes (e.g. the Theory of Relativity does not dispose of Newtonian physics, but reduces it to a special case). In contrast, philosophy has not been able to decisively resolve the dispute between, for example, Aristotelian and Platonic views for centuries.

SCIENCE AND MATERIALISM

Science is supposed to be free from prejudice, but in practice the majority of scientists harbour some taken for granted beliefs[1]. This is what links science to a particular ideological view, with the consequence that it can sometimes become dogmatic and impede rather than further the evolution of human knowledge. Not surprisingly, materialism is the usual choice.

Pioneering scientists, however, did not set out to promote materialism[2]. It became the prevailing ideology associated with science only in the second half of the 19th century (materialist beliefs, of course, had existed before and in other parts of the world, one example being the Carvaka doctrine in India). Most misconceptions about science arise because of this link. Reducing reality to the physical world is not the result of science, but the ideology that appropriates science. Materialism (which, significantly, fits well with the dominant socio-economic system in the West) has usurped science and technology which can and have coexisted with other perspectives. This makes some scientists behave unscientifically: they adapt observations and facts to their views and method, rather than the other way around. What does not fit such a lifeless world is chased out and declared illusionary. The following example may help clarify the difference between science and its ideological baggage:

> De Duve states, a scientific approach 'demands that every step in the origin and development of life on Earth be explained in terms of its antecedent and immediate physical-chemical causes.' (Hazen 1997, p.157)

This statement may look scientific but, in fact, it is an ideological statement that contradicts good science. An honest scientist should approach the subject of his research with an open mind, and try to find the most probable explanation for a phenomenon observed. A proper scientific approach cannot demand that phenomena fit into the pre-assumptions of the researcher. The quote shows that the author is more interested in confirming his own views than providing the best possible explanation. Such a demand is not based on any evidence or reasoning, but it presupposes where to look for answers and where not, and rejects *a priori* any other possibility. This attitude relies on

---

[1] As Brian Silver, a scientist himself (and an atheist), puts it: 'There is more faith involved in science than many scientists would be prepared to admit' (1998, p. xvi).

[2] In *The Ascent of Science* the above writer comments: 'Many of the heroes of the sixteenth- and seventeenth-century scientific revolution were deeply interested in the occult, in the so-called Hermetic writings, and in magic in general; one only has to look at the lives of John Dee, Boyle, Bruno, Paracelsus, Kepler, and many others... Newton, the herald of the Age of Reason himself, believed firmly in the mystic aspects of alchemy and of Pythagorean thought' (Silver, 1998, p.495).

faith as much as any religious attitude. There is nothing more scientific in *believing* that life is only a complex chemical reaction than in believing that life is more than that. Not surprisingly, materialistic ideology seems to inherit the framework of thinking established by its antecedents. The agency of God is replaced by the deity of chance, but neither of them have a significant explanatory power, they are just an easy way out of difficulties. A religious person may claim that a complex and intricate thing, such as a flower, was engineered by God, a materialist may claim that it is a result of chance mutations. Neither, in fact, explains much[1].

The above does not imply that proper scientific findings should not be taken seriously, far from it. However, it is important to realise that much of what is said in the name of science is not facts, but interpretations that fit a particular ideological view. Geneticist Richard Lewontin summarises this position:

> We take the side of science in spite of the patent absurdity of some of its constructs, in spite of its failure to fulfil many of its extravagant promises of health and life, in spite of the tolerance of the scientific community for unsubstantiated just-so stories, because we have a prior commitment, a commitment to materialism. It is not that the methods and institutions of science somehow compel us to accept a material explanation of the phenomenal world, but, on the contrary, that we are forced by our a priori adherence to material causes to create an apparatus of investigation and a set of concepts that produce material explanations, no matter how counter-intuitive, no matter how mystifying to the uninitiated. Moreover that materialism is an absolute, for we cannot allow a Divine Foot in the door. (1997, p.31)

The likely reason why so many scientists are prepared to accept materialistic ideology without much reflection is because it is convenient. Reducing all the phenomena to 'solid' matter makes their lives much easier. Otherwise, scientists would be forced to concede that their method is not always adequate or sufficient, and they are understandably reluctant to do so.[2] However, as with other rigid frameworks, materialism is not only restraining, but becomes restrictive, which limits science itself. The guardian (against superstition and prejudice) becomes a jailer.

---

[1] This may be contrasted, for example, with indeterminacy in quantum physics. Although the idea is not without controversy, it *does* have an explanatory power.

[2] This is reflected in the persistency of the mechanistic view of the world: 'With the Einsteinian revolution at the turn of the century physicists had moved irrevocably beyond the mechanistic paradigm. Then, some two decades later, with the advent of quantum theory, they abandoned the last vestiges of classical mechanistic thinking. Yet many scientists, especially in the human, social and engineering fields, remained fascinated by the simplicity and power of the Newtonian formulas' (Laszlo, 1993, p.35).

THE LIMITATIONS OF THE SCIENTIFIC APPROACH

Extrinsic limitations

Some limitations of the present scientific approach are imposed, as it were, from the 'outside'. They are a result of materialist beliefs not science itself.

Determinism - it is fair to say that determinism is not something that only materialists adhere to. There is a long history of this belief that includes thinkers from very different perspectives. Materialism has only defined determinism in terms of the natural laws. This not only precludes the possibility of purposeful causes, but also of choice and of creativity. Ironically, modern science itself has come to the conclusion that determinism does not fully reflect reality, and yet many, especially human science disciplines, are reluctant to give it up (most psychology text-books, for example, still recognise nature and nurture as the only factors that affect human behaviour).

Reductionism - one of the most stubborn beliefs of modern science is that complex phenomena can always be reduced to simpler, more fundamental ones and the laws that govern them. Mind can be reduced to biology, biology to chemistry, chemistry to physics. This is the essence of reductionism, adopted in the 19th century. However, this belief appears to be a dead-end even on the most basic level. It is already recognised that, for example, 'the macroscopic behaviour of a large ensemble of particles cannot be deduced from the properties of the individual particles themselves' (Silver, 1998, p.19). Many eminent scientists are ready to admit the improbability of reductionism[1].

Insisting on material evidence - a position that would always insist on material evidence, and automatically dismiss an argument that is not based on observable data is somewhat naïve. Even hardcore science inevitably operates with phenomena or principles for which material evidence does not exist (e.g. time or causality) or is based on stipulations that cannot be empirically verified (such as the ones linked to the theory of relativity). Also, many scientific concepts (gravitation being one example) cannot be known directly but only through their effects[2].

---

[1] Laszlo paraphrases the renowned physicist Stephen Hawking: 'Although the goal of physics is a complete understanding of everything around us, including our own existence, physics has not succeeded in reducing chemistry and biology to the status of solved problems, while the possibility of creating a set of equations through which it could account for human behaviour remains entirely remote' (1993, p.48).

[2] Neuroscientist Pribram writes: '…we think of the force of gravity as a thing. Actually, of course, all we have are the observations of actions at a distance… this means that we are inferring gravity from our observations: gravity is not an observable; as in the case of field concepts, gravity is inferred' (Laszlo, 1993, p.12).

The inertia of science has been criticised by a number of scholars (Kuhn, Feyerabend and Lakatos being probably the best known). It transpires in a rigid, absolutistic demand to adhere to certain views and self-imposed methods and criteria. Physicist Max Planck allegedly said that a new scientific truth does not triumph by convincing its opponents, but rather because its opponents die, and a new generation grows up that is familiar with it. This stifles rather than advances human knowledge. As Chalmers points out, 'we cannot legitimately defend or reject items of knowledge because they do or do not conform to some ready-made criterion of scientificity' (1980, p.169). The best scientists have always been on the front lines, prepared to sacrifice their pre-assumptions for the sake of better understanding. However, there is another, inevitably larger group of scientists that prefer to maintain the status quo[1]. Science writer Horgan comments that 'the scientific culture was once much smaller and therefore more susceptible to rapid change. Now it has become a vast intellectual, social, and political bureaucracy, with inertia to match' (1995, p.137). Both of these groups, progressive and conservative, may be necessary, the former to prevent the solidification of science, and the latter to prevent chaos. The problem is that the conservative stream often supports and perpetuates particular ideological views in order to maintain a special status and social power. The suspicion is that some scientists are more interested in advancing their careers than knowledge. Chalmers claims that '[ideology of science] involves the use of the dubious concept of science and the equally dubious concept of truth that is often associated with it, usually in the defence of conservative positions' (1980, p.169).

Bias - those phenomena to which the established scientific method can be applied are studied in greater and greater detail, often without any reference to a larger picture; whereas those to which it cannot be are ignored or are declared illusionary. *The Oxford Companion to the Mind*, for example, has entries such as 'Frankenstein' but not 'will'. The consequence of such an attitude is a distorted and impoverished picture of reality. Even if some phenomena or events cannot be explained, they need to be taken into account and acknowledged:

> Objectivism has totally falsified our conception of truth, by exalting what we can know and prove, while covering up with ambiguous utterances all that we know and cannot prove, even though the latter knowledge underlies, and must ultimately set its seal to, all that we can prove. (Polanyi, 1958, p.286)

---

[1] It has been observed that 'it is no coincidence that those who feel most certain of their grip on scientific method have rarely worked on the frontiers of science themselves' (Collins and Pinch, 1993, p.143).

Limitations of science as a social practice

Besides the above ideological limitations there are other self-imposed limitations to present day science that are the result of the social milieu within which it operates.

Specialisation is such an instance. The best specialisation can provide is a fragmented picture on reality, which leaves out the possibility of an overall, synthetic view. This can lead to 'not seeing the wood for the trees', and can have highly undesirable consequences. James Burke, a scientist himself, concludes that 'the reductionist approach, forcing people to be specialists, has got us into the mess we are in' (*The Sunday Times,* 1st of January 1995). The one who looks through a microscope all the time may not notice an elephant standing next to shim. Historian Zeldin proclaims:

> ...around the beginning of the eighteenth century... the ideal of encyclopaedic knowledge was replaced by specialisation. Withdrawal into a fortress of limited knowledge meant one could defend oneself on one's home ground; it gave one self-confidence of a limited kind... Now that the silences produced by specialisation have become deafening, and now that information fills the air as never before, it is possible to reconsider the choice, to ask whether many people might not be better off if they began looking again for the road which leads beyond specialisation, if they tried seeing the universe as a whole. (1994, p.197)

The insistence on observable, public and repeatable is still prevailing, although there are certain phenomena (in cosmology and the realm of sub-atomic particles, as much as in studying life and mind) that cannot satisfy these requirements. Any attempts to fit them within these criteria severely impoverish their understanding. The very existence of atoms was derided as metaphysical nonsense until barely a century ago. Leading scientists argued that it made no sense to talk of entities that could never be observed, which drove one of the most talented scientists at that time, Boltzmann, to suicide. His struggles against the scientific orthodoxy illustrate the dangers of allowing such a dogmatism to seep into the quest for knowledge, especially in the fields of human and social science (the mind is neither observable, nor public, nor repeatable).

Authoritarianism - to secure their special status, priests used to perpetuate a belief that their vocation made them somehow closer to God, so the best way for ordinary people to relate and be informed about spiritual matters was through them. Scientists nowadays acquire a similar aura of authority. The impression is that they are experts above others (fostered not necessarily by scientists themselves, of which some, in all fairness, are trying to break out of such an image). It surfaces in frequently heard statements in the media such as 'scientists claim that...', without saying who these scientists are and what these claims are based on. This makes science not only vulnerable to manipulation, but also alienates it from ordinary people.

Scientific detachment was introduced to ensure a higher level of objectivity and is often justified (e.g. to enable independent verification). However, it is sometimes taken so far that it becomes an obstacle and, in fact, leads to bias through the back door.

Intrinsic limitations

The above ideological and historical limitations are contingent, and should not be taken as detrimental. After all, they can be overcome in the future. However, there are some limitations of science that can never be surpassed, which is why the scientific approach cannot be sufficient on its own and needs to be combined with other approaches.

Dealing with complexity - scientific method is essentially analytic, which enables the simplification and generalisation of some phenomena. Yet, reality is complex, and if that complexity is disregarded, some important qualities can be missed. One of the world's most distinguished quantum physicists and a philosopher, Werner Heisenberg, warned: '...the scientific concepts are idealizations... But through this process of idealization and precise definition immediate connection with reality is lost' (1958, p.200). More heuristic methods are better suited to deal with complex systems. Human beings could not operate in the world if they only relied on science and excluded the common sense that is capable of intuitively grasping this complexity. Psychologists, for example, are not yet nearly able to provide the profound insights about the human psyche that can be found in the works of narrative writers such as Shakespeare, Dickens or Tolstoy.

Incompleteness - there are certain phenomena or questions that are beyond the reach of science. For instance, one of the dogmas of the present scientific ideology is that all the processes in nature are governed by physical laws. However, science seems at loss to explain where these laws come from. It is not only a question of why there is this set of laws rather than any other, but more fundamentally, why there are laws at all, why the universe is orderly, rather than chaotic and disorderly. Physicist Paul Davies speculates that attaining full knowledge through science is unlikely, given the limits imposed by quantum indeterminacy, Gödel's theorem, chaos theory and the like[1]. Mystical experience might provide the only avenue to absolute truth, he concludes (in Horgan, 1996, p.261).

A lack of criteria for interpreting facts - Henri Poincaré, one of the greatest mathematicians and physicists in the 19th century, wrote: 'Just as houses are made of stones, so is science made of facts; but a pile of stones is not a

---

[1] Quantum indeterminacy is the apparent necessary incompleteness in the description of a physical system; Gödel's theorem demonstrates that there are always undecidable elements within any formal system; and chaos theory sets the limit to the ability to predict future states from initial conditions.

house and a collection of facts is not necessarily science'. What sort of structure is created depends on the way scientists play with or interpret facts. Interpretations are important. Human understanding would be very limited if it was based only on descriptive statements. The laws do not have much explanatory power; they leave many questions unanswered. However, interpretations are not obvious, they are extrapolations that necessarily involve mental operations, not solely based on observations. So, many observable facts can give rise to a number of different interpretations, of which some may not be accurate even if the facts behind them are. A different set of criteria is needed for interpretations than for observations, but scientific method does not provide them. This is why it is easy to highjack scientific findings and present one's interpretations as scientific truths[1].

To conclude, the scientific approach is no doubt useful for examining natural phenomena, but it is not sufficient to explain reality as a whole. At its best, it can offer an incomplete account of reality. This is not the fault of scientists. After all, few of them have ever promised to provide a full and coherent picture of the world. However, a more comprehensive understanding requires a more comprehensive approach. A professor of Computer Science and Engineering, Joseph Weizenbaum summarises this point in the following statement:

> … some people have the same type of very deep faith in modern science that others do in their respective religions. This faith in science, grounded in its own dogma, leads to defence of scientific theories far beyond the time any disconfirming evidence is unearthed. Moreover, disconfirming evidence is generally not incorporated into the body of science in an open-minded way but by an elaboration of the already existing edifice (as, for example, by adding epicycles) and generally in a way in which the resulting structure of science and its procedures excludes the possibility of putting the enterprise itself in jeopardy. In other worlds, modern science has made itself immune to falsification in any terms the true believer will admit into argument. Perhaps modern science's most devastating effect is that it leads its believers to think it to be the only legitimate source of knowledge about the world… This is as mistaken a belief as the belief that one cannot gain legitimate knowledge from anything other than religion. Both are equally false. (in Singh, 1987, p. 281)

---

[1] 'More recent research (Pickering, Galison, Rudwick, and others) has added that scientific facts are constituted by debate and compromise, that they harden with the distance from their origin, that they are manufactured rather than read off nature, and that the activities that produce and/or identify them form complex and, with respect to theory, relatively self-contained cultures' (in Honderich, 1995, p.808).

THE SPIRITUAL APPROACH

There are diverse views on what spirituality means. In this context, 'spiritual approach' is used as a general term for those perspectives that do not adhere to strictly materialist or reductionist views. In other words, it includes attempts to reach beyond immediate sensory perception and make cognitive claims about that which transcends ordinary experience.

The spiritual approach starts from a sound premise that the physical world may be only a sub-set or one plane of reality. After all, it is impudent to believe that everything is accessible and explicable from data obtained through our five senses (even with the help of instruments). It makes sense to consider the possibility that there is more to it than meets the eye. The spiritual approach is concerned with that which is beyond the ordinary perception of reality and in which this reality may be rooted. It is characterised by a sense of 'otherness', 'something there' a sense that what we normally perceive is limited in its scope. So, the natural world is usually considered a part of a greater whole, and it can be properly understood only with reference to the whole. It would be a mistake to exclude this possibility outright, as long as the beginning, end and cause of the familiar world cannot be fully accounted for otherwise.

An attempt to expand beyond ordinary experience is not in itself something unique to spirituality. Science does the same (by using microscopes or telescopes, for example). What is specific to this approach is its method, which transcends normal perception by the means of personal transformation. Achieving such knowledge requires altering the level of awareness, which, in turn, necessitates at least a temporary personal change. So, whereas for scientific method the quality of an experiment matters (while the experimenter should be neutral, in the background), for these kind of insights the quality of the experimenter matters (while the 'experiment' is only a vehicle). Although they are not necessary, various techniques are traditionally used to assist this process: psychotropic substances, lucid dreaming, meditation, breath-control, repetitive sound or movement, trance, fasting, sleep deprivation and so on. They all have the same aim, to reach beyond the familiar constructs of reality. Therefore, spiritual experience may include, but nevertheless transcends, an experimental element. It provides 'knowledge by presence', a direct, unmediated mode of cognition. Thus, although spirituality is empirical in the sense that it is based on experience, it differs from conventional scientific empiricism in the objects of its enquiry and in its method.

It should be clarified though that spirituality is here distinguished from mysticism or religion (this, of course, is not to say that there are no grey areas and overlaps between them). Mysticism generally takes the stand that the riddle of reality is a mystery and will always remain a mystery – in other words it cannot be solved. The religious view, on the other hand, is that the mystery has already been solved in the past. Both, religious paths and mysticism are preparation rather than exploration. Their aim is to reach a particular state, which may have personal value and inspire others, but makes a limited contribution to the expansion of knowledge. Furthermore, mysticism is highly personal, which makes it incommunicado, while religion stresses socially shared constructs and easily becomes dogmatic. Spirituality does not need to be as strongly personal as mysticism, nor as strongly social as religion. Taking a middle ground in this respect puts it in a better position to make a bridge, integrate the larger perspective with the rest of life, and by doing so contribute to our knowledge and understanding.

SOME COMMON MISCONCEPTIONS ABOUT SPIRITUALITY

Spirituality is reserved for special or initiated individuals - spiritual experiences are not rare. Apparently, about 40% of people have at least one experience that they count as spiritual[1]. In fact, practically everybody who manages to move beyond the noise of everyday impressions can access at least some aspects of such experiences.

Spirituality requires the abandoning of autonomy - spirituality is very often associated with *surrendering*, the term usually poorly understood and occasionally abused by religious movements. Surrendering has no value if it is not accompanied by independence and autonomy. Therefore, it cannot be identified with the unconditional adoption of a system of beliefs, attitudes or conducts dictated by established teachings, theories or dogmas. It is not surprising that there is antagonism between spirituality and official religions. Robert Forman, an eminent researcher in this field, writes that 'Most often, by far, spirituality was opposed to the "stuffy old church" and its fixed +-dogmas' (2004, p.48).

Spirituality conflicts with empirical data - certain claims from this approach may indeed contradict scientific findings or common sense, but this is not the rule. In some cases, spiritual insights have even preceded science (see, for example, Capra, 2000). There is nothing inherent to spirituality that makes it incompatible with empirical facts. Assertions that do so, are likely to stem from an inauthentic experience or a mistaken interpretation. There is

---

[1] See, for example, Hay, 1990, p.79, and Forman, 2004, p2-3,

one legitimate difference though: while science attempts to be objective by detachment from the personal, spirituality aspires to achieve objectivity by transcending the personal.

Spirituality is incompatible with rationality - the spiritual approach may, in some instances, require a non-rational mode. But, this is different from being irrational (incompatible with the rational). Transcending reason is different from contradicting reason. Throughout history, many scholars with spiritual inclinations from various cultural and religious backgrounds have tried to square rationality with their insights (Plato, Ibn Sina, Abelard, Rudolf Steiner or Krishnamurti are just a few examples). Such attempts did not intend to undermine reason, but to extend it beyond the empirical phenomena of the material world.

THE RELEVANCE OF SPIRITUALITY

The major contribution of this approach to the understanding of reality is its exploration beyond immediate sensory perception. This enables a larger perspective, from which issues that would otherwise remain hanging in the air can be addressed. To clarify this point, a parallel can be drawn with a dream or computer game. They are self-contained to some extent, but can really be understood only with reference to reality outside the dream or game. This attempt to move beyond ordinary human experience and activities is important because it keeps alive the search for ultimate answers, however elusive they seem to be. It is perhaps not surprising that even more and more scientists are prepared to admit their spiritual inclinations.

The other significant input of the spiritual approach is an attempt to grapple with the question of meaning that has a profound importance for human life. The scientific approach is inadequate to deal with this matter (which is why some reductionists simply declare that the world and life are meaningless - not on the basis of any evidence, but simply because they do not have a way to address the issue)[1]. Philosophy may take up this subject, but is lame without experiences that would provide the substance for any such consideration.

Spirituality is also capable of transcending cognitive operational processes in a different way than common sense. While common sense can deal with complex situations for which thinking is simply too slow, in this

---

[1] Polanyi, who was trained as a scientist, recognises the value of this point too. He writes that 'the biblical cosmology continues to express – however inadequately – the significance of the fact that the world exists and that man has emerged from it, while the scientific picture denies any meaning to the world, and indeed ignores all our most vital experience of this world' (1958, p.285).

case it is a qualitative shift. Some experiences and insights may go beyond what reason would expect.

Finally, the spiritual approach is essentially holistic rather than a specialisation driven endeavour (see p.19). Although some individuals in this field focus on one procedure (e.g. 'shamanic journeys' or meditative practices) most of them acknowledge that no understanding can be complete without a reference to the whole. Such a perspective, on the other side of the spectrum from reductionism, can potentially be of a great value.

SPIRITUALITY AND RELIGION

Spirituality relates to religion in a similar way to how science relates to materialism. Religion is an organised set of fixed beliefs, while spirituality is empirical in a sense of transpersonal experiences and consequently more exploratory and less dogmatic. As the etymology of the word *religion* indicates, its purpose is to bind people together by a system of beliefs and rituals. Religions are characterised by their cosmologies, moral code, rituals, the architecture of their temples, their revealed literature, and so on. So, religion refers to more public (or *exoteric*) forms of spiritual practice, but there is also an *esoteric* core. The diversity of religions is a norm, while many spiritual experiences tend to be cross-cultural[1]. If the circumstances are favourable, if it is a historically ripe moment, some esoteric experiences can trigger a religious paradigm shift. They are adapted to particular circumstances as the means of (re)organising society or even achieving social control and power. If the new view is accepted, an official doctrine is created that becomes an established reference point for generations to come. In other words, another framework of social reality is formed. It provides a sense of security (to individuals), and also unifies by offering a common aim (to the society). However, as science does not need to adhere to materialism, spirituality does not require a religious framework. In fact, esoteric and exoteric aspects do not always go hand in hand. It is common that as soon as the latter (a new religion) reaches a point of power, it sees the former as a threat and tries to suppress it in order to preserve its status[2] (as materialist ideology often obstructs the development of science in order to preserve its

---

[1] An American mathematician, Jaya Srivastava makes an even stronger claim: 'Each great religion has two aspects, a spiritual part and a ritualistic part. As is very clear, the spiritual part of all religions is the same' (in Singh, 1988, p.176). Such an assertion is probably an exaggeration and can hardly be defended. A tendency towards universality does not presuppose the sameness.

[2] A poignant allegory about this strife between religion and spirituality can be found in Dostoyevsky's fable 'The great inquisitor', where even Jesus, who returned to the Earth, was prosecuted by the Church.

own privileged position). It is a misconception, for example, that in the past the Christian church fought primarily science. In fact, it first and foremost fought spirituality and mysticism (the craze of burning 'witches' and 'heretics' is one example among many) and eventually allowed the growth of science (within its ranks) to help in this fight. The importance of spirituality in challenging religious dogmas should not be undermined. There have been a great number of people who have put much courage, effort and self-sacrifice into exploring reality beyond accepted doctrines.

THE LIMITATIONS OF THE SPIRITUAL APPROACH

As other approaches, spirituality also has its limitations that can be grouped into the same three categories.

Extrinsic limitations

These limitations arise from the association of spirituality with the various religious frameworks within which it may be situated.

Infallibility - if spiritual insights are achieved through personal transformation, the issue for those who have not gone through such a process is how to decide which ones are valid. One possible solution is accepting 'truth by authority', which means that it is more important who does the saying than what is said. Indeed, religions rely heavily on authority, because the majority of people cannot personally verify spiritual claims. Chosen individuals or scriptures are given a special status (often reinforced by their alleged super-natural source) and their unquestionable acceptance is expected. Considering that spiritual experiences can be interpreted in various ways, 'truth by authority' can undeniably have a unifying purpose. However, the problem is that the demand to accept unconditionally and unreflectively certain assertions means that they cannot be challenged, which leads to stagnation. It is not surprising then that there are growing discrepancies between religious claims and recognised facts, and also that there are contradictions within religious interpretations, too[1]. Psychologist Csikszentmihalyi is right saying that '…a vital new religion may one day arise again. In the meantime, those who seek consolation in existing churches often pay for their peace of mind with a tacit agreement to ignore a great deal of what is known about the way the world works' (1992, p.14).

---

[1] This applies to moral matters as well as factual. Subjecting Job to suffering (and his first wives and offspring to annihilation) simply to win a bet, or ordering the Israelites to destroy other tribes, does not seem compatible with an image of a God that is good.

Dogmatism - although religions must adapt to new circumstances to some extent, most of them are essentially conservative rather than progressive. This is because they rely on the teachings and experience of significant figures inevitably from a distant past (the further from the present and more obscure, the more authority they seem to have). However, not allowing interpretations to evolve can be cripplingly restrictive and misleading.

Moreover, despite being supposedly based on transpersonal insights, religions usually discourage direct experience, for fear that those who have them would not conform to an already established credo. So, in fact, religion in most cases, stalls the development of spiritual knowledge, which leads to an increasing discrepancy: while other aspects of human life have been evolving, official religions rely on anachronistic interpretations from a few thousand years ago. This is regrettable and unnecessary. People still respect old scientists or philosophers and build on their insights and theories (of which many, as for example Pythagoras' theorem, remain valid). However, it would be absurd to consider them absolute authorities and to reject further developments because of them.

Limitations of spirituality as a social practice

Locality - the heightened awareness that enables spiritual insights is typically unstable. So, even those who reach that point, quickly fall back into a socially shared reality and often try to situate the experience within an existing framework. Yet, as long as spirituality is embodied in local traditions, it can hardly claim universality.

Ineffability - even if one maintains the clarity of an experience, the problem remains how to communicate so gained insights. Considering that they are beyond ordinary experiences, something 'out of this world', they do not fit comfortably with the usual perception of reality. A common language often lacks the words to express them adequately, there is little to connect to, and any attempt to verbalise them may sound shallow or plain weird. This is why analogies or metaphors need to be used, but they can be variously interpreted. Others may choose to understand them in a way to suit their own purposes, which inevitably leads to further distortions. It is not surprising that religious or esoteric texts often stray in attempts to conceptualise spiritual revelations.

The issue of proof - another difficulty with spiritual insights is that they are not publicly verifiable. Nothing solid can be brought back as evidence. An analogy can be made with an explorer who comes across a 'lost tribe' without bringing any modern gadgets. S/he may try to explain to those people that there is a different world outside, s/he may speak about cities, cars, computers, TV, airplanes, but cannot prove to them that they exist (even if they may occasionally see some strange shiny 'birds' in the sky).

S/he will most likely be considered a mad person, a crank[1]. Not surprisingly, many spiritual people choose obscurity – hence the term esoteric knowledge. Yet, the fact that, by default, it is impossible to provide material evidence for non-material phenomena does not invalidate such knowledge *per se*. Other approaches are not immune to this problem either. Silver admits that also 'many of the basic concepts of science cannot be verified either logically or by observation' (1988, p.503). Nevertheless, some ways or criteria that can render spiritual claims at least plausible are still needed.

Intrinsic limitations

Non-testability - one difficulty with this approach is that following the same procedure will not necessarily produce the same results. The content and the quality of experience are to a large extent unpredictable. Even the timing is difficult to determine. For this reason it is hard to separate such insights from wishful thinking, fantasies, superstitions and other products of one's mind. This is why a spiritual path requires a high degree of personal discipline, but discipline, on its own, cannot provide a foolproof guarantee that an experience is genuine. So, although it is meaningless to demand material evidence, any claims need to be checked against recognised scientific findings. They do not need to be reduced to these findings, but they should not contradict them either. Spirituality is not about burning the bridges between the two worlds but making them.

Convolution with other altered states - not all altered states of consciousness lead to valid spiritual insights. Some of these states can be on the other side of the 'bell curve' (a normal state of mind) – namely madness, hallucinations. Distinguishing between these two opposites may not always be possible within a spiritual framework and needs to be validated by other approaches. For example, if it may not be straightforward to scientifically challenge (self-)destructive 'messages' from God, they can be dismissed as poor candidates for genuine spiritual experiences by common sense.

Fragmentation - although spiritual insights may contribute to a more holistic view (by interpreting them with reference to the whole), they are usually based on isolated and disconnected pockets of experience. These experiences may yield glimpses of a transcendent realm, but they cannot, on their own, provide a full picture. Reasoning is required to make sense of them. And reasoning is *not* a part of the experience.

---

[1] A similar situation is vividly described in H. G. Wells' story *The Country of the Blind.*

THE PHILOSOPHICAL APPROACH

For centuries philosophy was an umbrella term for all the methods of rational enquiry. Gradually, however, more and more disciplines gained their independence. Especially after the apparent failures of grand philosophical systems (such as Hegel's), its field was rapidly shrinking. On the one hand, philosophy could not compete with science in studying the natural world. On the other hand, any turn to the subjective experience would blur its boundaries with the mystical or religious with which few philosophers wanted to be associated - for fear of losing credibility. Philosophers tried to develop logic into an elaborate system, an exact meta-language that could rival mathematics, but this endeavour hit a dead-end when it transpired that logic can never be completely logical (only shortly before it happened to mathematics itself). So, they focused on the relationship between subject and object, the so-called 'human condition'. The domain of philosophy became *relations* not particulars that relate, which freed philosophy from being bound to a specific subject. It is now considered to be a method of enquiry that develops defensible arguments based on reason (rather than observation or experience). The aim of philosophy is understanding, which necessitates the examination of the relation between awareness of the world and the world as the material of awareness. For example, philosophy is not primarily concerned with the question 'does God exist?', but rather 'does the idea of God make sense?', or 'does the concept of reality without the idea of God make sense?' This is why philosophy can never be conclusive - people are changing, so their understanding is changing too.

A COMMON MISCONCEPTION ABOUT PHILOSOPHY

It is irrelevant - the inconclusiveness of philosophy has led to a widespread belief that philosophy does not matter. Yet, throughout history philosophy has influenced every sphere of life, from science and religion, to education, politics, economics, art and even fashion. Stoicism served as the working ideology of the Roman Empire, the writings of Plato and Plotinus were instrumental in transforming an intellectually rudimentary offshoot of Judaism into one of the dominant world religions. Descartes and Leibniz directly contributed to the 17th century rise of science, while Voltaire and Rousseau inspired the French Revolution. More recently, the philosophy of Marx and Engels' stirred political changes from Cuba to China, while existentialism and later post-modernism shaped Western culture.

THE RELEVANCE OF PHILOSOPHY

The most important value of philosophy is that it utilises reasoning as the method of rational enquiry. Reasoning provides a basis for independent judgement (because its criteria can be internal, and therefore less prone to distortions). This method can avoid some of the pitfalls that spirituality and science are vulnerable to. On the one hand, reasoning is not so difficult to verify as spiritual insights. On the other, reasoning is not limited only to observation, and therefore it has potentially unlimited scope (can deal with non-observable, abstract issues). Indeed, philosophy often addresses problems lying beyond the reach of scientific investigation. So, this approach can have several roles:

It can examine the coherence of concepts, frameworks and existing practices within any individual discipline (for example, whether the concept of learning makes sense in computer science, or programming in biology).

Other approaches have their own ways to validate their findings, but they rarely have criteria for *interpreting* these findings. This is another sphere where philosophy can make a significant contribution.

One potential problem with any discipline is that its theoretical foundations are usually taken for granted. Thus, besides critical analysis of existing practices and theories, philosophy can make distinct contributions by focusing on the meta-level. In other words, it can tease out and examine assumptions that any particular discipline or method is based on. No individual discipline can do so, because it already operates within its own framework, which requires accepting its presuppositions.

Finally, philosophy can have an overarching, synthetic function. Cross-disciplinary subjects and themes that need a synthetic approach are largely neglected. Whereas scientists tend to become more and more specialised in their interests, philosophers generally stand back from the details of particular research programmes and concentrate on making sense of the overall principles and on establishing how they relate to each other. This can be essential in determining the way all the components function together: the practical aspects in relation to its theoretical premises, as well as the findings of different approaches. Thus, even if some epistemic categories require contributions from specialised disciplines, it is philosophy that can provide the perspective from which they are not only examined, but also combined. Such a contribution is significant because it gives hope that a coherence and completeness of human understanding can be achieved.

PHILOSOPHY AND IDEOLOGY

Many philosophical ideas have given rise to or been associated with various ideologies. A radical example is dialectic-materialism based on the philosophical work of Marx and Engels, which became the official credo of communist countries in the 20th century. Another instance is Nietzsche's philosophy, distorted to such an extent that it was linked to movements such as Nazism. These may be extremes, but other philosophies have also been used to justify ideological ends - for instance, an impoverished interpretation of Adam Smith's work (via economist Milton Friedman) was popular during Thatcherism. As in the other cases, such ideologies are usually distortions and simplifications of the original thought that contradict the impartiality of philosophical argument and severely restrict its independence. Philosophy properly conceived should not be one more form of power, but a counter to external power.

THE LIMITATIONS OF THE PHILOSOPHICAL APPROACH

As with the other approaches, philosophy also has its limitations.

Extrinsic limitations

Relying on authority - although less so than religion, philosophy can also suffer from an over-reliance on authorities (e.g. Aristotle, Kant, or Marx). The weight of an argument is sometimes based on who has said something, rather than on the reasoning strength of what has been said. This is reflected in the extensive use of references to other philosophers that may have an aura of authority, but mean little to those who are not initiated. Such a trend contributes to solidifying particular views into ideologies. Many philosophers have given their allegiance to various '-isms' and felt obliged to remain true to these frameworks.

Limitations of philosophy as a social practice

Focusing on the language - examining the relationship between the subject and object, between human beings and reality, degenerated in the main stream philosophy of the mid-20th century into examining only the means by which the constructs of reality are made: the use of words and language. The clarification of language (getting rid of ambiguities) was considered a proper way of formulating the truth, despite the fact that the futility of such an endeavour was realised very early[1].

---

[1] As far back as 1902 Charles Pierce wrote in the *Dictionary of Philosophy and Psychology*: 'Think of arm chairs and reading chairs and dining-room chairs, and kitchen chairs, chairs that pass into benches, chairs that cross the boundary and become settees, dentist's chairs, thrones, opera stalls, seats of all sorts, those miraculous fungoid growths that cumber the floor of the art and crafts exhibitions, and you will see what a lax bundle in fact is this simple straightforward term. I would undertake to defeat any definition of chair or chairishness that you gave me.'

Intrinsic limitations

Abstractedness - one of the problems with philosophy (which is, to some extent, a consequence of focusing more on relations rather than on that what relates) is that it is divorced from everyday experiences. Philosophers often indulge in attempts to outwit each other by building more and more complex arguments, while examining in minute detail the arguments of their opponents, which only moves them further away from the subject at hand and contributes little to its real understanding. This is why there is a saying that philosophers live in ivory towers, and the term 'philosophising' sometimes has a derogatory meaning. Philosophical theories that entirely flout common sense tend to forfeit a connection with ordinary life and become too abstract.

Groundlessness - reasoning can be so proficient that it can prove almost anything, which easily leads to relativism. Sufficiently complex systems allow endless combinations and permutations, so even radically opposed views may seem reasonable. Hence, philosophy can become a game and, therefore, in effect unreliable. To relate to the real world, some other constrains or tests of acceptability are needed besides the internal criteria. In other words, reasoning needs to be grounded in hard facts that can be supplied by methods usually associated with science.

Speculativeness - philosophers are in a good position to deal with universals, but philosophical method cannot provide content (without taking into account experience, reasoning is nothing more than speculation). And if the full picture, aspired to by philosophers throughout the centuries, is ever to be reached, philosophy cannot rely only on everyday life. It would be difficult to avoid drawing from, and taking into account, what can be broadly called spiritual practices and experiences, as these can supply the raw material needed for a metaphysical framework.

THE SYNTHESIS

All the above approaches contribute in their unique ways to the understanding of reality, but none of them is likely to provide a full picture. Not only are they incomplete and insufficient on their own, but they also seem to be stuck in ostensibly irresolvable conflicts with each other. Francis Bacon and Descartes (who are considered the founders of opposed factions in philosophy, *viz.* empiricism and rationalism) agreed on one point: to separate religion and the study of the natural world. They may have been right to do so at the time when the Church was all-powerful, but this does not mean that scientific and spiritual approaches are inherently in conflict. They appear so only because of ideological prejudices in both campuses. Many scholars seem to be arriving at the same conclusion starting from different perspectives[1]. Reality can be interpreted as meaningful without conflicting with empirical facts. Polanyi and Prosch make the point stating that 'the religious hypothesis, if it does indeed hold that the world is meaningful rather than absurd, *is* therefore a viable hypothesis for us. There is no scientific reason why we cannot believe it' (1975, p.179).

This is not only of theoretical significance. Our very survival may depend on an ability to transcend what is superfluous and synthesise what is important in these approaches. Human society cannot long afford to live in a world in which philosophy is disparaged, religion contradicts science, and science contradicts common experience and social practice (e.g. democracy assumes choice, and legal systems personal responsibility - both are based on the notion of free will that is not upheld by science). Such antagonisms must be reconciled in order to produce a more adequate and complete interpretation. This does not require the abandonment of the current methods (they have contributed to knowledge and continue to do so), only a recognition that they have limited value in isolation and that, in some cases, it would be beneficial to combine them[2]. In order to do so, there are two obstacles that must first be overcome:

---

[1] For example, Schrödinger, who formulated the fundamental equation of quantum mechanics, espoused in his book *Mind and Matter* (1958) a spiritual view that he identified with the 'perennial philosophy' of Aldous Huxley, and expressed his sympathy for the *Upanishads* and Eastern spiritual thoughts.

[2] It has been recognised that 'objections to novelty and to alternatives come from particular groups with vested interests, not from science as a whole. It is therefore possible to gain understanding and to solve problems by combining bits and pieces of 'science' with prima facie 'unscientific' opinions and procedures' (Honderich, 1995, p.809).

34

Exclusiveness stems from a belief of 'insiders' that their perspective can grasp and explain everything on its own[1]. This is, however, highly unlikely. For example, science has a reliable method but a limited scope. Spirituality, on the other hand, can perhaps reach what is not accessible to science, but its insights cannot be easily verified and are prone to distortions. As Albert Einstein famously put it, 'science without religion is lame; religion without science is blind' (Einstein was not practising any religion, so in this statement he most likely referred to spirituality). It is not surprising then that the frameworks they are associated with are not satisfactory. While religious interpretations are generally outdated, materialist interpretations are fragmented and incomplete. In other words, religion on its own provides an irrational interpretation, while materialism on its own provides a meaningless interpretation.

Ideological baggage - history shows that when one of these approaches takes over and starts dominating, it easily becomes a form of ideology with undesirable consequences. The canonisation of religious ideologies has frequently led to the slowing down of individual and social development, and also (with a few exceptions) created a state of permanent conflict and bigotry between different faiths – without change there is no hope for reconciliation. There is a profound awareness that an overgrowth of materialistic science and technology could also have a potentially devastating outcome if it is not paralleled with the development of other ways of knowledge. The aviator Charles Lindbergh made this poignant comment: 'I have seen the science I worshipped and the aircraft I loved destroying the civilization I expected them to serve.' This, of course, does not refer only to the destructive power of machines, but also to zealous attempts to implement scientific methods in life, especially human life (eugenics and social Darwinism being two examples). An even more pervasive consequence of materialism is a climate in which technocracy, meaninglessness, selfishness, competition and consumerism dominate, which also prevents further progress and ultimately leads to a dead-end. With equally disastrous consequences, cultural frameworks and philosophical ideas can be turned into a tool of repression (nationalism and Marxism may be prominent but certainly not unique examples[2]). Even if the

---

[1] Scientists are most susceptible to this belief nowadays because their approach is dominant. But, as the philosopher of science Feyerabend points out, defenders of science typically judge it to be superior to other forms of knowledge without adequately investigating those other forms.

[2] Nietzsche's own sister revised his writing to provide support for the ideology of racial supremacy. Philosopher Heidegger advised his students in 1933 to abandon doctrines and ideas and salute Hitler.

above cases are considered historical aberrations, there is a more subtle but enduring problem with ideology of any kind. Ideologies are linked to social power and control. However, power unlike knowledge is finite. Giving knowledge to others does not decrease the knowledge of the one who gives, but giving power to others does. Therefore, unreflective faith in an ideology, regardless of whether it has a spiritual, scientific or philosophical basis, decreases the power of individuals. This in turn limits the fluidity or flexibility of society, which are essential in times of rapid changes.

Overcoming these obstacles would make a synthesis possible, but this does not mean only refining and combining the methods embedded in the above approaches[1]. It also implies a synthesis between several complementary perspectives.

First of all, the bottom up direction (reductionism) needs be combined with the top down direction (holism). Reductionism attempts to explain complex phenomena by their components, while holism claims that the significance of the parts can only be understood in terms of their contribution to the whole and that the latter must therefore be epistemically prior. Most approaches have a tendency to favour one of these perspectives (e.g. reductionism in science), but this does not need to be the case. It is possible to recognise the value of both.

The synthesis also requires reconciling two ways of enquiry: one that examines the objects of experience (experimental), and the one that examines the experience of objects (experiential). A comprehensive and accurate interpretation must rely on both, objective knowledge derived from manipulating reality (e.g. by creating controlled conditions in a laboratory) and objective knowledge derived from manipulating the experience of reality (through personal transformation). *Objective* means, in this context, avoiding collective bias (ideological constraints) or personal bias (prejudices, preferences) respectively.

Finally, empiricism (in a broad sense, that includes common sense and transpersonal experiences) needs to be combined in a meaningful way with rationalism. This can surely be more productive than relying solely on either experience or reason.

---

[1] Of course, there are already grey areas and points of contact among them. Philosophy of religion and philosophy of science are well established disciplines. Some theologicians have thought that a scientific approach is the best means to understand God, while others have resorted to philosophy. However, these are rarely efforts in synthesis, but rather attempts to use one approach to support (or discredit) another. For example, Logical Positivism, a highly influential philosophical movement of the 20th century, was largely created by scientists with a certain ideological bent in order to steer science in their preferred direction.

When the approaches discussed above are separated from their ideological baggage and the spurious ways used to support their claims, a small number of methods remain. Three methods that relate to three types of experience as a knowledge source (personal, impersonal and transpersonal) can be discerned: *phenomenological, inductive-deductive* and *transpersonal*. However, none of them is infallible and fully sufficient, so another method, *reasoning*, that can serve as a link between them is also needed. Of course, not all of these methods must always be combined (there are some areas where only one is enough), but their synthesis is likely to produce a more complete picture. Before they are described though, it should be underlined that any method is only a tool, not an end in itself. Some scholars emphasise a form and correct procedures because this gives their work an aura of seriousness and credibility, but it also often kills enthusiasm and creativity.

PHENOMENOLOGICAL METHOD

This method can be used to achieve greater objectivity in relation to personal experiences (linked above to common sense). It has been already recognised that scientific observation, as a method, is somewhat limited. It cannot penetrate 'below' the surface of the observable. This is a statement from mathematician Srivastava:

> Gödel's theorem states that, loosely speaking, in any mathematical system which has the natural numbers (the numbers 0, 1, 2, and so on) as a subset, questions exist which cannot be answered yes and no... What all this means is that science is basically handicapped or limited in its capabilities. It is not possible by a series of experiments and related analytical reasoning to fathom the depth of the universe. To fathom the universe, man has another tool: direct perception, direct experience of reality (in Singh, 1988, p.177-178).

The problem is, however, that this 'direct experience' typically remains on the surface of personal bias, and cannot claim universality. If there is any 'essence', it has to lie below the objective surface of the reality and the subjective surface of individuals. So, only in the depths can the dichotomy between objectivism and subjectivism be overcome. Such objectivity is not based on facts 'out there' or on a social consensus. It is not achieved by moving outwards and away from oneself, but by moving inwards, reaching underneath personal subjectivity, finding what is universal in one's experience[1]. This is achieved by submerging oneself below interpretations based on superficial perception, collective pre-assumptions or one's own prejudices and preferences.

---

[1] Polanyi makes the same point: '...man can transcend his own subjectivity by striving passionately to fulfil his personal obligations to universal standards' (1958, p.17).

The method that can assist this process is called phenomenological reduction. The term was coined by philosopher Husserl at the beginning of the 20th century, but interpreted in a broad sense (as a method rather than a philosophical doctrine) it has been practised since ancient times. This is its clearest and shortest definition:

> Phenomenology is [...] a turn to subjectivity with the intention of arriving at objective truth. (Solomon, 1988, p.130)

The aim is to get insights about essence from experience alone rather than through the veil of existing mental constructs. In other words, the object of phenomenological description is 'to... go beyond the various 'facts' of experience and the reality of theories and practices to those features of experience which are "absolutely given in immediate intuition"... Not the evidence of the senses but of the consciousness as such' (Solomon, 1988, p.131). In fact, all personal experiences are phenomenological and as such they are real and true. What, however, can be distorted (intentionally or not) is their interpretations. An extreme example is hallucination, where an internal experience is interpreted as an external event. Interpretations are, of course, necessary and useful, but they are usually contaminated by past experiences, expectations, judgements etc. Phenomenological method means being able to examine experience as it is, prior to these possible distortions[1]. To achieve this, one needs to become aware of what comes from the phenomena experienced and what does not. This is not as easy as it may seem. It requires vigilance and discipline in 'bracketing' (putting aside) any pre-assumptions that are added to an experience.

Phenomenological method is indispensable if insights from personal experiences are to have a degree of universality (a greater level of objectivity). However, it falls short of providing a way to construct reliable interpretations from them (to bring them back to the surface). And yet, interpretation is necessary in order to communicate these insights. Furthermore (as already pointed in *The limitations of common sense*, p.9), personal experiences are somewhat limited in their scope. So, this method is insufficient on its own and needs to be combined with others.

---

[1] To quote again the historian of philosophy, Solomon, 'it is... a description of experience and a philosophy that is without presuppositions, and experience of experience as such, an opportunity to see clearly and without doubts the essential structures of not only one's own consciousness but of every possible consciousness' (1988, p.138).

INDUCTIVE-DEDUCTIVE METHOD

Inductive inferences are based on observations and controlled experiments. To minimise bias and achieve a greater objectivity, a degree of personal detachment and independent verification is required. However, this should not lead to an objectivism that demands a researcher to be entirely neutral. Detachment, taken too far, can become an obstacle rather than an advantage. Positivistic science has conflated two different meanings of objective: 'unbiased' and 'external'. This is not only unnecessary, but also mistaken: perception of the external can be biased and of the internal can be impartial. By explicitly excluding the subject, reality can never be captured in its totality. Besides, scientific detachment can be only an ideal. Researchers cannot completely avoid bringing themselves into the story. So, distancing seems a more realistic attitude than detachment. While detachment strives to achieve objectivity by eliminating the subject, distancing does so by including and maintaining a larger perspective.

In any case, the value of empirical research cannot be denied, findings based on impartial observation and experimentation can greatly contribute to the understanding of physical reality. However, as already pointed out, it has been recognised that induction is not infallible, and should not be taken for granted. Moreover, some phenomena cannot (or at least not yet) be directly examined; they can only be deduced from their consequences. This is nothing new. For example, Silver writes that 'molecules were part of the scientist's explanation of nature long before we could observe them. Their existence was *deduced* from the behaviour of matter' (1998, p.18). Through deduction we can arrive at certain knowledge that would not be accessible otherwise. Of course, it is important to go as far as possible in providing empirical support, but some conclusions will always have to be inferred.

There are several tools that can be used to assist this process, such as mathematics, geometry or theoretical (logical) conjectures. Nevertheless, even with the help of such systems, however stringently applied, deductive conclusions are not completely safe. In the 19th century non-Euclidian geometry was constructed, shortly before logic appeared to be not completely logical, and Gödel's theorem (mentioned above) showed that even mathematics is not foolproof. Furthermore, deduction cannot prove that its conclusions are true, because they depend on their premises that cannot be deduced.

To conclude, although this method can contribute to better understanding and finding more probable or plausible explanations, it should be recognised that both its components, induction and deduction, have their limits. This may not matter in some relatively simple cases, but more complete interpretations would again require the combination of inductive/deductive inferences with other methods.

TRANSPERSONAL METHOD

This method refers to transcending the personal, either in terms of perception (e.g. awareness of or sensitivity to phenomena beyond their physical manifestations), or by the way insights are arrived at (illuminations, visions, revelations). Such transcendence is often associated with mysticism, esoteria and a non-rational aspect of the mind, but, in fact, it can be relevant to any subject of enquiry, even those that are traditionally the domains of philosophy or science. Socrates habitually communicated with his 'daemon', mathematician Gauss claimed that the answer to some of the riddles with which he was struggling was given to him by God. Chemist Kekulé discovered the structure of benzene (which was the beginning of modern organic chemistry) in a vision of a snake swallowing its tail, while neuroscientist Otto Loewi found how to conduct experiments on neurotransmitters thanks to a dream.

Transpersonal method is based on manipulating the experience of reality, rather than the objects of experience, so it requires an, at least temporary, altered state of consciousness (the most common being dreams). These shifts do not need to be something radical and can happen spontaneously, but to have any value, they require an opening up, moving beyond common perception and existing constructs. Polanyi claims that scientific discovery would not be possible without these excursions outside the pre-established framework. The same applies to religious insights: a vision of Jesus or Shiva can have an epistemic value only if the images of Jesus or Shiva are transcended, by focusing on the essence beyond the culturally specific representations (in other words, taking such images symbolically).

Most of these experiences, however, are subtle and often pass unnoticed because people usually associate them with something special and grand. To use an analogy, when a tourist arrives in a foreign country s/he is unlikely to bump into the president or the Queen first. Tiny expansions of awareness or shifts of focus are what matters in most cases. This may be compared with listening to a faint radio station that is normally muted by a stronger one. Such 'signals' are accessible to practically everybody, but are subtle and fleeting, so effort needs to be put into stabilising them. A number of techniques can be used for this purpose (meditation being one, although not every type of meditation has such a function and would necessarily lead to it). Furthermore, isolated pockets of experience are meaningless. It is like when an untrained person looks through a microscope or telescope. S/he is unlikely to discern any meaningful information. To get a coherent picture, to make sense of such experiences, training, discipline, and dedication are necessary, as well as an altered state of mind.

Verification

The focus here is not on personal transformation as a 'technology' (making life better) but as a way to knowledge and understanding. So, the verification of such experiences, rather than their effects, matters. For example, seeing fairies may be psychologically beneficial to some, but it does not have a universal value unless certain criteria are observed that will bear out the perception and enable situating it within a larger context. The same applies to the qualities of experience such as elation or a sense of unity with the universe. They are elements of personal experience, so phenomenological reduction is more relevant in such cases than transpersonal method.

Transpersonal inferences are notoriously difficult to empirically verify (in the same way that many scientific findings can be). The scientific criteria that currently dominate are mostly inadequate when applied to this field. 'Truth by authority', as is widely used within religious frameworks, also suffers from well-known shortcomings. Yet, to achieve a degree of universality and objectivity, transpersonal experiences need to be distinguished from purely subjective ones. There are other altered states of consciousness such as illusions and hallucinations (triggered, for example, by mental illness or intoxication) that are entirely fictional and do not have an element of the transpersonal. Thus, what needs to be verified foremost is the source: whether the experience corresponds to something real or is entirely the product of one's mind. There are several criteria that can be used to test if such experiences are genuine:
• A lack of other plausible explanations. This means that all other reasonable possibilities have to be examined and eliminated (applying the *Ockham razor*[1]).
• As with scientific experiments, the quality of the process or procedure leading to an experience also needs to be taken into account (e.g. possible contamination by the influences of one's surroundings if using psychotropic substances).
• Logical consistency: knowledge progresses through checking reason against experiences, and checking experiences against reason (e.g. can the question 'why would real angels need wings?' have a logical answer?).
• There are certain qualities that characterise such experiences (although not all of them have to be always present). These include a maintained awareness of the parameters of ordinary reality, commonly indicated by an element of surprise (in ordinary dreams even the most bizarre events do not seem surprising); non-attachment, low excitability (even if intense emotions

---

[1] Ockham razor states: 'plurality is not to be assumed without necessity', which in this case means that a transpersonal element should not be invoked if a whole experience can be reasonably explained without it.

may be present); serenity. In short, transpersonal experiences mean perceiving normally inaccessible aspects of reality with a clear mind.

• Phenomenological criterion: '…from a subjective perspective [these experiences] feel truer, more real than dreams, hallucinations, even ordinary perception, they seem to represent "a more fundamental reality than the baseline reality"' (Horgan, 2003, p.78, quoting Andrew Newberg, a researcher in mystical experiences). The genuine conviction that what one has experienced is real should persist after the experience, when one returns to the usual state of mind (after a hallucination the person is normally aware that s/he was hallucinating).

• Maintaining relative control, agency and choice (e.g. an ability to remove oneself from the situation experienced). Transpersonal experiences can be spontaneous, but are extremely rarely imposed to a degree that one feels trapped in them.

• The object of the experience has to have a relatively independent existence from the experiencer. For example, if an observed phenomenon moves as one moves shis eyes, it is likely that it is a product of the observer's mind.

• Although such experiences can sometimes refer to the person involved, their meaning usually has a more impersonal, general nature (whereas a schizophrenic, for example, sees everything as a personal message intended for shim alone).

• An experience is likely to be real if others have independently had similar ones. Considering the possibility of collective bias, fantasies or even hallucinations, arriving at them independently is of the utmost importance.

• Correspondence: the perception of somebody's energy field, for example, can be validated by correlating so gained insights to the emotional, physical or mental state of the observed person. Or, the legitimacy of non-rationally derived predictions can be verified by systematically recording the actual future events.

• It should be possible to interpret an experience in such a way that it makes sense in relation to other transpersonal experiences.

• Usefulness: experiences that can lead to explaining or understanding certain phenomena better can be cautiously taken as probably real.

• Finally, these experiences should not be in breach of accepted empirical facts or basic common sense, and should not be self-contradictory. The only meaningful way to go beyond reason is to climb the ladders of reason. In other words, if a transpersonal conjecture is valid, combining it with the findings of other methods should be not only possible, but also beneficial. Mystics cannot bridge the gap created by the ineffability of their experiences, and religions are hopelessly stuck with outdated interpretations within the narrow range of existing social constructs. As with other methods, the fallacy of self-sufficiency has to be overcome to move forward.

REASONING

Inferences based on the above methods need to be connected to make a meaningful whole. Reasoning can serve this purpose. To preserve its independence and allow an unbiased verification, it must be governed by its own internal criteria. Four of them are suggested below. A number of examples, further in the text, show that existing scientific, religious and philosophical interpretations occasionally breach one or more of these (they are not brought up here in order to avoid repetition).

Congruence means that reasoning should not contradict accepted facts (facts are already statements, which is why congruence can be an internal criteria). This is not to say that facts are rock solid; they can change too. Congruence allows facts to be challenged, but not ignored. Therefore, if a statement contradicts commonly accepted facts, a valid justification needs to be provided. In this context, besides observable facts, plausible deductive and phenomenological ones are also recognised. For example, mathematical inferences and some historical events for which there may not be direct evidence (e.g. the existence of a proto-language deduced from similarities in existing languages) can be considered facts. On the other hand, theories based on an interpretation of facts do not have the status of a fact[1]. This does not mean that every claim has to be empirically proven. As already mentioned, proofs based on induction are not always reliable and can be limiting. So, no claim should be rejected outright unless and until it can be refuted[2]. In this way congruence resembles Popper's falsification method (see p.13) although it could not be identified with it: disregarding automatically an assertion just because it is not empirically falsifiable can be in some cases premature. In any case, it is sometimes difficult to pinpoint incongruences, and it is also possible to interpret facts incorrectly without contradicting them. For these reasons, other criteria are needed.

Consistency means that individual statements that are part of the same explanatory structure should not be in conflict with each other. In other words, an interpretation must not contradict itself. Circumventing this criterion by claiming, for instance, that a 'higher state of consciousness' transcends the contradictions is not considered justified because it is an external validation that cannot be challenged.

---

[1] Silver makes this point clear: '...most scientists believe in the theory [of evolution], but it has not been *proved*. Facts may be regarded as indisputable; theories are not' (1998, p.19).

[2] The Principle of Credulity may be relevant here: '... it is a sound principle of reasoning to suppose that things are as they seem to be, unless and until proved otherwise' (Swinburne, 1991, p.145).

Completeness requires that an interpretation should be able to account for all the cases relevant to the subject. This does not mean that every detail needs to be addressed, but that no fact at the same level of interpretation can be ignored. 'At the same level' is a caveat implying that if an interpretation is general, it is not necessary to discuss some anomalies and aberrations that may be a result of specific circumstances or features. However, even small exceptions need to be taken into account if they cannot be explained at the lower interpretative levels. If this had not been the case in the past, we would not have the theory of relativity or quantum physics nowadays. The criterion of completeness is important because without it congruence and consistency can be achieved within a limited scope, by simply excluding those phenomena that do not fit.

Cohesiveness means that all the parts of an interpretation should be meaningfully connected. This implies that all its elements should relate to each other and are necessary. Nothing can be redundant; every part should have its place, purpose and function within the whole (it must effect the whole somehow). Cohesiveness is similar to Ockham's razor[1]. Its main purpose is to prevent *deux ex machina* explanations. It also guards against jumping to conclusions, when the path from the given premises is unclear. Cohesiveness can compensate for not requiring material evidence to prove that something exists. Rather than asking for proofs, this criterion demands that something may be included only if doing so provides a more cohesive or more probable explanation than if it is not. For instance, the existence of unicorns cannot be refuted (only evidence for their existence can be). However, because there are no consequences that cannot be explained without involving unicorns, their existence can be considered irrelevant, and therefore unnecessary (until shown otherwise). Science and common sense already use this criterion. For example, the physical forces, energy, or even human thoughts are not self-evident and their existence cannot be falsified. But, they offer the best explanation for certain phenomena at the moment, so they are widely accepted.

---

[1] The difference between the Ockham razor (see p. 40) and cohesiveness is in a degree: cohesiveness allows the introduction of a new element if an explanation which includes it is substantially more likely, even if it is not absolutely necessary. For example, a meaningful word made of small stones could be the result of chance, a random falling and rolling of the stones, but this is extremely unlikely. A far more plausible explanation requires a new factor that may not be present or detectable any more in a direct way: an intelligent being that deliberately made the word from the stones.

THE MODEL

The diagram below represents the above methods and their relations:

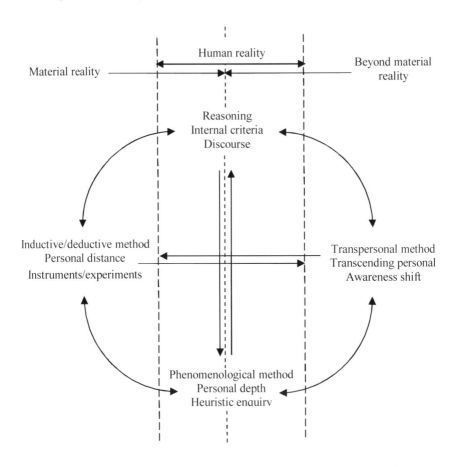

Approach:	Method:	Objectivity:	Expansion
Common sense	Phenomenology	Personal depth	Heuristic enquiry
Scientific	Induct./deduct.	Distancing	Instruments/experiments
Spiritual	Transpersonal	Transcending personal	Awareness shift
Philosophical	Reasoning	Internal criteria	Discourse

• The first column refers to the approach with which these methods are associated.

• The names of the methods are given in the second column.

• In order to reach a certain level of a universal validity, each of these methods needs a degree of objectivity. The truth itself cannot be a guide in this case (if we knew the truth, the whole process would be unnecessary). Hence, the third column is best qualified as commitment to objectivity that can be facilitated by the above procedures. Of course, absolute objectivity cannot be achieved, so *striving* for objectivity is what matters.

• Besides striving for objectivity (that leads to improving the existing knowledge) it is also important to expand, to face the unknown and try to incorporate it. The fourth column indicates the ways such expansion can be achieved. In the first case, heuristic or intrapersonal enquiry is suggested (already used in qualitative research, for example)[1]. It leads to developing non-algorithmic, tacit understanding and requires a willingness to get personally involved with the subject of enquiry. Transforming the perception of reality (object manipulation) through using instruments and conducting experiments is already well practised in science. Manipulating experience (subject manipulation) through shifts of awareness is a recognised path of enhancing transpersonal experiences. The interpersonal means (dialogue, discourse) has been used since Plato, but was significantly refined in the 20th century (through the work of Buber, Bohm, Bakhtin, Gadamer and others), and can too contribute to expansion.

The following allegorical example may help in recognising the unique qualities of each of these methods, and how they can be combined. Let us imagine that four individuals come across a river, and each of them has a preference for one of these methods. The first person may attempt to experience the river directly. S/he may taste the water or even swim in it (immerse shimself in it). Phenomenological reduction could assist in determining the extent to which such an experience can have a universal value. The second person, in contrast, may stand on the bank and use, for instance, geometry to measure the width of the river, or bring some instruments to determine its chemical composition. The third person may sit by the river and try to merge with it on a non-material level, seeking the meaning of the river beyond shis immediate experience. The fourth person, using reason, may try to conceptualise the river, probably by pacing up and down its banks and possibly by entering into dialogue with others (in an attempt to see how their experiences can make rational sense). Now, we could imagine that one person can do all of the above. This, however, is not necessary, as long as those four do their work with integrity and are open-minded and willing to put their findings together. On first sight, trying to synthesise a chemical analysis of water with a Siddhartha-like experience of the river, may seem odd, but it is not impossible. The rest of this book is an attempt to interpret reality by doing just that.

---

[1] Heuristic enquiry asks: 'What is *my* experience of this phenomenon and the essential experience of others who also experience this phenomenon intensely?' (Patton, 1990, p.71).

THE MEANING

THE ORIGIN OF THE PHYSICAL WORLD

THE EXISTING VIEWS

Religious - the origin of the world in most religious texts is described in essentially teleological terms, which means that this subject is intertwined with the issue of meaning or purpose, and usually implies the involvement of an agency. Such views are possibly based on genuine spiritual insights, but they are interpreted within historically and culturally specific constructs. So, it is not surprising that religious explanations often appear to be in conflict with facts and reasoning. To bring just one example, in *Genesis,* it is claimed that the Sun was created after the planet Earth, contrary to the accepted fact that stars must have appeared before planets. Nor does the image of an anthropomorphosised creator and his actions seems to be helpful. Of course, these descriptions can be taken as merely metaphorical expressions, but it is not clear what these metaphors stand for, beyond acknowledging the necessity of an agency.

Philosophical - philosophy seems at a loss regarding the question of the beginning. Aristotle and other Greek philosophers believed that the universe is infinite and therefore does not have a beginning, it has existed and it will exist forever, but this standpoint has been heavily criticised from both rational and empirical perspectives[1]. Philosopher Kant called the question of origin an antinome because apparently both possibilities, that the universe has the beginning and that it does not, seem to contradict reason (this is true, however, only under certain assumptions, such as that time continues back for ever in each case).

Materialistic - science has avoided the incongruences present in religious interpretations, but some fundamental questions, such as how and why the universe came into existence and why it has certain properties, may not been within the reach of its method. Starting from an *a priori* assumption that the whole of reality can be reduced to its physical aspect (which is required in order to fit the materialistic framework) may lead to an impossible situation. It is comparable to a chick inside an egg that tries to find out how the egg

---

[1] Not all these criticisms have been justified, though. For instance, philosopher Heinrich Olbers' objection that an infinite static universe would have so many stars that the sky should be bright at night as if it was daylight, does not hold water: the light of far stars would be in the invisible infra-red spectrum. This example is worth mentioning because it highlights the need for philosophy to pay attention to science.

was created, ignoring the possibility that anything outside the egg may exist. The commonly accepted interpretation in scientific circles at the moment, that everything came from nothing, in no time and for no reason, and yet in a very orderly and precise manner, seems as absurd as the claim that an all powerful anthropomorphic being created the universe in six equal time periods[1]. The Big Bang and quantum singularity (a single point of infinite compression from which the Big Bang started) do not dispose of the questions of how and why the universe was born - only of science as it is, because the laws of physics break down near a singularity. And, closing the case just because of methodological limitations cannot be justified. Some scientists try to get away with the answer that nothing could have existed before and caused the Big Bang because time itself started with it. Even if time, as presently conceptualised, had not existed (the idea first expressed by theologian St. Augustine) this 'solution' is not satisfactory. Imagine that you dream two people discussing how the dream came to existence. One may claim that because the 'dream-time' started with the dream, nothing could exist before the dream and therefore cause the dream. But this, of course, would be mistaken. The starting premise only implies that dream-time is different from awake time. By the same token, it can be postulated, for example, that the universe is contained in reality with a different time (e.g. non-entropic one) or more radically, that in reality without matter, movement may not be bound to the concept of time at all. In other words, movement may exist without time - recognised as such in relation to other events, rather than to an abstract notion of time. There is also another problem. It is probably true that if one starts from a mathematical description of the universe as it is and goes backwards, everything *can* lead to a point from which the process began. However, that the universe can be traced in such a manner does not necessarily mean that the events unravelled forward in the same way. For instance, a glass can be mathematically traced back to the chemical components of the material and the way they combine, without taking into account that, in order to produce a glass from these components, a glass maker is necessary.

Neither of the above viewpoints seem to offer a fully satisfactory interpretation. This is probably the case because they stick to ideological frameworks that are inherently limited. Before considering an alternative though, certain features of the physical world need to be examined first.

---

[1] The advocates of both views can claim that they seem absurd only to outsiders because they lack a full understanding. This would mean though, that one has to accept a certain framework first, to become a believer (in materialism or a monotheistic religion). But, why would anybody wish to do so, if these frameworks do not look credible in the first place?

SOME CHARACTERISTICS OF THE PHYSICAL WORLD

The issue of the origin of the physical world is important, because it can cast the light on the question of whether it is purposeful. A purposefulness would imply that sentience is not only necessary to investigate reality, but is also its essential ingredient. On the other hand, if the universe is the result of random meaningless events, sentience may be only an accidental by-product. Examining some characteristics of the physical world can help in determining the likelihood of the above possibilities.

One striking feature of the universe relevant to this question is its orderliness, conformity to formula and rational laws perfectly suited for life. It is often (somewhat inaccurately) referred to as the *Anthropic principle*. The universe could have been chaotic, but it is not – it is very orderly. The Big Bang theory does not predict that all its properties have to be so finely tuned. There are infinite possibilities of bad balance that were far more likely to emerge if it was only down to chance. Any of them could have produced a universe that was incapable of generating stable stars, planets and life. Some examples will be highlighted to bring home how remarkable this is.

The Big Bang

To have a universe that will sustain galaxies, stars, planets and life, the conditions at the beginning must be right within very narrow ranges. The universe had to start with the right density, amount of inhomogeneity of radiation, and the initial rate of expansion.

Apparently, there was a slight excess of matter over antimatter (baryons over anti-baryons, electrons over positrons, etc.) at the initial stages of the universe. If this excess had been smaller, there would have not been enough matter for galaxies and stars to be formed. If it had been greater, there would have been too much radiation for planets to emerge.

The initial inhomogeneity ('lumpiness') in the distribution of radiation was also necessary for the appearance of stars and galaxies. However, too much inhomogeneity would have led to black holes being created before stars.

If the original velocity of expansion had been one millionth greater, the heavier elements and stars would never have come into existence; if it had been one million millionth smaller, the universe would have collapsed before it was cool enough for the elements to form.

The present theories do not imply that this set of conditions had to exist. There are many other possible combinations that would not support stars, planets and life.

Subatomic particles

Each particle has a few defining properties which determine its behaviour. These properties are always and everywhere the same. For example, all electrons have a charge of –1 and a spin of ½; all positrons have identical properties to electrons, but a charge of +1; all protons have also the same charge and spin, but a much greater mass. There are a countless number of particles with these characteristics, but no known particles with intermediate features between the two kinds. Moreover, their features seem to be *mutually* tuned. For example, despite their huge difference in mass, for a reason unknown to science, the electrical charges of electrons and protons match precisely. If they did not, all material configurations would be unstable and the universe would consist of nothing more than radiation and a relatively uniform mixture of gases. This can hardly be just an accident. The celebrated scientist Hawking writes:

> The remarkable fact is that the values of these numbers seem to have been very finely adjusted to make possible the development of life. For example, if the electric charge of the electron had been only slightly different, stars either would have been unable to burn hydrogen and helium, or else they would not have exploded... One can take this either as evidence of a divine purpose in Creation and the choice of the laws of science or as support for the strong anthropic principle[1]. (1988, p.138-139)

Four forces

Present day science claims that the four forces (gravity, electromagnetism, strong and weak nuclear forces) govern all events in the physical universe. These too are, for inexplicable reasons, finely tuned. If any of them was slightly different, the universe (and, therefore, life) could not exist.

If gravity was just a little bit weaker, galaxies would fly apart and stars would burn out prematurely. There would not be enough gravity to pull the debris from dead stars into new interstellar dust clouds. The formation of new suns and planets would be impossible. On the other hand, if gravity had started out even a fraction stronger, then the rate of collisions between stars would have been so great that any typical solar system, such as this one, would not have survived long enough to produce stable planets and life.

If the exertion of electromagnetic force altered in any way, chemistry would not exist, which again means no stars and planets, and no physical life.

The same applies to the strong force that holds the core of atoms together. If it was slightly weaker, the particles would not be able to form the nucleus

---

[1] The strong anthropic principle implies in this case the multiple universes hypothesis, which will be discussed later on.

of an atom. If it was a little stronger, protons would coalesce without the necessity of neutrons being around. The single proton that forms the nucleus of hydrogen, would be unstable. So, hydrogen, one of the basic building blocks of the universe, would not exist. Moreover, in the first case the stars would not be able to shine, and in the second they would inflate and explode before there was any chance to form planets and life on them.

If the weak nuclear force (responsible for various forms of radioactive decay) had slightly different properties the stars could not burn and the elements necessary for life, such as carbon, oxygen and nitrogen, could not be formed inside them.

This is not all. If these four forces were not *mutually* aligned in the way they are, the universe also could not exist. Any change in the relationship between these forces would result in the complete impossibility of material reality.

Stellar objects

Supernovae, or stellar explosions, are important for life. All the necessary elements (carbon, nitrogen, oxygen, iron, etc.) are manufactured in the interior of the stars. If these elements are to accumulate in planets such as the Earth, they must be released from the stellar interiors and disperse throughout the cosmos. This is one of the results of supernova explosions (moreover, the shock waves that they generate are probably important in initiating the condensation of interstellar gas and dust into planetary systems). However, supernovae are also highly destructive. If they were too close to a planetary system, their radiation would obliterate any life. So, supernovae must occur at a very precise rate, and the average distance between them and between all stars must be within a relatively narrow range. The distance between stars in this galaxy is about 30 million miles. If this distance was smaller, planetary orbits would be destabilised. If it was greater, the debris thrown out by a supernova would be so diffusely distributed that planetary systems (like this one) would never be formed. Interestingly, as a great number of stellar objects have been created, the universe appears to be speeding up (the present science cannot explain why), which minimises the destructive effects of supernovae.

The same precision is also apparent with regard to the ratio of longevity between galaxies and stars. Galaxies last several times longer than the lifetime of an average star, which allows the atoms scattered by an earlier generation of supernovae within a galaxy to be gathered into second-generation solar systems.

Complex structures

Not only are the properties of the universe precisely ordered to allow the formation of stellar bodies, but they are also synchronised to allow the formation of complex structures, such as molecules (which, of course, must come later). If this was not the case, the creation of the chemical compounds instrumental for life and planetary systems capable of sustaining life would be impossible. Here are some examples:

Chemistry is the process of building up different molecular structures that need to be relatively stable to interact and to form new structures. This could not have happened if some nuclear constants such as the fine structure constant (α) and the electron-to-proton mass ratio (β) were slightly different. If these constants had a higher value, the long chains of molecules such as DNA, could not be formed; if they had a lower value, atoms would not be stable.

Other constants are also crucial: the fact that protons and neutrons have almost, but not quite the same mass, also turns out to be essential. If this value was much different, protons would decay before they could form stable nuclei. A neutron is heavier than a proton by 0.14%, but this small difference is important because it exceeds the total mass of an electron. If it had not, electrons would combine with protons to form neutrons, leaving no hydrogen. Moreover, if the neutron did not outweigh the proton in the nucleus, the active lifetime of the sun and similar stars would be reduced to a few hundred years, not enough for the formation of planets and life. Similarly, that electrons weigh so much less than protons or neutrons is crucial for the existence of chemicals essential for life. Otherwise, molecules like DNA could not maintain their precise and distinctive structures (the electron mass determines the overall size of atoms, and the spacing between the atoms in a molecule).

If the nuclear constant force increased by only 0.3%, it would bind two neutrons; an increase of 3.4% would bind two protons, in which case all the hydrogen would have burned to helium in the early stages of the Big Bang, and so no hydrogen compounds or stable stars could have been formed. On the other hand, a decrease of 9% would unbind protons and neutrons, which would prevent the formation of elements heavier than hydrogen. The consequence of either variation would be that larger elements, including carbon (the basis for organic life), could not exist. A small increase in electromagnetic force would have the same effect.

There is exactly the right amount of heavy subatomic particles (baryons) in the universe to allow the formation of planets. If this amount was marginally greater, the higher density of stars would substantially increase the probability of interstellar encounters that would affect the stability of planetary orbits and by doing so destroy any possible life.

The creation of complex atoms and molecules was also only possible because the properties of the basic elements were well synchronised, and there is no known reason why it should be so. The first nuclei to be formed were those of hydrogen and subsequently helium, but they are too inert to create more complex atomic structures. Carbon served as a catalyst enabling the formation of heavier elements. This required large amounts of carbon in the first place. If two helium nuclei react, they can produce a nucleus of beryllium, a highly unstable isotope that almost immediately disintegrates into helium. To produce carbon, beryllium needs to enter into reaction with helium, which is only possible because the combined energy of the beryllium and helium nuclei is slightly smaller than the energy of carbon - the product of that reaction. However, if so produced carbon reacted with helium, it would be reduced to oxygen. This does not happen because their combined energy is slightly higher then that of oxygen, so it is not a 'resonance reaction'. Here again is a most improbable fine-tuning of energy levels for four entirely different elements, but without it, more complex structures (including planets, and life forms) could not emerge.

Symmetries

The very existence of consistent and rational physical laws (that follow certain mathematical rules) is not something that should be taken for granted and begs a question. But this is not all. Precision and regularity does not apply only to physical laws. Physicist Murray Gell-Mann discovered that when the properties of sub-atomic particles like protons and neutrons are plotted on graphs, they take the form of hexagons and triangles, with the known particles sitting at various points within them. Gell-Mann predicted other sub-atomic particles that science had yet to discover, on the basis of gaps in these patterns. He also predicted that particles in fact consist of 'sub-sub-atomic' particles (now known as quarks). All his predictions proved correct. Similar patterns, generally know as 'symmetries', have since turned up often in successive theories of physics.

POSSIBLE EXPLANATIONS FOR THE 'ANTHROPIC PRINCIPLE'

The above examples show that the universe has some striking properties, discovered but not fully explained by science. At present, some scientists are hoping that GUT (Grand Unified Theory) may provide an answer to the above consistencies, but this is not likely. Even if found, the cosmological constant makes it doubtful that GUT will yield an explanation for the precision and elegance of all these laws and features. Moreover, as the systems theorist and writer Ervin Laszlo points out, '…the problem with GUTs is that they cannot satisfactorily explain the progressive structuration of matter in space and time' (1993, p.66).

There are several speculative attempts to account for at least some of these regularities, for example, various inflationary models (that propose rapid expansion of the universe in its initial stages). These models do not always fit well with some observable facts though, and also, as Hawking points out, 'the inflationary model does not tell us why the initial configuration was not such as to produce something very different from what we observe' (1988, p.148). Hawking proposed his own theory that disposes of singularities and boundaries and involves imaginary time, so the universe 'would neither be created nor destroyed. It would just BE' (*ibid.,* p.151)[1]. He concludes: 'So long as the universe had a beginning, we could suppose it had a creator. But if the universe is really completely self-contained, having no boundary or edge, it would have neither beginning nor end: it would simply be. What place, then, for a creator?' (*ibid.,* p.157). It is interesting that not only does such a universe in imaginary time make mathematical sense, but is also remarkably similar to descriptions of 'the other world' found in various spiritual traditions from Buddhism to Christianity (stripped, of course, from their anthropomorphised embellishments). The problem is, however, that the universe familiar to human beings and that operates within real time, still exists. Hawking admits: 'When one goes back to the real time in which we live, however, there will still appear to be singularities…' (*ibid.* p.154). The question is then, what is the factor that brings about the transition from the 'time-less' universe to the familiar one? In other words, why did the universe with singularities, the Big Bang, and the time that goes only in one direction come to existence? If the above view is correct, it seems that there still might be a place for a 'creator'.

---

[1] Some theologicians seized upon this hypothesis to conclude that the creator is also the sustainer. If the beginning has no special status, the creator creates/sustains the universe at all times. But this is unnecessary. The creator would need to sustain the universe only up to the point when time separates from space and starts behaving 'normally' (which is until the size of the universe reaches 10^{-33} cm).

Another attempt to explain the above regularities is the 'evolving universe' proposed by cosmologist Lee Smolin. It claims that new universes are created on the other side of black holes. Our universe has black holes and life, and therefore black holes are supposed to be able to produce new universes with the right properties. 'Bad' universes will not be able to form a black hole and therefore not 'reproduce' – similar to natural selection processes. However, this concept has some fatal flaws. There is not any indication that these universes exist. They may be in different dimensions, but there is no reason why they should be, if created by black holes in this universe. Secondly, it seems that the energy trapped in a black hole does not go anywhere, but in fact eventually gives birth to galaxies in *this* universe. And finally, the concept in fact does not provide an answer, only moves the question further down the line. The issue remains where the first ancestor universe came from to start this reproductive cycle.

There are, however, two other interpretations of the 'anthropic principle' that are both rationally consistent, although one operates within the materialistic framework, while the other does not.

The multiple universes theory (advocated, for example, by David Deutsch) can account for the precision and regularity of physical phenomena, and is consistent with materialism. The idea is that universes are constantly formed independently from each other. It is possible that a practically infinite number of universes come into existence. Most of them instantly collapse, but a few survive. If there is an infinite number of universes in becoming, some of them are bound to have the right properties however unlikely they are. The additional advantage of this interpretation is that it can explain some seemingly illogical experimental data in quantum physics. Although a speculation (multiple universes can never be empirically proven), this interpretation is a valid rational candidate to explain why this universe has the features that it has[1].

The teleological interpretation - considering all the above mentioned regularities, the other possibility, that the physical universe is intentional, needs to be take into account. This is called the teleological (not to be confused with theological) interpretation which implies purposefulness. The universe is as it is in order to enable the development of phenomena such as

---

[1] This is not to say that this hypothesis is without controversy. For its criticism see, for example, Davis, 1992, p.215-221, and more recently *ibid.*, 2007, 295-304, where the author evaluate the above two and some other possibilities. Those that Davis himself favours are not included here because of their bizarre and paradox prone requirements (e.g. backwards causation or causal loops).

life and consciousness. Materialism has not yet come up with a convincing argument about why chemistry emerged from physics, why biology emerged from chemistry, and why the brain and the mind emerged from biology. A teleological view is that a particular type of physics emerged in order to enable the development of chemistry, a particular type of chemistry emerged in order to enable the development of biology, a particular type of biology emerged in order to enable the development of the brain, a particular type of the brain emerged in order to enable the development of the mind. Teleological interpretation (although as speculative as the 'multiple universe' one) is not irrational, so it should not be discarded outright. The materialistic perspective rejects this possibility for ideological reasons, not because it conflicts with reason or evidence. The statements below show that some contemporary theologians, philosophers and physicists have come to remarkably similar conclusions. The theologian Swinburne writes:

> That there should be material bodies is strange enough; but that they should all have such similar powers which they inevitably exercise, seems passing strange. It is strange enough that physical objects should have powers at all – why should they not just be, without being able to make a difference to the world? But that they should all, throughout infinite time and space, have some general powers identical to those of all other objects (and they all be made of components of very few fundamental kinds, each component of a given kind being identical in all characteristics with each other such component) and yet there be no cause of this at all seems incredible.' (1991, p.145)

This statement comes from philosophers Polanyi and Prosch:

> ...our modern science cannot properly be understood to tell us that the world is meaningless and pointless, that it is absurd. The supposition that it is absurd is a modern myth, created imaginatively from the clues produced by a profound misunderstanding of what science and knowledge are and what they require, a misunderstanding spawned by positivistic leftovers in our thinking and by allegiance to the false ideal of objectivity from which we have been unable to shake ourselves quite free. These are the stoppages in our ears that we must pull out if we are ever once more to experience the full range of meanings possible to man. (1975, p.181)

The physicist Paul Davies makes a comparable point:

> ...certain crucial structures, such as solar-type stars, depend for their characteristic features on wildly improbable numerical accidents that combine together fundamental constants from distinct branches of physics. And when one goes on to study cosmology – the overall structure and evolution of the universe – incredulity mounts. Recent discoveries about the primeval cosmos oblige us to accept that the expanding universe has been set up in its motion with a cooperation of astonishing precision.' (1982, foreword)

THE SYNTHESIS PERSPECTIVE

One implication of both possibilities, the purposefully created universe and multi-universes, is that there is 'supra-reality' containing the physical world (and possibly other worlds). Thus, it is proposed that physical reality is only one level, a sub-system of a larger framework (multiple universes must be created in some other reality that contains all of them[1]).

This view is supported by universal (in the sense that they appear in practically all cultures) spiritual experiences of a greater whole within which the material world is embedded. Although its glimpses may be fleeting and difficult to interpret, they seem to be in the root of all religions, even non-theistic ones. It is true that religion sometimes serves a purpose to alleviate fears and increase sense of control, but these factors cannot be a full explanation for the ubiquitous nature of this belief. A human need to reach beyond immediate sensory experience (that often finds its expression in fantasies, art or mythology, but is also related to genuine transpersonal insights) cannot be easily dismissed as a sort of psychological defence mechanism. There are other (even more conducive) ways to produce similar results, and yet they have not rendered beliefs in supra-reality redundant. By claiming that there is nothing beyond, that humans live in a meaningless self-sufficient bubble, materialism closes the window for satisfying this need. There is no reason to deny the possibility that at least some of these experiences are genuine and correspond to something real. This, of course, does not mean that their various interpretations are valid, but the core of these interpretations should not be undermined.

Some scientists have also come to the conclusion that reducing everything to the world of matter is inadequate, that reality stretches beyond the physical. It is implied for example, in Bohm's theory of 'implicate order' and earlier, in De Broglie's model. The latter proposed that reality is built in levels of size and organisation, each level containing its own causal and statistical laws. As already mentioned, some implications of Hawking's theory also hint in this direction.

---

[1] Nothingness is non-referential and cannot be an option (vacuum is not nothingness, it only lacks matter). Empty space, if such a thing exists, is also not an alternative because, as science teaches us, space was created in the Big Bang, so it could not have existed before. It is possible that cosmological constants and some laws of nature vary within physical world, thus creating may universes. However, in this case they would all still depend on the specific mathematical and theoretical model, so the problem would not be resolved, just moved on a different level. If this theory is to be taken as a serious candidate, it must be assumed that multi-universes are created in reality that does not dependend on the rules that operate within them.

So-called realistic sceptics, of course, might not be satisfied, because it is not possible to provide material evidence for this aspect of reality, which can only be extrapolated or experienced (in terms of transpersonal experiences). However, those who demand such evidence neglect the fact that solipsistic and historical sceptics can use the same argument against the existence of physical reality. Ultimately the existence of the material world cannot be proven either. It cannot be proven (to a solipsistic sceptic) that the world is not just a figment of one's imagination as a dream is, or (to a historical sceptic) that it existed a moment ago, and yet these are accepted as facts. Thus, material proof is here not considered decisive. However, there is indirect support for this notion. For instance, some findings in quantum physics suggests that 'the world of matter-energy appears to float, rather as a thin precipitate, on a deep sea of almost infinite energies' (Laszlo, 1993, p.87). This is not the same kind of energy that forms matter. The energies in question, also known as zero-point energies, although not 'real' undoubtedly exist and cannot be ignored. The following may be a case in point. Electromagnetic fields propagate in a vacuum, but there is not an obvious source for this field (the electron cannot be a field source). Nevertheless, the field in which the electron appears stores a large amount of energy. That energy must be, as it were, non-material (meaning without a mass) because otherwise it would have created a gravitational potential that would have collapsed all matter in the universe to a singularity shortly after the Big Bang. And yet, the universe is still expanding. In fact, the very existence of matter can be questioned. What appears as matter are in effect highly condensed (and relatively unstable) energy fields. Popper writes:

> Matter turns out to be highly packed energy, transformable into other forms of energy; and therefore something of the nature of a *process*, since it can be converted into other processes such as light and, of course, motion and heat... The universe now appears to be not a collection of things, but an interacting set of events or processes... [atoms have] a structure that can hardly be described as 'material', and certainly not as 'substantial': with the programme of explaining the structure of matter, physics had to transcend materialism. (Popper and Eccles, 1977, p.7)

This all indicates that if the methodological and ideological limitations of scientific and spiritual approaches are overcome, there is no insurmountable conflict between them. They both point at the possibility that reality is made of at least two levels or planes. The familiar one, consisting of a huge amount of very dense and relatively slow energy that appears as matter. It can be defined as an aspect of reality determined by the physical laws. In other words, physical reality and the laws that govern it can be considered a special case, a subset of a larger reality (as Newtonian physics is assumed to be a special case of Einsteinian physics, and valid within a limited range). The boundaries of physical reality are twofold: on one hand, singularities, allegedly in the centre of black holes where the laws of physics break down, so they can be taken as 'out of this word'; and on the other, the speed of light - anything faster than the speed of light would violate the General Theory of Relativity and therefore be again 'out of this world'. Considering that the material reality includes entities of maximum density and minimal movement (black holes) it is likely to be the lowest possible level. It is proposed that the other reality consists of faster, less dense but more refined energy, not bound by all the laws of physics applicable in the material world. Although this may be difficult to imagine, all the evidence suggests that energy is best conceived as the process itself, pure movement (without necessarily something that moves). In this case it is possible that there are movements with speed beyond that of light. A science and spiritual writer, David Ash, who advocates this view, writes:

> Modern physics may have established that particles cannot move faster than the speed of light, but this does not mean that movement is constrained to this speed. The speed of light is the upper limit of velocity if it is assumed that movement can only exist as the property of particles. However, this classical assumption of the atomic hypothesis is merely a reflection of outmoded materialism.' (1995, p.139)

The implication is that such energy does not operate within the space-time continuum (which is relative to the speed of light) and it can consist only of forms that do not have mass, so it can be called non-material reality[1]. Such reality has no stable ground state, no equilibrium condition, no space-time framework; hence, there is no beginning and there can be no end[2].

This is not to say that this realm can be interpreted in such a way to allow the breaking of the laws that operate *within* the physical world (as the Theory of Relativity would not have been valid if it had contradicted Newtonian physics within its range). Even fields and waves, as long as they are linked to physical objects and their interactions, have to be interpreted in compliance with the laws of physics. Nevertheless, on the level of sub-atomic particles (that can be conceived as waves too) some strange behaviour can already be detected: for example, if two photons that have been 'entangled' (meaning essentially that they spin in the same direction)

---

[1] Even in the material universe not everything has to have mass; fields do not have mass as well as light and other waves, and they may play an essential role in linking the two realms. However, electro-magnetic or gravitational fields are vector fields (having both, magnitude and direction) rather than standing scalar fields, so they really belong to the world of matter.

[2] Note that if the beginning is not required, the problem that the Big Bang theory faces in relation to the material world, namely what was before, is not an issue anymore.

are separated, and one of them changes the direction of the spin, the other will also change direction irrespective of their distance – and instantaneously, indicating that they are still somehow connected and that the space-time framework is already losing its grip.[1]

It is likely that these two realties are in constant interaction. After all, subatomic particles seem to appear from 'nowhere' and disappear all the time, but this interaction can be ignored in most of cases (except perhaps in the sub-atomic sphere and in complex wave generating systems such as the brain). Human beings normally perceive only the material world. Phenomenologically, the relation between reality as a whole and the material one can be compared to the relation between an awake state and a dream – regarding inclusiveness and non-presence. A dream state is situated within a larger framework of the awake state, but while in a dream, the dreamer is usually not aware of it (except in so-called lucid dreams). Of course, this parallel has its limits. A dream is typically subjective – meaning that dream events depend on the dreamer, while the material world is objective - other agents and objects exist independently from the observer. Nevertheless, it may not be completely off the mark to say that in this world all sentient beings share a collective dream.

The question may be asked why one should be concerned with reality beyond our immediate reality. In most situations, indeed, it does not need to be taken into account (as, for all practical purposes, Newtonian physics suffices and Relativity can be ignored). However, if non-material reality is in a causal relationship to the physical world - in other words, if the physical world is rooted in it, non-material reality is necessary for the existence of material one. Therefore, only a larger perspective that includes the notion of such reality can offer some hope of finding a rational explanation to some fundamental questions relevant to this world.

The real issue, however, is not the existence of this supra-reality. What separates the materialist perspective from the non-materialist one is that the former denies the role of an agency and purpose, while the latter accepts this possibility. Thus, what needs to be considered is whether the necessity of sentience makes sense and can be justified.

---

[1] This *does not* violate the General Theory of Relativity that claims that nothing can travel faster than the speed of light, because it is not an informational exchange – there is no cause and effect.

THE ONE

We do not only make constructs but also discover them, so it seems that reality itself is, to a degree, constructed. This begs an even more fundamental question than why the properties of the universe are finely tuned; namely, why there are laws at all, why the universe is orderly, rather than chaotic and disorderly. The principles of constructing reality (such as the laws of physics) could not emerge spontaneously unless there were certain pre-set conditions that severely limit all possible options. If one of the basic such laws, the second law of thermodynamics, is correct and universal (and there is no reason to believe that this is not the case) entropy or disorder constantly increases, which implies that the universe was at the beginning even more orderly then now. High entropy is completely random, a state of zero information. The universe, therefore, could not have started from a high-entropy state, or it would not have its present complex structure. It had to begin as a low-entropy, high information state (entropy and information are inversely proportional). This means that a great amount of potential information was condensed in an extremely small space. That would make the spontaneous formation of the laws of physics through the interplay of matter and forces as they go along, extremely unlikely. These configurations must have already been in-built (as a potential) at the beginning. The physicist and philosopher Edward Milne concludes:

> One cannot study cosmology without having a religious attitude to the universe. Cosmology assumes the rationality of the universe, but can give no reason for it short of a creator of the laws of nature being a rational creator. (in Hazen, 1997, p.31)

The orderliness of the universe renders the possibility that reality is purposeful and that some sort of sentience is involved conceivable. However, this by all means should not be interpreted as a definitive proof (such a proof would not be conducive any way, which will be elaborated shortly). It only shows that a belief in a meaningful reality is rational and at least as plausible as a belief in a meaningless one. Neither the teleological nor multiple universes explanations can be proven; nor is one less reasonable than the other. So, the answer to the question of whether the universe was purposefully built or not, remains in the realm of personal choice (it is significant that reasoning does not remove choice). True, if the high improbability of an accidental occurrence of the other events that enable human beings to contemplate these questions (the onset of organic life, the process of biological evolution and the appearance of consciousness) is added to the above, the teleological interpretation may seem more plausible – but the other one is not impossible.

There is, of course, the third standpoint of an agnostic, undecided (the one who is waiting for a proof). This position is, however, highly problematic and inconsistent. One inconsistency is between the belief and action. Although the person may claim to be undecided, shis actions, at least in some instances, have to be either congruent with a meaningless reality or a meaningful one (this is because either possibility eliminates some rational choices). So, even if s/he refuses to take a stand, s/he must act *as if* s/he believes that life is either meaningful or meaningless (it cannot be neither or both at the same time). Furthermore, the immediacy of the material world (within which meaning remains elusive) creates an asymmetry that in practice often reduces this position to an unacknowledged materialist one. And this is not all. Many propositions have their roots in and can be traced back to this fundamental question, and therefore cannot be justified unless one of the options is accepted. The bottom line is that neither of the above two positions can be definitely proven, so there is no point in waiting for a proof. A materialist and a non-materialist may be right or may be wrong; an agnostic cannot be right in any case.

Given that both explanations cannot be logically or empirically excluded, a modified version of *Pascal's wager* may be relevant here. Assuming that both options are rational and possible, it can be deduced that a person who errs in shis belief that reality is not purposeful loses more than a person who errs in the belief that reality is. By the same token, a person who is correct believing that reality is purposeful gains more than a person who is correct believing that it is not[1]. Thus, it is sensible to consider the option that reality is meaningful. If the other one is taken, nothing more needs to be said. It can be left to scientists to fill in any gaps that they can, and ascribe to chance or ignore those aspects of reality that are inaccessible to their method. This would, however, go against common sense. Humans have an inherent need to interpret their existence in a meaningful way, and although such a coherence may be an illusion, the need cannot be. Therefore, all plausible avenues that could meet this need should be explored. First though, a possible objection that purpose violates the criterion of cohesiveness needs to be addressed. If a cohesive interpretation can be provided without it, then purpose is superfluous. Yet, this does not seem to be the case. Both interpretations that offer a rationale for origin and orderliness of the universe involve an additional factor. Materialist interpretation relies on chance (and infinity that makes chance plausible), while a teleological interpretation

---

[1] These losses and gains do not refer to material or possible after-life losses and gains, but losses and gains related to the understanding and conceptualisation of human existence in a coherent way. The original Pascal's wager is criticised by Dawkins (2006, p.103), but his argument does not apply in this case.

implies purpose. Chance, however, has a lower level of explanatory power than purpose (in fact, chance has an explanatory power of next to nothing). So, all other things being equal, incorporating meaning is likely to provide a more cohesive interpretation than otherwise.

The purposeful universe has to be intentional, therefore it requires intent, and intent requires awareness (it does not make sense to consider intent without awareness). Both require *that* which is aware and intends. In other words, there must be a source of the intent and the awareness. Experience of any kind can hardly be of much help in contemplating such an entity. Throughout history people may have been able to intuit but, as most theologicians agree, not directly experience the existence of such a source, even in the context of transpersonal experiences that in the best case may be limited to 'emanations' or associated feelings of bliss or unity[1]. Thus, any conjectures in this respect can be only deduced.

If intent is instrumental for the birth of the universe, its source cannot be in material reality, so it must be in non-material reality. It is reasonable to suppose that the energy in non-material reality has the focal point. Movement is always relative to something, either a medium or a point (e.g. the movement of a car is relative to the road or to a starting point). Considering that non-material reality does not operate within the space-time framework (it is accepted that time and space started with the Big Bang), it can be concluded that energy must have at least a reference point[2]. In other words, because in that realm there is no medium (such as space), the pure movement, which is arguably the best description of energy, starts from and converges on one point. That point can be called the One. Even polytheistic religions, such as the Hindu and the Ancient Greek, are familiar with this concept. The One can be conceived as the indivisible, non-dimensional (meaning of no size, infinitely small) focusing point of non-material energy that, in turn, makes 'the body' of the One. The One and the associated energy are, therefore, two aspects of the same. Thus, the One is not just another object that can be discovered, found or proved. As already recognised in many spiritual traditions, the One is beyond words and images (a point cannot be defined, and even a drawn point is a crude approximation consisting of an infinite number of points).

---

[1] This is not to say that such experiences are irrelevant. Einstein himself acknowledged their value. He writes that 'scientist's religious feelings take the form of rapturous amazement at the harmony of natural law, which reveals an intelligence of such superiority that, compared with it, all the systematic thinking and acting of human beings is an utterly insignificant reflection' (1949, p.29).

[2] Space too depends on a point. As represented in a coordinate system, it requires three dimensions that cross at one point (0, 0, 0).

So, what would be the necessary characteristics of the One? The One resembles the notion of God. The concept of God can be, indeed, seen as the imaginative expression of an intuition about the existence of the One[1]. Traditionally (especially in Christianity) the following properties are put forward: omnipresence (all present), omnipotence (all powerful) and omniscience (all knowing). However, this seems to contradict common sense and in some instances even logic[2]. Something else is necessary though: that the One is and that the One does - in other words, existence and agency. This is the basis for the two properties already mentioned: awareness and intent.

Awareness generally can be considered an ability to focus possibilities or actualise potentials (as, for example, in the case of the collapse of the quantum wave function). Considering that in this instance there is no distinction between the subject and the object (awareness amounts to self-awareness), the minimum requirement is that the focused energy is aware of its own being, its own existence. Thus, it can be postulated that awareness is an intrinsic property of focused energy or energy 'loops', as gravitational force is, for example, an intrinsic property of matter (in the physical world energy can only be transformed from one form to another, it does not have the focus or source, hence no awareness). Awareness does not presuppose and cannot be equated with the mind and its materials (conceptual knowledge, thoughts, language, memory, imagination etc.). These are all normally indirect constructs that are not necessary (for example, it is possible to be aware of a change, without having to conceptualise what is changing). Metaphorically speaking, awareness can be compared to the light from a movie projector, that enables the materials projected (a movie) to be distinguished or actualised, but it cannot be identified with them.

Intent is another essential property. It also does not require the mind and thinking in human terms. The universe that operates on the basis of finely tuned and consistent laws and principles does not necessitate theoretical knowledge, it only necessitates an intent. To make an analogy, when a

---

[1] The term God is avoided because it is too firmly imbedded in existing religious interpretations, which has undesirable implications: it is difficult to avoid anthropomorphisation, and certain attributes that are commonly ascribed to God can hardly be justified (such as that God is the judge of human acts, open to direct communication, and mostly concerned with human affairs).

[2] Here are some examples: omniscience implies knowing the future, including God's own future interventions; but this would mean that God cannot change his mind and choose to act differently, which means that he is not omnipotent. Omniscience also does not go well with the notion of free will, important in all monotheistic religions, while omnipotence cannot be easily reconciled with the suffering of innocent. Omnipresence too conflicts with the traditional view that God is outside time.

person moves shis arm, a set of relatively regular principles and alignments are involved that can be rationally discerned. However, s/he does not need to know them in order to move shis arm, s/he only needs the intent to do so (providing that the muscles, nerves, brain and bones are functional, which is in this case beside the point). Similarly, directing the flow of water does not require knowing and positioning every water molecule, but only setting the boundaries to its flow. As Polanyi and Prosch put it, '... some sort of intelligible directional tendencies may be operative in the world without our having to suppose that they *determine* all things' (1975, p.162). This global directional tendency can be called the Intent[1]. The Intent does two things: it provides direction by setting the boundaries and also encourages energy to move in that direction. To make a parallel with the above mentioned example, this is similar to what a river-bed and gravitational force do for water. The Intent sets, to use Polanyi's term, the 'boundary conditions' that are conducive to the purpose, and like a funnel, forces energy in a certain direction (in fact, a more accurate analogy would be a reversed funnel that starts from a very narrow point and then gradually expands). Therefore, the One does not need to create the individual laws of physics and material objects (galaxies, stars, planets etc.). It is sufficient to intend the particular behaviour of energy, and the physical laws are spontaneously created and tuned to accommodate the Intent[2]. Because the energy can be considered 'the body' or 'the mind' of the One (there is no separation between the subject and the object) it is enough to intend and that intent becomes realisation - intention is creation. Like when a person chooses to imagine something, it immediately appears in shis mind and becomes a mental event. Many spiritual traditions are familiar with the notion of the Intent. What is common to Brahman in the Upanishads, Rita in the Rig Veda or the Chinese concept of Tao is the notion of a dynamic force that permeates reality.

---

[1] Capitalisation is used to distinguish this term from other possible intents.

[2] This means that miracles, if they are defined as violations of the laws of nature by an intervention of a supernatural being, are out of question. If the natural laws are not created individually, they cannot be broken individually. However, some so-called miracles (e.g. certain forms of healing), may not violate natural laws, but only limited interpretations of these laws.

THE TWO

Just saying that there is a purpose is not enough. Any teleological explanation would be incomplete if a possible purpose itself is not examined. A reasonable starting point in this case is to consider what the One could possibly seek. To address this issue adequately, two fundamental principles, *static* and *dynamic*, need to be brought to attention first. States and processes, rather than matter, seem to be fundamental properties of reality, and they are manifestations of these two underlying principles. They are widely recognised in spirituality (e.g. yin and yang in the East) and permeate every aspect of reality. In human life, for example, static and dynamic principles are manifested as tendencies towards security and freedom (but apparently even subatomic particles, such as electrons, get agitated, speed up, when they are confined to a small region of space). Not any movement, though, represents the dynamic principle. A degree of indeterminacy or change must be involved. Predetermined, regular movements are essentially static. For instance, if the rotation of a planet around a star is observed from a four dimensional perspective (including time), it will look like a relatively stable spiral (although even this movement is to some extent chaotic and not fully predictable). From this perspective, it could be said that Newtonian physics is essentially static, while modern physics takes into account the dynamic principle.

The static and dynamic principles are intrinsic characteristics of non-material energy and must be in a relative balance. This necessity for balance indicates that there are limitations to the One. The One is not born and cannot die (energy did not at one point *become* focused, but simply is). However, if the static principle prevails, it could lead to stagnation and uniform movement only, which would be an equivalent of death. On the other hand, if the changes involved are completely chaotic, the dynamic principle could take over, which could lead to disintegration (resembling, in human terms, madness). But everything the One *does* becomes straight away *is*, so the static principle is likely to dominate[1] (the nearest phenomenological parallel in human life would be the sense of boredom). One way out of it could be to act in an unpredictable manner, but that would lead to chaos and the prevalence of the dynamic principle. So, in order to strengthen the dynamic principle in a non-chaotic way, something that is *not* the One is needed. A non-chaotic, and yet not completely predictable entity that will be able to enter into an interaction with the One. Therefore, another agency is necessary, something that can be pro-active not only reactive, something that

---

[1] If everything one wants immediately became reality, it would eventually lead to a cessation of wanting.

has freedom (otherwise *doing* turns into *being*). Something that will develop its own independent awareness and intent and will eventually grow to be an active counterpart to the One. This could establish a permanent balance between the dynamic and static principle. In other words, *the Other* needs to become. The One is one, and the only thing that the One may seek is the Other. Thus, the purpose of life can be formulated as the development of the Other that will enable an infinite interplay with the One. From this perspective, humanity presents one form, at one stage, in this process. This purpose was already recognised at the dawn of spiritual development. One of the oldest Hindu myths (Hinduism being one of the oldest religions) is that the world was created because the original being was lonely. The ancient Egyptian religion makes a similar point.

How infinitely creative this solution is can only be grasped if it is considered that the 'otherness' does not exist at all to start off. The question may be asked, though, why the One simply does not split into two. However, in such a case every part would be fully aware of the other (like looking at a mirror), and because these parts could only interact with each other, the dynamic principle would not be strengthened[1]. The Other, the counterpart, must start from the state of minimal awareness and intent.

Before moving on, it may be worthwhile to briefly consider alternative propositions regarding the meaning. The most popular one, even nowadays, is the attainment of unity with God in one form or another. But this proposition neglects that such a solution still refers to the 'meaning in life' rather than the 'meaning of life'. In other words, even if it is accepted that such unity may provide the meaning in the lives of human beings, why would God want unity with vastly inferior creatures? And even if this question is somehow bypassed, would such a state be desirable at all? Not even Dante managed to make heaven appealing. A non-theistic equivalent, nirvana, may be free from pains, but it seems unbearably dull. It is unlikely that the end of everything is some homogeneous state. However, this notion does not miss the target completely. It may reflect the longing for lost unity, but it may also be based on a recognition that transcending the separation between individuals is necessary before The Other is fully formed.

Another proposition is linked to the idea of evolution (which existed well before Darwin). Its relatively recent proponent was a maverick theologician Teilhard de Chardin, but perhaps the best known case is the philosopher Hegel's evolution of the absolute spirit. He lucidly married the evolutionary

---

[1] For the same reason, polytheism of any kind is not an option, for without a difference that can come only from different experiences or processes, it would be reduced to cloning the same.

process with dialectics (popularised since as 'thesis – antithesis – synthesis', although Hegel himself rarely used these terms). Hegel's philosophy is too complex to be analysed here, a general comment will have to suffice. The final goal of evolution, according to Hegel, is that *Geist* (Mind or Spirit) understands itself, in other words, a full self-actualisation. Hegel has been often seen (by Popper and others) as overly optimistic, but the real problem is that this view is ultimately pessimistic. Even if the absolute spirit (or the collective mind) cognises itself, what then? Lacking an answer to this question renders this possibility, in fact, meaningless. However, as in the first case, it seems that the above proposition also contains something important. Where else could this evolutionary process head if not towards creating a god? But a lonely god indeed.

To summarise, although both above possibilities make some significant points, they are incomplete. While in the first case the relation is overemphasised (at the expense of the evolutionary process), in the second the relation is neglected. Perhaps combining them, the synthesis between being and doing, would be closer to the mark.

To achieve the purpose, the development of *independent* awareness and intent is needed. This requires alienating, separating some energy so that it can grow on its own. A direct influence would be counterproductive. If the One interfered directly, such a development would be reduced to mere conditioning, which would constrain awareness and intent beyond the pale. Aligning with the purpose must be an act of free choice, rather than the result of the fear of punishment or the expectation of a reward. Thus, the One must stay mostly hidden, providing only a possibility (symbolised, for example, by the tree of knowledge in the biblical tradition). For this reason the One cannot even be conclusively proven - that would remove the choice, which would not be conducive to the Intent. Even if the meaning of life is accepted, separateness and uncertainty are still necessary in order to recognise the ontological independence of the One (and oneself). Otherwise the whole process could amount to a blind and lazy following. The importance of separation, God's withdrawal, was already hinted at in some spiritual traditions such as the Cabalist doctrine of tsimtsum.

However, separation cannot be enough. To prevent the prevalence of the dynamic principle, to prevent freedom from becoming a chaos, the separated energy must be restricted and protected until it matures. This 'slowing down' enables a gradual gaining of self-control. Such a restriction cannot come directly from the One though, so it must be embodied in the environmental conditions. This is the purpose of the material world: to enable the separation of some energy from the One and to provide the stage for the gradual development of awareness and intent independent from the One. As poet

John Keats eloquently put it, 'call the world if you please "the vale of soul-making" then you will find out the use of the world... How then are these sparks which are God to have identity given them – so as ever to possess a bliss peculiar to each ones individual existence? How, but by the medium of a world like this?' (from the letter to George and Georgiana Keats, 14th of February – 3rd of May, 1819).

So, in order to eventually strengthen the dynamic principle, the static principle is, in fact, first maximised by condensing and slowing down some energy to the point of nearly absolute stillness. This is the parent Black Hole that spontaneously bursts out into the physical universe (the Big Bang) following the flow determined by the Intent[1]. The two principles (static and dynamic) can be imagined like the sides of a seesaw. Instead of adding weight to the 'lighter' side (by increasing uncertainty and chaos), the other side is pushed down to the lowest point, so that the seesaw bounces back into a balanced position. This is why the material world, as we know it, is as it is. It is best perceived as a sheet or plane (known in physics as the M-brane) that separates some non-material energy from the rest. To use an analogy, matter is like a balloon, while the air in the balloon is energy separated from the rest (the air outside the balloon). The basic constructs of the world (its coordinates) on which all the others rely, are time and space. Time does not really exist, it is derived from the relation between the dynamic and static principle (as in the formula $t = v/l$)[2]. Nevertheless, time and space construct reality, and by doing so protect and at the same time limit freedom, that would have otherwise been an unbearable burden. The best boundaries are infinite boundaries.

The above indicates that not only the physical universe but also life is intended. The next chapter will examine this possibility.

---

[1] The tendency of energy trapped in matter to return to its 'natural' (non-material) state is expressed as an attempt to escape gravitational force (that is a property of matter). The weaker the gravitational force is (with distance), the stronger this tendency is, which is maybe why the universe expands faster and faster.

[2] No-time is often confused with ever lasting present, but the present is still a concept of time, not no-time. In fact, a process can exist without time altogether. However, this is difficult to imagine. The best way to do so is to think that such processes happen in an imaginary time (as proposed by Hawking).

THE ORIGIN OF LIFE

THE EXISTING INTERPRETATIONS

Creationism (reinvented recently as 'Intelligent design') that adheres to the Biblical account of the origin of life is still seen in some places as an alternative to the materialist view, so it is worth briefly addressing this position. Creationists are very good at criticising the opposite standpoint, but not in providing a coherent support for their own. Genesis is clear that the creation of life is a deliberate act, but the way it is presented has many problems. Without getting into details, a general one is the claim that an agency assembled various species as discrete units. This does not seem plausible. All paleontological and micro-biological evidence indicates that life, in all its diversity, originated from very simple forms and evolved through a long period of time. Contrary to the creationist account, it is evident that more complex organisms have derived from simpler ones, and that there are big time gaps between the appearance of various species. This is not to say that life is an accident, as materialists would like to believe. The following is an attempt to show that such a claim is also problematic.

Materialism - from the materialistic perspective, the origin of life is explained as a chance event that occurred through the interplay of physical forces and chemical reactions. The idea that life came about accidentally from inanimate matter should not be taken for granted, though[1]. Contrary to popular belief, this account is not proven, empirically or rationally. It has never been demonstrated in a laboratory or anywhere else that a complex structure such as a living cell could arise spontaneously (or through human intervention) from inorganic stuff. Honest scientists are ready to admit this:

> We have not yet come up with a convincing mechanism for abiogenesis…
> And we have come nowhere near creating life in the laboratory. (Silver, 1998, p.339)

In the 1950s Stanley Miller recreated the conditions believed to exist on prebiotic Earth (a mixture of methane, ammonia, hydrogen and water was exposed to heat and occasional spark-discharges). In a relatively short time

---

[1] Silver, a biochemist himself, comments: 'One can believe that a complex system like the living cell is capable of manufacturing large, complex molecules from small, simple precursors, but the original manufacturing mechanism has to come from somewhere' (1998, p.340).

Miller found some amino-acids in the apparatus (amino-acids are the building blocks of proteins that are in turn the basis of organic life). Recent findings suggest, though, that life arose in an environment far less hospitable than Miller's glass apparatus. Moreover, many experiments since have not gone much further. Apparently, some researchers managed to create a synthetic organic molecule that could replicate itself, but this should not be confused with procreation. They only replicate in highly artificial, unnatural conditions, and they reproduce only exact replicas. Yet, without mutations the molecules could not evolve.

Not only has materialism failed to produce a convincing support for its position, but it is also internally inconsistent. Biogenesis is an accepted doctrine in biology, which states that living organisms are produced only by other living organisms, and that the parent organism's offspring are always of the same kind. Abiogenesis (the notion that life can appear from non-life) is only assumed for the beginning of life, when apparently the first living organism was accidentally generated from inanimate matter. This inconsistency is accepted not because the available data is in its favour, but because it fits current ideology. In his book *The Intelligent Universe* mathematician and astronomer Fred Hoyle asks:

> '…there is not a shred of objective evidence to support the hypothesis that life began in an organic soup here on the Earth. Indeed, Francis Crick, who shared a Nobel prize for the discovery of the structure of DNA, is one biophysicist who finds this theory unconvincing. So, why do biologists indulge in unsubstantiated fantasies in order to deny what is so patently obvious, that the 200 000 amino acid chains, and hence life, did not appear by chance?' (1983, p.21)

Indeed, it has been calculated that accidental abiogenesis is extremely unlikely, even if millions of years were available (see, for example, Overman, 1997). According to palaeontologist Fondi, 'a spontaneous assemblage of molecules driven by chance cannot account for the emergence of complex organisms — even the oldest algae and bacteria are too complex to have resulted from chance processes in the observed time frames' (in Laszlo, 1993, p.100). In order to survive and reproduce, a one-cell organism, however simple, requires at least several components, RNA, (and/or DNA), some proteins and a cell membrane. Furthermore, they all need to function in a synchronous way. Let us consider how likely this is if left to chance.

THE NECESSARY CONDITIONS FOR THE CELL FORMATION

Molecular properties – a functional cell requires many polymers, large long-chain molecules, built from a number of simple molecules (monomers). These molecules can hardly form spontaneously for several reasons. The formation of polymers requires bifunctional monomers (i.e. those that can combine with two others), and can be stopped by a small fraction of unifunctional monomers (those that can combine with only one other, thus blocking one end of the growing chain). Prebiotic simulation experiments produce five times more unifunctional molecules than bifunctional ones. Furthermore, many polymers (such as proteins, DNA or RNA) come in two forms, 'left-handed' and 'right-handed'. The building blocks of polymers essential for life need to have the same 'handedness' – proteins consist of amino acids that are all 'left handed', while DNA and RNA contain sugars that are only 'right-handed'. Under the right conditions, an undirected environment that operates solely on the principles of physical chemistry can produce amino acids, but they are wrong for life. So created molecules are a blend of left and right hand forms, not the pure ones needed in living things. They could not form the specific shapes required for proteins, and DNA could not be stabilised in a helix and support life if just a small proportion of the wrong-handed kind was present. To produce the correct types of amino acids and sugars, life requires a certain type of proteins called enzymes. However, these complex molecules do not appear spontaneously, they can only be manufactured in a living cell. An equivalent of such a molecular machinery though, did not exist in the pre-life environment.

The cell components - even if all the right ingredients are present, there is still the problem of forming a functional cell components by random processes. Proteins and other structures necessary for life consist of many building blocks which must be instantly put together in a *certain order*. Out of a total number of possible protein structures (within an appropriate size range) only a tiny set have the correct properties from which a simple bacterium can be successfully built. The odds that they will be formed purely by chance is infinitely small. Let us consider the above mentioned enzymes. Just one is typically comprised of 300 amino acids. Even if it is assumed that a much smaller number of amino acids is needed to form a 'primitive' enzyme, the probability of the required order in a single functional protein molecule arising randomly is estimated at 10^{43} (this is a modest estimate, some go as far as 10^{195}). The simplest living cell must have at least several hundred enzymes and other proteins, which makes a chance arrangement of these molecules extremely unlikely. Silver writes that 'the probability of a crowd of small molecules forming the needed large molecules to start the long, complex path to a single cell seems to be almost zero' (1998, p.349).

The cell membrane - the other necessary component of a living cell is the cell membrane. A universal ingredient of all cell membranes is the phospholipid molecule. This molecule can spontaneously form vesicles in water ('bubbles' that resemble in shape the cell membrane), but no one has managed to reproduce this in the experiments that attempt to simulate conditions on the Earth when life began. Moreover, the cell membrane does not only maintain the physical unity of the cell, but also performs other vital functions (e.g. allowing energy exchange)[1]. This all requires a relatively complex structure even for the simplest imaginable functional cells that is highly unlikely to be a result of random chemical reactions.

Functioning of a cell - the above evaluates only the necessary parts, not a functional arrangement, i.e. one that works. Even if it is accepted that the components of a living cell were somehow formed accidentally, that would not be enough[2].

The simplest one-cell organism represents a level of complexity not found anywhere in the inanimate world including that created by humans (viruses, that are, roughly speaking, DNA coated in a protein, do not count, because they need other more complex cells to reproduce, so they could only appear or degenerate to this simplicity later in evolution).

All the components of a living cell need to be synchronised, to act in a union in order to maintain a cell. So, a cell cannot be built piecemeal, all the major constituents must have been created and assembled instantaneously for the cell to function. Without elaborate mechanisms that enable energy intake, chemical distribution, processing of proteins, and storing of genetic information to be passed on to the next generation, life could not exist.

So, the components on which these processes depend could not have evolved separately. Proteins cannot form without DNA, but neither can DNA form without proteins. Moreover, they could not exist independently for very long:

---

[1] Some of its properties seem to even anticipate complex life forms: '...the cell membrane is uniquely and ideally fit for its role of bounding the cell's contents and conferring on the cells of higher organisms the ability to move and adhere selectively to one another. These critical properties are also dependent on the size of the average cell being approximately what it is and on the viscosity of cytoplasm being close to what it is. The membrane is also fit, in that its selective impermeability to changed particles confers additional electrical properties, which form the basis of nerve conduction' (Denton, 1998, p.209).

[2] To quote Silver again, 'the basic problem facing anyone who is looking for the origin of life is to account for the formation of a complex, *very highly organized, self-sustaining* and *self-replicating* system out of a mixture of chemicals that, certainly in the early days of the soup, displayed none of these characteristics' (1998, p.340).

> The large and complex molecules essential to life – proteins with dozens of
> hundreds of amino acids, RNA and DNA formed with long chains of
> nucleotides – do not appear spontaneously, even in carefully devised
> environments with high concentrations of monomers. Indeed, these
> macromolecules appear to be quite unstable. Even when two monomers link
> up or polymerise, they often will just as quickly disintegrate or depolymerise
> under water-rich conditions. (Hazen, 1997, p.165)

Most nucleotides (essential cell components) degrade fast at the
temperatures that apparently existed on the early Earth. Polymers also
quickly break down in water (water absorbing chemicals or evaporating
water by high temperature would require either unrealistic conditions or
would lead to the destruction of the polymers necessary to form a cell). This
means that not only did they all need to be produced close to each other, but
also within a very short period of time. DNA (and/or RNA), some proteins
and cell membrane need to be formed at the right time and place and under
the right conditions. However, as Silver point out:

> It stretches even the credulity of a materialistic abiogenesis fanatic to believe
> that proteins and nucleotides persistently emerged simultaneously, and at the
> same point in space, from the primeval soup. We are in trouble enough
> without adding events of an astronomical improbability (1998, p.347).

Even if this was the case, many of the important biochemicals would, in fact,
destroy each other (i.e. sugars and amino acids mutually react). Living
organisms are well-structured to avoid this, but the 'primordial soup' would
not be. In other words, the cell is born out of co-ordinated complexity, not
out of chaotic complexity.

The above indicates that an accidental beginning of life is implausible. Even
a hard-line materialist, such as Crick, admits that 'the origin of life appears
to be almost a miracle, so many are the conditions which would have had to
be satisfied to get it going' (in Silver, 1998, p.349).

Some current hypotheses

The popular argument is that, given a very long period of time, life would
occur, even if the chance of its appearance is minuscule. However, 'it seems
that life appeared almost as soon as the planetary hydrosphere had cooled
sufficiently to support it. The time available is certainly short – nothing like
the supposed thousands of millions of years that was once assumed to be
available' (Denton, 1998, p.295). Not surprisingly, many scientists are at a
pain to find an explanation which would overcome the problems that the
above facts create for the materialistic perspective. Crick, for example,

hypothesises that life came from outer space (as the Sumerians and a Greek philosopher Anaxagoras believed much before him). Even if this is true, it does not solve the problem, but only moves it elsewhere. Some scientists speculate that the original cell or cells were much simpler than the simplest existing one-cell organisms. For example, it could be the case that RNA at one point was not only a messenger but also a replicator (therefore assuming the role of DNA too). However, this possibility faces several difficulties. RNA is hard to synthesise even under controlled circumstances, with all the help of scientists, let alone in the conditions in which biological life was formed. Even when RNA is manufactured, it requires much tinkering to make new copies of itself: '...the synthesis of RNA *by chance* is a highly improbable process, and as yet no one has presented a mechanism by which it might have occurred... even when you do have RNA, the process of self-replication in the laboratory is not at all straightforward, and it requires considerable intervention on the part of the experimenter' (Silver, 1998, p.348). Intervention, however, is exactly what materialists deny in regard to the origin of life. There are a number of other alternatives, but none of them is very credible. It is not possible to examine all of them here, so the final comment is left to an evolutionary biologist who already did so:

> Although many exotic hypotheses far more speculative than the RNA world have been proposed to close the gap between chemistry and life, none are convincing. (Denton 1998, p.294)

That an accidental appearance of life is extremely unlikely seems to be the inevitable inference. Polanyi and Prosch conclude that 'every living organism is a meaningful organization of meaningless matter and that it is very highly improbable that these meaningful organizations should all have occurred entirely by chance' (1975, p.172). The above does not, of course, provide a definitive proof that a teleological explanation is correct. This is not essential though. Declaring that life must have come about by chance simply because there is no concrete evidence for an agency, would be like declaring that a sculpture is the result of a natural process because the sculptor cannot be seen. In the words of the astronomer Carl Sagan, 'absence of evidence is not evidence of absence'. On the other hand, however dismally small the chance of accidental abiogenesis is, it is not entirely impossible that such a fluke may have happened. There might be some purely physical factors, not yet discovered, that could greatly increase the probability of a spontaneous formation of life. Thus, although the involvement of an agency seems a more plausible explanation, it cannot be conclusively proven, so the choice to accept this possibility or not is preserved. What is important, however, if a teleological position is to be taken seriously, is to examine whether it can be interpreted in a rational way.

THE SYNTHESIS PERSPECTIVE

It seems equally unlikely that life was created accidentally and that an agent acted/acts like an engineer, putting various parts together or programming DNA sequences. A more plausible explanation that combines spiritual and scientific insights (without their religious and materialistic baggage) is that life was *intended*. As suggested earlier in relation to the tuning of the four forces and other physical properties, 'design' or the direct involvement of an external agency need not to be invoked. In accord with the criterion of cohesiveness, it is sufficient to postulate as the most likely explanation an intended abiogenesis. The Intent acts, on one hand, as a driving force pushing the matter into more complex organisation and, on the other, as a restricting force, a 'funnel' that converges a huge number of possibilities into one point – the appearance of life[1]. Of course, there could not be direct evidence for such an intent (it cannot be expected that the One would leave 'fingerprints'). However, there are some suggestive indicators, making this explanation more likely than highly improbable chance. They include the distinctive properties of the building blocks that enable the formation of complex forms conducive to life, and finely tuned (physical, chemical and environmental) conditions. Several examples will be brought up to illustrate this.

It is not only the physical forces, constants and solar objects that are precisely adjusted to enable life, but also many physical and chemical properties, established much before life appeared, are uniquely fit for carbon-based organisms. Biologist Denton (who is not associated with Creationism or similar movements) should be credited for collecting comprehensive and compelling evidence that life is unlikely to be an accident. He points out that life could not exist if 'various constituents – water, carbon dioxide, carbon acid, the DNA helix, proteins, phosphates, sugars, lipids, the carbon atom the oxygen atom, the transitional metal atoms and the other metal atoms from groups 1 and 2 of the periodic table: sodium, potassium, calcium, and magnesium – did not possess precisely those chemical and physical properties they exhibit in an aqueous solution ranging in temperature from 0°C and about 75°C' (1998, p.382).

Let us consider water, for example, arguably the most important substance for life. Water is very unusual. While most substances shrink when cooled, water starts expanding (below 4°C) so solid ice is atypically less dense than

---

[1] Later on, in evolution, a divergent process takes place (analogous to the Big Bang explosion, after the energy had been first compressed into singularity). So, different principles govern the proliferation of various life forms (see chapter 16).

liquid water. Water is also extraordinary slow in warming up - another anomaly. What is amazing is that all this and many other characteristics of water (e.g. the low viscosity, the surface tension, the capacity to dissolve a vast number of different substances, etc.[1]) are beneficial to life. For example, if ice was heavier (more dense) than water, the oceans would have frozen completely, killing all marine life; the slow warming up of water protects organisms against massive swings in temperature, and so on. Scientists find it hard to explain many of these properties. They are most likely linked to hydrogen bonds between water molecules, and they again depend on zero-point vibration energy – energy from 'nowhere'.

Many other physical and chemical features are also well adjusted for life. For example, carbon (the building block of organic matter) has a whole range of such properties: maximum utility of both the strong covalent bonds (that keep atoms together) and the weak bonds (e.g. hydrogen bonds) in the same temperature range at which water is fluid; the perfect fit between the α helix of the protein with the large groove of the DNA; the relative stability of organic molecules below 100^0C; the relatively un-reactive nature of oxygen, a source of energy for carbon-based life, below 50^0C; the fact that carbon dioxide is a gas (which enables the excretion of the products of carbon oxidation); the sufficient strength of hydrogen and other weak bonds to hold proteins and DNA at temperatures conducive to life, and so on. Moreover, atmospheric gases (including water vapour) and liquid water, absorb virtually all the harmful radiation from space and transmit only a tiny band that is of visual range and is at the same time, fit for photochemistry. Also, all the classes of atoms in the periodic table play a harmonious role in the formation and sustenance of life. Adaptation of life to these circumstances is not a sufficient explanation. If only a few of them had not been already there, life would not have had a chance to adapt to anything. In addition, these properties are not only conducive to the appearance of microorganisms, but seem to anticipate more complex multicellular life forms. To quote Denton again:

> Many of the properties and characteristics of life's constituents seem to be specifically arranged for large, complex, multicellular organisms like ourselves. The coincidences do not stop at the cell but extend right on into higher forms of life. These include the packaging properties of DNA, which enable a vast amount of DNA and hence biological information to be packed into the tiny volume of the cell nucleus in higher organisms, the electrical properties of cells, which depend ultimately on the insulating character of the cell membrane, which provides the basis for nerve conduction and for the coordination of the activities of multicellular organisms; the very nature of the cell, particularly its feeling and crawling activities, which seem so ideally

---

[1] Professor Martin Chaplin listed over 40 anomalous characteristics of water.

adapted for assembling a multicellular organism during development; the fact that oxygen and carbon dioxide are both gases at ambient temperatures and the peculiar and unique character of the bicarbonate buffer, which together greatly facilitate the life of large air-breathing macroscopic organisms. (1998, p.381-2)

One can also add to the list the decrease in the viscosity of the blood when blood pressure rises, which increases the blood flow to the metabolically active muscles of higher organisms (without it, the circulatory system would be unworkable); the quite slow hydration of carbon dioxide, which prevents a fatally high level of acidity in the body of complex organisms in anaerobic exercises (that require increased pace or greater effort). Curiously, only atmospheres with between 10 and 20% oxygen can support an oxidative metabolism in a higher organism; and it is only within that range that fire – hence technology – is possible. As Denton puts it,

...for every new constituent we required, there was a ready-made solution that seemed ideally and uniquely prefabricated, as if by design, for the biological end it serves... (1998, p.230)

Even those phenomena that are taken as calamities, are, in fact, often purposeful. For example, volcanic eruptions bring water and metals to the surface, contribute to the atmosphere, regulate heat, and finally, fertilise the land, enabling agriculture.

Without going into further details, it can be concluded that it is consistent with the Synthesis perspective that life started from very simple forms, as scientists claim too. Whether it originated in a 'primeval soup', in hot-water vents at the bottom of the ocean, in clay sediments, or on Mars, is a technical issue that does not affect the basic assertion, which is that life being intended is not only congruent with the known facts, but highly probable. The above indicates that life could hardly appear by chance, and that the funnelling of randomness was necessary.[1] This is all that can be claimed at this point (the *process* that led to the beginning of life will be considered on p.149). To make further inferences about the appearance of life as we know it, the question of what life is, what it consists of, needs to be addressed first. This issue (that will require the examination of some complex aspects of human life) will be the subject of the following part.

---

[1] It is sometimes claimed (e.g. Dawkins, 2006, p.138) that even if the chance is one in a billion, providing that there are a billion planets in the universe, life will appear at least on one of them. This argument is based on either misunderstanding or misuse of statistics, so it does not deserve a serious consideration.

THE BEING

THE 'MIND–BODY PROBLEM'

The previous part hints that life may have a non-material aspect to it, but the criterion of coherence demands more direct support for such an assertion. Although it may apply to other life forms, the most conducive way to approach this issue is by focusing on human beings. This has the advantages of being able to refer to one's personal experience and to utilise the ability of language. So, examining the so-called 'mind-body problem' (how mental processes are related to bodily states or processes) seems the best starting point. An additional benefit is that this 'problem' is also democratic. Unlike the mysteries of the universe or subatomic particles that require equipment available only to a few specialists, everybody has access to shis own mind.

Before the various options are considered though, a modern myth related to this subject must be addressed. It consists of the claim that science has already solved or is close to solving the riddle of consciousness and its relation to the brain. The myth is perpetuated by some scientist (e.g. professor Semir Zeki) but more often by non-scientists (such as philosopher Daniel Dennett) or the media. It is true that science has made a great contribution in recent years to understanding the structure and functioning of the brain, but this is a different matter. In fact, science is no closer to solving this problem than it was fifty or more years ago, when the interest in the subject re-surfaced. The consensus of the speakers at the 1995 conference in London, *Consciousness – its place in contemporary science*, was that 'science really did not understand *anything* about consciousness – what it is, how it evolved, how it is generated by the brain, or even what it is for' (Sutherland, 1994, p.285). The issue is not that science is not there yet, and that only more study and more sophisticated instruments are needed. More fundamentally, with the current methodology, science is unlikely ever to address this problem fully and adequately. The commonly accepted criteria for data in a scientific analysis are that they are objective, public, and replicable (leading to predictability). However, consciousness has some unique characteristics that render these criteria inadequate:

The first person perspective - the present scientific methodology favours observation, but the mind is not open to external observation. The mental is private, non-accessible to the outside, objective, public sphere, unlike physical objects or phenomena. It is intimately and directly accessible to its 'owner', but not to others (a report is already second hand data). Güzeldere, a professor of Psychological and Brain Sciences, writes (1995b, p.116):

...from the outside, the first-hand exploration of the consciousness of others just seems to be out of the reach of ordinary scientific methods, others' experience being neither directly observable nor non-inferentially verifiable.

Non-spatiality - the other problem is that the materials of consciousness are non-spatial. They are not located in any specific place nor do they take up a particular volume of space; they are not made of spatially distributed parts nor have they spatial dimensionality; they are not solid and some of them don't even have a shape (e.g. the ideas of love or freedom). Since they are non-spatial, they are in principle unobservable. The view of some scientists that the appearance of non-spatiality is a kind of illusion seems so far to be baseless. It was discovered a while ago that certain sets of neurons process lines, angles or simple geometrical forms, but this is a far cry from even the simplest mental images. Nobody has yet managed to find in the brain anything that even remotely looks like a house or the grandma that one can imagine or remember. It has been proposed that the brain, in theory, can produce something similar to holograms, but this has never been detected, so its spatiality cannot be taken for granted even if the premise is correct. Thus, it is reasonable to accept that mental events as such are unobservable from the third person perspective, and for all practical purposes, non-spatial until shown otherwise.

Qualia (qualities that experiences such as feeling pain, seeing the colour green, or smelling a flower consist of). There is clearly a difference between the particular behaviour of nerve cells associated with pain for example, and the actual experience of pain. Even materialists such as Koch, admit that 'there seems to be a huge jump between the materialistic level, of explaining molecules and neurons, and the subjective level' (1992, p.96). To paraphrase philosopher Chalmers, however much knowledge neuroscience gains about the brain, there will still be an 'explanatory gap' between the physical and subjective realms. Experimental work on perception, for instance, only relates to the *contents* of consciousness, not to the experience itself. Neuroscience can explain, to some extent, how sensations can be 'translated' into electro-magnetic impulses, but it does not say anything about how these impulses are translated into images, thoughts, feelings (not to mention that humans are able to create them too). Put simply, science has not found mental events in the brain. The best it can do is to provide a detailed map of the physical processes that correlate with specific subjective states. No neurological theory explains *why* brain functions are accompanied by them.

The contribution of science should not be underestimated, but the inevitable conclusion is that science, on its own, cannot truly solve the mind-body problem. Bearing this in mind, various possibilities of the relation between the brain and mind can be examined.

MATTER EXISTS, MENTAL DOES NOT

This view is known as reductive materialism or materialistic monism. It is based on the belief that the mind can either be identified or reduced to the brain (or body) activity. For a true materialist the 'mind' is nothing more than a way of describing certain electrical impulses and chemical processes in the brain and the rest of the body. Thoughts or emotions are just a mere folk terminology for them. Consequently, the laws of nature govern these processes, and freedom of choice is merely an illusion.

Arguments for materialism do not amount to much. Some of its proponents admit that they are motivated by such considerations as Occam's razor (see p.40) and a general belief that everything is reducible to one kind of entity. The reason why this perspective seems plausible to many is that brain injuries or chemicals can alter mind states. However, although this proves that the brain affects the mind, it is not evidence that the mind *is* the brain. To make a comparison, if a car breaks down or runs out of petrol, the driver is forced to stop shis journey. This is not a proof, though, that the driver does not exist, or that s/he is identical to or a product of mechanical processes in the car's engine. Yet, materialistic interpretations make comparable claims in an attempt to explain the mind solely by brain processes. One thing is, however, clear. There is no scientific evidence that the mind is only a product of brain activity:

> …connection is not enough. To say that rain is connected with a fall of the barometer is very different from saying that rain *is* a fall of the barometer; and the same is true of sensations and brain-processes - even assuming that they could be correlated in the same sort of way. To go from correlation to identification requires a further step. Is this further step also a matter of science? (Hanfling, 1980, p.52)

Materialism looks attractive because it offers an easy solution to the problem that bedevils dualism: how states of the mind (expectations, volitions, feelings) can initiate physical movements. If the mind is identified with the brain this issue becomes trivial: the one part of essentially the same system affects another in a way that a car engine affects the wheels (dualists would comment that it is not the car-engine, but ultimately a driver who initiates the movement, and s/he is not a part of the system). The materialist solution, however, creates even bigger problems and requires sacrificing much of what it tries to explain. The mental must be completely eliminated because if it is acknowledged, it must be material, and therefore spatial and accessible from the third person perspective. Yet, this does not seem to be the case. So, there are several attempts to sidetrack this essential aspect of human experience (the irony is that there is so much bickering about the best way to do so, that materialists appear to be the best critics of each other).

Behaviourism

The eagerness of psychologists to present themselves as objective and show that the third person perspective can be employed to study the mind too, resulted in the theory of behaviourism that reigned for fifty years (roughly between 1915 and 1965). A radical form of materialism, it reduces all mental states to phenomena that can be observed and measured (i.e. behaviour). A particularly influential form was the 'logical behaviourism' espoused by philosopher Ryle in his book *The Concept of Mind*. He also coined a disparaging phrase for dualism - 'the dogma of the ghost in the machine'. Once the mental is identified with behaviour, it is easy to discard the mind altogether. Ryle, for example, argues that one cannot expect to find a mind over and above all the various parts of the body and its actions, for the mind is just a convenient label for certain physical actions. He uses the metaphor of a university that does not exist out and above the buildings and people that make a university. So, as university, the mind does not really exist, it is only a different level of description. There are many objections to this perspective:

• Ryle may be right to compare the mind with the concept of 'university' in so far as the mind does not exist independent from its constituents (it is just a name for a sum of mental processes). However, identifying these processes (thoughts, images, feelings, desires etc.) with the description of behaviour leads to some absurd consequences. For example, from this perspective, no distinction can be made between the person who is really in pain and the person who acts convincingly that s/he is in pain. Also, what about those who do not show any external expressions of mental events (e.g. a person who is paralysed or meditating)? Although public evidence for one's thoughts or feelings must indeed come from shis observable behaviour, it is a real leap of faith to assume that they can be reduced to it.

• By identifying mental events with behavioural tendencies this doctrine leaves qualia out of the equation. The experience of being in pain cannot be simply reduced to a disposition to scream, wince or say 'I am in pain'. *Feeling* the pain is too important to be ignored. Philosopher Kripke argues that the behaviourist account of the mental fails because the subjective character of an experience (or 'its immediate phenomenological quality', as he calls it) is the essential property left out by such analyses.

• Behaviourism naturally does not allow the possibility that behaviour can be caused by mental events such as beliefs for example. According to this view, such events do not exist independently of behaviour, they are just dispositions to behave in a certain way. For example, one does not take an umbrella because s/he believes that it is going to rain, but because s/he has a disposition to take an umbrella. This, however, blatantly contradicts common experience and common sense.

• Behaviourists' claim that an individual learns about shis own beliefs by monitoring shis behaviour and by listening to what s/he says, also seems absurd. It would mean that we cannot have any beliefs that we have not first acted upon or verbally expressed.

• A logical consequence of such a position is that the mind is fully determined by its environment ('nurture'), but this does not leave any room for choice, creativity and other common phenomena (and if they did not exist on the first place, they could not even be invented, since invention involves creativity).

Not surprisingly, behaviourism was eventually rejected even by those who subscribe to materialism, so other ways have been sought to dispose of the mental.

Eliminativism

Eliminativism is an extreme materialist doctrine that attempts to solve the 'mind-body problem' by completely eliminating the mind. It simply denies the existence of the phenomena that cannot be explained from a materialistic perspective. Eliminativists maintain that mentality is nothing more than folklore, and advocate the replacement of everyday psychological concepts (such as feelings, desires, beliefs, intentions etc.) in favour of neuro-scientific ones. This position was championed by Patricia and Paul Churchland and Daniel Dennett. The latter, in his rather over-confidently entitled book *Consciousness Explained,* asserts that consciousness – and our sense that we have a self – is an illusion. This, however, cannot be justified for several reasons:

• A claim that common mental phenomena are illusions - similar to optical illusions, is not only unsubstantiated, but also misleading. Unlike perception, which is mediated by the senses that can play tricks on us, phenomenological experience is direct and cannot be an illusion. Only its interpretations can be, because they require a correspondence to events or objects outside one's mind. However, being aware, intending or the sense of self are not interpretations (we do not project them onto or seek correspondence with something 'out there'). They are prime examples of unmediated experiences. So, we may be wrong believing that they are in the brain (or not in the brain), but they cannot be dismissed as an illusion. For instance, if a person says that s/he feels pain, s/he may be wrong about many things (e.g. where that pain is coming from) but not that s/he is experiencing, is *aware* of pain. Saying 'No, you are mistaken, you are not aware of any pain' simply does not make sense (unless it is suspected that the person is deliberately lying, but this is beside the point).

• The complex organisation of a brain is merely a mechanism, and being a mechanism it cannot be sufficient to account for what Chalmers calls the 'hard problem'. He points out that '…it is conceptually coherent that brain processes could be instantiated in the absence of experience' (1995, p.208). Therefore, if they may happen without experience, referring to the physical processes alone cannot adequately explain why experience arises.

• Qualia cannot be eliminated without losing the essential quality of consciousness. A particular part of the brain may be active when one feels sad, for example, but this electro-chemical process (even if it was the physical cause of the experience) is not the same thing as a phenomenological experience of sadness.

• If the mind *is* the brain, no discrepancies between these two should be possible. Yet, there are several empirical findings of dis-synchrony, such as temporal discrepancies between neural events and the related experiences apparent in backward masking, antedating and a commonly perceived slowing down of time in acute emergencies (see Popper and Eccles, 1977).

The conclusion is that although eliminating the mind would make life easier for those who study consciousness, it does not seem to be a viable option. Roger Sperry, one of the most distinguished neuro-scientists in the second half of the 20th century, declared in his paper 'Changing priorities':

> Current concepts of the mind-brain relation involve a direct break with the long-established materialist and behaviourist doctrine that has dominated neuroscience for many decades. Instead of renouncing or ignoring consciousness, the new interpretation gives full recognition to the primacy of inner conscious awareness as a causal reality. (1981, p.7)

Identity theories

Identity theories, a variant of the above, claim that mental events and brain processes are identical, just different descriptions. The oldest version is the so-called *type-identity theory*. It states that mental events and physical ones are just two ways of looking at the same thing (like H_2O and water). The fact that many people have no knowledge of brain processes but know intimately their own thoughts and feelings is not a problem *per se* (they are contingently identical). However, there are several other reasons why this theory does not seem plausible.

• The identity theory fails to explain why a particular neural activity causes a certain experience (e.g. why the excitation of C-fibres is associated with pain, not itching).

• Logical differences between propositions about the mind and propositions about the brain pointed out by many philosophers cannot be ignored. Brentano's *intentionality* is one example: mental states are about something, while brain states are not, they just are.

• Another problem is that the same kind of a mental event can correlate with different neural mechanisms. It is hard to believe that the same mechanism underlies pain for all the different actual and possible pain-capable organisms. Thus, it seems that there is no single physical kind with which pain, as a mental kind, can be identified.

• If thoughts and brain states are identical, they should share the same properties and be located in the same place (as water and H_2O do). However, mental events have attributes that physical events do not have (and vice versa). Brain-processes are very different from mental images, thoughts, experiences, intentions, beliefs, etc. These differences cannot be seen as only different descriptions. A mental image, for example, cannot be described in terms of brain activity without losing the essential qualities of that image. Philosopher of mind, Thomas Nagel, writes:

> The idea of how a mental and physical term might refer to the same thing is lacking, and the usual analogies with theoretical identification in other fields fail to supply it. They fail because if we construe the reference of mental terms to physical events on the usual model, we either get a reappearance of separate subjective events as the effects through which mental reference to physical events is secured, or else we get a false account of how mental terms refer (for example, a causal behaviourist one). (1981, p.401)

• If H_2O is just a different name for water, water must be always present when H_2O is present. This is not the case with the brain and the mind. There are brain processes that do not have corresponding mind events, and arguably *vice-versa*, as neuroscientist Libet claims: '…it is possible that some mental phenomena have no direct neuronal basis' (2004, p.184).

• It is hard to explain from this position why we are aware of some brain processes and not others, or how we can alternate between being aware and not being aware of certain neural events without altering them (e.g. the sensations associated with sitting).

• The implication of this theory is that the brain processes would always produce the same mental events, and that mental events are always associated with identical brain processes. Yet, this is unlikely. A thought today may involve a different brain state than the same thought one had a day before. Mental events cannot be segmented and isolated from general experience as physical processes can. To overcome this problem, a so-called *token-identity theory* was developed. Unlike type-identity theory, this one allows that mental events of the same type need not all be brain states of the same type. The theory however does not explain how it is possible, which makes the relationship between the physical and the mental even more mysterious than dualistic interpretations.

Functionalism

Functionalism became a popular theory of the mind in the late 20th century, not only because it looked more promising than identity theories and behaviourism, but also because it could be linked to the development of Artificial Intelligence that was gathering momentum at that time. It claims that a functional role, rather than the intrinsic features of a system, determine a mental state. Mind events can be observed in terms of the relation between input, existing brain state and output. In other words, the mind is a name for the various functions that the brain performs, and the brain can be seen as a sophisticated and complex computer (the organic basis, therefore, is not necessary and can be replaced, for example, with a silicon one). Although an improvement to the previous theories, functionalism can also be criticised on several counts.

• Searle's famous mind experiment, known as the 'Chinese room', highlights the difference between processing information, and thinking and understanding in human terms, that the proponents of functionalism tend to neglect. The person in the room does not understand Chinese. Through a letterbox come various Chinese characters printed on cards. On a table in the room is a book, and the task of the person is to match the Chinese character on a card with a Chinese character in the book. The book will then indicate another, different, Chinese character which is paired with the first one. The person takes this other character from the pile of cards that s/he has and pushes it back out through the letter box. The cards coming into the room are questions written in Chinese. Those the person pushes back out are shis answers, also in Chinese. Even though s/he does not understand Chinese, it appears from outside that s/he is giving intelligent answers in that language. Yet, the person does not have any relevant experience or understanding; s/he is simply manipulating what for shim are meaningless characters. Artificial Intelligence is in the same position as the person in the 'Chinese room'. Like shim, it just manipulates symbols without genuinely understanding what they refer to. Thus, functionalist model does not capture a complete picture of the mind. Güzeldere writes:

> Something essential to (at least our common sense conception of) consciousness, it was largely believed, was necessarily left out in characterizing consciousness only by specifying its functional role in the cognitive economy of human mentation and behaviour. (1995a, p.49)

• The other way to pinpoint the inadequacy of the functionalist account is to compare human behaviour with the behaviour of purely mechanical complex systems such as machines, robots or 'zombies' (a term used in this area of study to signify something that looks like a human, but does not have conscious experience or freedom of choice). Any significant differences would indicate that a living organism cannot be reduced to the functions of shis physical component. The obvious one is a lack of two essential characteristics of life: experience and agency. Let us consider pain again. Pain is functional in many ways. In principle, a machine may be programmed to process or react to the same stimuli in a similar fashion, without, in fact, experiencing pain. Yet, human beings do not react only functionally to pain, they do a lot of things that are not functional: they may jump up and down, bite their hand, swear, or even masochistically enjoy their pain. These may not all be functional in respect to the body, but serve some purpose for the one who is *experiencing* the pain (these are reactions to experience, rather than to an informational aspect of the pain or its cause). There is not any need for robots or 'zombies' to exhibit such reactions, and therefore they would not be present if living organisms were the same. Moreover, humans reactions are far less causally determined than what one would expect from machines:

> If our brain operates like computers, appropriate behaviour to avoid harm and remedy damage could simply be the output of unconscious computation, and pain would be superfluous. As it is, pain gives us notice of the desirability of such behaviour, and a motive to engage in it; but it leaves us with a choice to do something else if we judge other considerations to be more important. (Hodgson, 1994, p.213)

There are many other manifestations of human behaviour that are unlikely to be found in inanimate systems: self-determination, insecurity, anticipation, curiosity, intolerance of boredom, creativity, surprise, choice based on future perspective (e.g. expectations), guessing, indecisiveness, or desire to survive often irrationally expressed in acute situations (robots would have no use for panic, and such a reaction is too complex to spontaneously occur as a result of their malfunctioning). Of course, theoretically it may be possible to make a machine that could simulate these characteristics, but this would be only a form without a content[1]. Chalmers concludes:

> the explanation of functions does not suffice for the explanation of experience. Experience is not an explanatory posit but an explanandum in its own right... (1995, p.209)

---

[1] Writer Lem makes this point in a more descriptive way: 'One can, to be sure, program a digital machine in such a way as to be able to carry on a conversation with it, as if with an intelligent partner. The machine will employ, as the need arises, the pronoun "I" and all its grammatical inflections. This, however, is a hoax! Nothing will amuse such a machine, or surprise it, or confuse it, or alarm it, or distress it, because it is psychologically and individually No One... One cannot count on its sympathy, or on its antipathy. It works towards no self-set goal; to a degree eternally beyond the conception of any man it "doesn't care", for as a person it simply does not exist... It is a wondrously efficient combinatorial mechanism, nothing more' (1981, p. 306-307).

Functionalists, of course, may disagree, but, as Alwyn Scott puts it,

> Computer functionalism is a mere theory of the mind, and our experiences of qualia and free will are widely observed facts of nature. What are we to believe – our own perceptions or a belief handed to us by [reductionist] tradition? (1998, p.76)

Conclusion

It seems that reductive materialism cannot find a plausible way to exclude the mental from the equation without losing what is essential:

> None of these theories can count as solutions to the perennial mind-brain problem; they are rather, evasions of the problem. They provide various linguistic formulae for sustaining the pretence that there is no problem as traditionally supposed. However, since they all involve a denial that subjective experience constitutes an irreducible datum, they must be deemed to fall at the first post. (Beloff, 1994, p. 33)

It may be worthwhile to summarise the problems with this perspective in relation to the criteria of reasoning specified in the first part (p.42).

Incompleteness - materialism leaves out the essential elements associated with the mental: awareness (experience, qualia), intent (initiating mental acts that can affect the body, too) and self (as that which is aware and intends). The philosopher Schopenhauer described such a view as the philosophy 'of the subject who forgot to take account of himself'. More recently, the neuroscientist Nunn (1994, p.127) makes a similar comment:

> Recognising the incapacity of ideas of this sort to account for qualia, Dennett took the desperate, and in our view mistaken, step of arguing that they do not really exist in quite the way that everyday introspection suggests.

Materialism cannot acknowledge qualia because they would have to be material, which would mean that we should be able to find them. This would also imply that there are physical events that have that property and some that do not, which leads to property dualism that is hard for a materialist to accept and justify. Yet, the subjective cannot be reduced to the objective without losing its essential character. Nagel writes:

> Any reductionist program has to be based on an analysis of what is to be reduced. If the analysis leaves something out, the problem will be falsely posed. It is useless to base the defence of materialism on any analysis of mental phenomena that fails to deal explicitly with their subjective character. For there is no reason to suppose that a reduction which seems plausible when no attempt is made to account for consciousness can be extended to include consciousness. Without some idea, therefore, of what the subjective character of experience is, we cannot know what is required of physicalist theory. (1981, p.392-393)

Creativity (e.g. finding original solutions, or simply formulating a new sentence) is another phenomenon that materialists cannot adequately explain, considering that the brain processes, according to them, should be solely governed by natural laws[1].

Inconsistency - biologist J. B. S. Haldane was first to point out that materialism is self-defeating, it cannot claim to be supported by rational argument. If materialism is true, we cannot know that it is true. If opinions are nothing more than the electro-chemical processes going on in the brain, they must be determined by the laws of physics and chemistry, not logic. Developing this argument further Popper concludes:

> Materialism… is incompatible with rationalism, with the acceptance of the standards of critical argument; for these standards appear from the materialist point of view as an illusion, or at least as an ideology. (1977, p.81)

Even illusions themselves are a discretely mental category (computers do not have illusions), which is what materialists deny. In other words, they claim that having an illusion is itself an illusion – a contradiction in terms.

Incongruence - materialistic interpretation also cannot adequately account for some experimental data, such as split brain experiments (forebrain commissurotomy - the removal of the corpus callosum), blind sight, temporal discrepancies between neural events and mental experiences, intentional activation of a brain module without corresponding action, and binding (integrated character of the experience that is not reflected in the brain)[2]. An eminent scientist and brain surgeon, Penfield, concludes:

> Because it seems to me certain that it will always be impossible to explain the mind on the basis of neuronal action within the brain, and because it seems to me that the mind develops and matures independently throughout an individual's life as though it were a continuing element, and because a computer (which the brain is) must be programmed and operated by an agency capable of independent understanding, I am forced to choose the proposition that our being is to be explained on the basis of two fundamental elements… mind and brain as two semi-independent elements. (1975, p.80)

Materialists are right that the brain has an essential role in mental processes, but they do not provide convincing support for the claim that the mind can be fully reduced to it. As Scott points out, '…this chasm between the details of a mechanistic explanation of the brain and the ever-present reality of conscious awareness, has continued to yawn… Reductive materialism fails to bridge that gap' (1995, p.101).

---

[1] One should bear in mind that the unpredictable and chaotic behaviours of some complex natural systems are not the same as creativity.

[2] These empirical findings will be addressed in more detail later on.

MENTAL EXISTS, MATTER DOES NOT

This position, known as idealism or transcendental monism, is advocated by a number of scientists and philosophers (e.g. A. S. Eddington, J. Jeans, G. F. Stout, W. Harman). In conversation with Einstein, a famous Indian poet and philosopher Rabindranath Tagore defended, rather successfully, a ('weak') version of idealism against realism. Idealism is not so absurd as it seems at first glance (especially if it is considered epistemologically rather than ontologically). In the end, what we know is the content of our mind (our perceptions are part of our mind not reality). And that content does not necessarily correspond to something 'out there'. For example, the experience of solidity is only a mental product. As science confirms, a stone that appears solid is in fact mostly empty space. The usual refutation that goes something like 'if you hit a table, the pain will be an obvious proof that it is real', does not, in fact, hold water. There is no reason why pain cannot be an established reaction to mental representations as much as material objects that have an independent existence. After all, we can experience pain in a dream as a result of hitting a dreamt table that is evidently not material.

A more serious problem that this position faces is how things unknown and unperceived by anybody can still exist. For example, somebody hides a treasure and subsequently dies. Nobody knows about it, but years later it is accidentally found. It makes sense to think that the treasure has existed all the time (although it was not in the mind of anybody). Bishop Berkeley, a philosopher often associated with this perspective, argues that reality is coherent and has continuity because it is in the mind of God – an omnipresent observer. Husserl also suggests in *Cartesian Meditations* that the transcendental ego would remain in existence even if the entire universe was destroyed. However, even if God or transcendental ego as a universal observer is accepted, another fundamental issue still remains. Whatever is called matter in our mental representations is distinct from non-matter (a dreamt table is, for all practical purposes, different from what is normally considered a real table). So, even if they are both subgroups of the mental, there is still a need to find out how these two subgroups relate to each other (e.g. what are hallucinations?). In other words, assuming that this perspective is correct would still leave the mind-body problem largely unresolved.

It can be concluded that neither materialist or idealist monism provide helpful arguments to overthrow the common sense assumption that both matter and mind exist and cannot be reduced to each other. This however, does not preclude the possibility that one causes the other, which is considered next.

MATTER CAUSES MENTAL

Although the starting point is matter, this is a very different perspective from reductive materialism. Its proponents acknowledge that the mind is irreducible even if it is the result of the brain. Therefore mental, as something distinct from matter, exists, which already makes this position a form of ('weak') dualism[1]. The most popular view, asserting that the mind arises from the brain complexity, is called *emergentism* (advocated by Sperry, Popper, Scott and many others). The assumption behind this is that a combination of simple structures can give rise to some qualities that their constitutive elements do not have. A simple example is the wetness of water that emerges from non-wet molecules of hydrogen and oxygen. More generally, the idea is that physics gives rise to chemistry, chemistry to biology, biology to the brain and the brain to consciousness, but none of them can be reduced to their precursors. This is a big improvement on reductive materialism because it can account for subjective experiences and perhaps even for the non-physical properties of the mental, but it has some other shortcomings.

• Emergentism does not explain why and how the brain gives rise to mind, but simply assumes that it happens. Not only does the question why the complexity of the brain would lead to consciousness remain unanswered, but also why the complexity increases at all. Considering that emergent systems are always open systems, it is possible that factor(s) external to the system force this increase. If this proposition is taken onboard, what these conditions and factors that contribute to the emergence of consciousness are, would need clarifying.

• The assembly of neurons and other cells that make up the brain undoubtedly produce some new qualities (e.g. an equivalent to the wetness of water would be the sponginess of the brain). However, the mind is different. Its phenomenal properties appear sharply dissimilar to those of the brain. It can be expected that the increased complexity of the nervous system would allow more complex processes in the brain to occur, but it seems implausible that sentient, experiencing entities could spontaneously evolve at one point out of wholly insentient, non-experiencing substance.

• There is no reason to believe that these properties are specific to human beings. True, the mental life of other organisms may be much more limited, but that does not mean that they are just carbon based robots that don't have any experience. In fact, as far as observation can be relied on, it seems that

---

[1] The word 'dualism' is at present ostracised to such an extent in the academic world that some scholars (e.g. John Searle) would counter-intuitively try to avoid this conclusion at any cost.

even some one-cell organisms exhibit behaviour hinting that they are capable of experience and that they can be pro-active. If this is true, then the ability to experience and some other mental qualities cannot be the result of the brain complexity. Seager concludes:

> If consciousness is not reducible then we cannot explain its appearance at a certain level of physical complexity merely in terms of that complexity and so, if it does not *emerge* at these levels of complexity, it must have been already present at the lower levels. (1995, p.279)

• Even if it is accepted that consciousness emerges from brain complexity, how the matter affects the mind needs an explanation. There is no reason to believe that physical-to-mental causation is easier to understand than mental-to-physical causation.

This last point leads to the issue of *mental causation* (which true materialists could avoid by simply denying that the mental exists). Many scholars recognise that a materialist perspective is too narrow and mistaken to exclude the mental. Yet, they feel the need to deny that the mental can be causal because it would conflict with the assumption that the universe only operates according to physical laws. This is called *epiphenomenalism*. In this view, the unique properties of mind are accepted, but mind is considered a result of brain activity, and therefore determined by natural laws. Mind does not influence the body in any way, so choice and agency are illusions. Qualia are acknowledged, but rendered irrelevant. All the processes within an individual and global processes such as evolution would take place anyway, whether living organisms were aware or not. There are several difficulties with this view:
• If mental events are just epiphenomena that do not have any effect, if they are ephemeral, it is hard to understand why it *seems* that they play such an important part in evolution, human society and the lives of every individual. It is incredible that human beliefs and desires have nothing to do with actions, that civilization would have developed even if no human had ever acted upon shis conscious thought.

• The brain cannot be determined by future projections. Yet, at least some actions seem to be based on decisions that rely on predictions and expectations, and they are of a distinctly mental character. If this is just an epiphenomenon, the question can be raised why would the mental process of making a choice (e.g. when faced with two alternate means to achieve a goal) exist at all.

• To broaden this question in the context of the evolutionary perspective, if consciousness is an epiphenomena, why would it appear in the first place? The mind has too important a role to be seriously considered just as an accidental by-product.

• Besides common experience, there is also substantial empirical evidence (which will be considered later) that clearly shows that mental events can affect the brain and body.

Some emergentists (e.g. Popper) accept that the mind can affect the brain, but this has an overtone of circular causation: the brain creates the mind that in turn affects the brain. This would necessitate that the mind (although the result of the brain) has a relative independence from the brain. Properties that are intimately related to an object (e.g. the colour of a flower or music from an instrument) cannot affect this object above and beyond what it already is or does. How it is possible for the mind to be created by the brain and then sufficiently separated so that it can influence the brain, remains mysterious. This issue will be further discussed within the causal dualism perspective.

Conclusion
Although it is based on an assumption rather than explanation, and despite the above contentious issues, emergentism can still be a highly useful concept. The main charge against this perspective is not so much in what it claims, but its incompleteness. It can be accepted that the complexity of the brain enables some processes associated with mentality. It is even plausible that such processes can have qualities that appear non-physical. Pribram, for example, convincingly argues that brain waves may create something like holographic images. However, even if this is accepted, it is not enough. TV stations are also complex systems that produce wave forms that can be transformed into images, but nobody seriously considers that they are conscious. Moreover, what would their use be if something else does not exist to 'pick up' these waves? This is missing in emergent theories. Their world looks like a place with a lot of radio or TV transmitters without radios or TVs to receive their signals. Considering all these points, the conclusion seems inevitable that if the idea of emergentism is pushed far enough, it is likely to end up in one form or another of either dualism or materialism, with all the additional problems that these theories have.

MENTAL CAUSES MATTER

Although this position may seem counterintuitive, the support for it may be found in some interpretations of a particular strand of modern science - quantum physics. Home and Robinson comment that 'Bohr's quasi-positivistic, essentially subjective view of nature.. taken to its logical extreme, denies the existence of the physical world – or at least its dynamical properties – until they are measured' (1995, p.175). Bohr is not alone in taking this view. For example, Hameroff, who believes that the solution to the mind-body problem lies in quantum physics, writes: 'When *unobserved*, an atom or sub-atomic particle behaves as a 'wave of possibilities'; *observation* in effect 'collapses the wave function' and a particle appears' (1994, p.100). One of the founders of quantum physics, Heisenberg, stressed that physicists no longer deal with elementary particles, but with our knowledge of these particles – that is, with the contents of our mind. Schrödinger and Wheeler have a similar view. Morowitz rightly concludes that 'such interpretations moved science towards the *idealist* as contrasted with the *realist* conception of philosophy' (1981, p.38-39). This perspective may be attractive as an antidote to the prevailing materialism in scientific circles, but it too faces a few uncomfortable issues.

• First of all, this particular interpretation of quantum physics is not the only possible interpretation. Bohm for example devised a system that is compatible with experimental results and yet does not necessitate an observer to make matter real.

• It is ridden with paradoxes. Einstein, who was one of the founders of quantum physics but firmly held the realist view, designed mind experiments, trying to show the apparent absurdity of such a position. For example, he asked, would a mouse that accidentally observes an experiment change the outcome? This difference is what created the rift between him and the other originators of quantum physics.

• Even if this position is correct, it does not seem to be very helpful with regard to the mind-body problem. A notorious issue in quantum physics is an inability to 'translate' or make a bridge between the micro level (the realm of subatomic particles) and the macro-level (the realm of everyday reality). In other words, although the theory may work on the micro level, different rules of the game operate on the macro level – and many issues concerning the mind-body problem relate to that level of organisation.

The above does not mean that quantum physics cannot contribute to a better understanding of the relationship between the brain and the mind, only that it is unlikely to provide the solution on its own.

It can be concluded that although evidently there is a connection between matter and mind, it is not likely that the one is fully the result of the other. So 'hard' dualism, as a possibility, needs to be considered, but there are various options there too.

MENTAL AND MATTER EXIST AND INTERACT

Dualism is based on a belief that there are two qualitatively different entities that interact with each other. Even if a number of scientists and philosophers in the 20th century were acutely aware that the physicalist perspective is inadequate and advocated various forms of dualism, this view is now largely abandoned, mostly because it does not fit the dominant ideology. Very few are prepared to publicly support such a position and risk their academic or scientific careers, be exposed to ridicule, and diminish the chance to publish their work. So, only already well established figures (e.g. Eccles, Popper, Wigner) have dared to argue in its favour. Common sense, however, never fully abandoned this idea. Descartes was the first who tried to establish it on a rational basis in the 17th century, which became the dominant view for a few hundred years. He envisaged two entities, one consisting of the immaterial mind (with properties such as thinking, feeling, willing), and the other of the material body with physical properties (shape, size, mass). By recognising the specific quality of mental states, dualism can account for many phenomena that are an insurmountable challenge for materialists. However, it has its own problems.

• The first difficulty is the very existence of mind. Brain, as a material substance, can exist independently from brain processes (as in the case of a corpse). However, this does not seem to be the case with the mind. One subjectively experiences mental events, but not the mind independent from those events. An individual in a deep sleep, for example, is aware of nothing, rather than an 'empty' or stagnant mind, indicating that the mind is just a term for the conglomerate of these processes. However, if this is the case, the mind cannot exist on its own and cannot interact with the brain. It can only be either a product of the brain activity or a product of an interaction between the brain and something else (this option will be considered later on).

• Descartes would not allow the possibility that animals have minds. This begs the question how and why would simple organisms (without mind) evolve into creatures that have it. And where from and why has this mind substance suddenly appeared?

• Classic dualism also fails to explain how qualitatively different entities can interact (mental causation). Descartes suggested that all mental events are part of the soul, and that the connection between soul and body is in the pineal gland (the only part of the brain that is not duplicated). However, the pineal gland is definitely a part of the body, so the question remains how its physical nature can respond to that which is not physical. Popper proposes that it is a pseudo problem: after all it is accepted that 'non-material' gravitation affects material objects without needing further explanations. This may not be a satisfactory answer in the case of mind-body interaction, though. Gravitation is a force, or a way of describing how large bodies influence each other at a distance. Every force (or energy field), as far as we know, requires a source (in the case of gravitation, a physical object). However, from the dualist perspective matter is not a source of the mind, so in order to interact the body and the mind would require a common medium and such a medium cannot be just assumed and left unexplained.

MENTAL AND MATTER EXIST, BUT DO NOT INTERACT

In order to avoid the interaction problem, some philosophers took the position that both, immaterial (mental) and material (brain) substance exist independently, but they do not interact. This view is called *parallelism* and was first formulated by a follower of Descartes, Geulinx, but is more often associated with the philosopher Leibniz. The obvious problem here is that it certainly *appears* that there is a causal relation between body and mind (it is normally assumed that an injury is the cause of the subsequent pain, and that feeling pain makes one scream). To explain this, Leibniz proposed that God arranged this in advance, so that the mind and body act synchronously (the so-called doctrine of pre-established harmony). Thus, the experience of pain is not caused by the injury, it is prearranged that one event parallels the other. Such a 'deus ex machina' explanation seems highly implausible. One would expect that a being capable of instituting 'pre-established harmony' would also be able to find a way to allow the interaction between mind and body – surely a more elegant solution. A similar (but perhaps even more bizarre) view is known as *occasionalism*, proposed by Malebranche. He suggested that whenever he wanted to move his arm, for example, it was actually moved by God rather than his volition. This would make God very busy indeed.

The virtue of dualism is that it is less reductive than materialism and corresponds better to common sense. It can account for the qualitative difference between mental processes and brain processes as commonly experienced. Yet, dualism also seems to be a dead-end in many respects.

ONE GIVES RISE TO TWO

There is another way to deal with the problem of causation, commonly known as *dual aspect theory* originally espoused by the 17th century philosopher Spinoza. It ascertains that mind and matter are both manifest aspects of a more fundamental property of the nature, which appear to interact by virtue of some unfolding, grounding process within nature itself. So, the experiential aspect is inseparable from its physical correlate, but neither of them can be analysed in terms of the other. There have been recent proponents of this view. For example, physicist Pauli writes:

> It would be most satisfactory of all if *physis* and *psyche* (i.e., matter and mind) could be seen as complementary aspects of the same reality. (Jung and Pauli, 1955, p.210)

A consequence of this perspective is that everything, including objects such as a stone or stick, has both a mental and a physical aspect. A modern version of this view is developed by Charlmers, who claims that the fundamental feature behind mind and matter is information. Some objections to this view can be raised too.

• Dual-aspect theory seems more an attempt to avoid the problem than to solve it. The issue of how such apparently different phenomena could be aspects of one thing remains obscure. Let us consider information, as Charmers proposes. The fundamental problem here is that an event becomes information only if it is cognised. An ability to experience must be already present for anything to be information. Therefore, either the experience is prior to information, or information, experience and its physical correlate appear at the same time. In the former case information cannot be a fundamental feature, while the latter endorses *panpsychism* (as argued by Whitehead and more recently Seager). This view would allow even a thermostat (as Chalmers tentatively suggests) to have, albeit a very primitive, experience. But this is incohesive. Inanimate objects can be fully explained by physical principles, so granting them another fundamental feature seems unnecessary. The behaviour of a thermostat can be satisfactorily accounted for without it having experience. The metal in a thermostat expands because of its intrinsic qualities and the laws of physics, not because it receives (feels) the information that the temperature has changed. Becoming aware and acting upon information is a very different matter from an automatic reaction, and this distinction is not only blurred, but difficult to explain from this position.

• As with some other already mentioned models, dual aspect theory is also unable to adequately explain certain discrepancies between neural events and its phenomenal correlates (e.g. antedating that will be discussed below).

THE SYNTHESIS PERSPECTIVE: TWO GIVE RISE TO ONE

It does not seem that the above possibilities provide an adequate explanation for the relationship between the brain and the mind. Although many of the theories have some elements that ring true, none of them are fully satisfactory. To summarise the main problems, materialism does not adequately explain experience and agency, while dualism cannot explain the interaction between mind and matter. A fresh look at the issue is required. As philosopher McGinn puts it, 'consciousness is an anomaly in our present world-view and, like all anomalies, it calls for some more or less drastic rectification in that relative to which it is anomalous.' (1995, p.226)

The model described below is based on the following postulates:
• The mind heavily depends on the nervous system (including the brain) and its development. This is not controversial, so it does not need further discussion.

• As the above criticism of the materialist perspective shows, the mind, however, cannot be identified with the brain. Even Aristotle argued that the mind must be immaterial on the bases that a material organ could not have the range and flexibility that are required for human thought. Similarly, in modern times, mathematician Gödel, for example, believed that his famous theorem showed that there are demonstrably rational forms of mathematical thought that humans are capable of, which could not be exhibited by a mechanical or formal system of the sort that mind would have to be if only physical. Brentano's notion of the irreducible flexibility of intellect, points in the same direction.

• Rather than being a discrete entity (as a brain is), the mind is considered a convenient name for the sum of mental *events* belonging to one person. These mental events must be interactive processes, otherwise the mind would be an epiphenomenon. And, if this interaction is only between the environment and the body/brain (behaviourism), the mind would be again just a passive observer in the best case. The mind cannot be reduced to the interaction between the various parts of the brain either, because it has certain features that the brain in all its complexity does not have[1]. A direct interaction between the brain and the mind (dualism) is also implausible, because it would make the mind too independent from the brain. To make a parallel, if the brain is a car, a road the environment, the journey itself can be called the mind. The journey does not interact with the car - it is the result of an interaction between the car and the road, and also between the car and the driver.

---

[1] Some of them have already been mentioned and will be further discussed below.

To follow up the above analogy, in order to account for qualia and agency, an equivalent of the driver is indeed necessary. Something that is not an integral part of the car, but interacts with the car and by doing so, affects the journey. Its existence is not only supported by common sense and transpersonal experiences, but also (contrary to popular belief), by findings from contemporary experimental research. For example, the already mentioned *temporal discrepancy* between neural events and conscious experiences indicates that something else is involved:

> The cortical activities evoked by some sharp stimulus to the hand in conscious human subjects took as long as half a second to build up to the level for giving consciousness; yet the subject antedated it in his experience to a time which was the time of arrival of the message from the periphery onto the cerebral cortex, which may be almost half a second earlier. This is an extraordinary happening, and there is no way in which this can be explained by the operations of the neural machinery. (Popper and Eccles, 1977, p.476)

Considering all the above, it is not surprising that such an entity is not and cannot be found in the brain (the point of agreement between materialists and dualists). In fact, non-physical properties of consciousness (e.g. non-spatiality) strongly suggests that a non-material component is involved, which may even, as McGinn puts forward, pre-date the matter:

> ...the origin of consciousness somehow draws upon those properties of the universe that antedate and explain the occurrence of the big bang. If we need a pre-spatial level of reality to account for the big bang, then it may be this very level that is exploited in the generation of consciousness. That is, assuming that remnants of the pre-big bang universe have persisted, it may be that these features of the universe are somehow involved in engineering the non-spatial phenomenon of consciousness. (1995, p.224)

Of course, there cannot be material evidence for this non-material aspect, its existence can only be extrapolated through its consequences (as with gravitation and the other forces). However, including it can provide a more complete and coherent interpretation than reductive approaches. The Synthesis model is, therefore, tripartite: the mental (or the mind) is considered *the result* of an interaction between the two qualitatively different aspects of a living being: one material and one non-material, but it cannot be identified with either of them[1]. This model differs from materialism because it acknowledges the existence of a non-material element and differs from dualism because it does not equate the mind with this element. In other

---

[1] It is worth noting that these three constitutes have been recognised in a number of spiritual traditions. For example, this was a dominant view in Christianity (using the term spirit instead of mind) until the year 869, when the Church reduced them to body and soul. Vedanta also recognises three 'bodies'.

words, the view is that materialists are mistaken to identify the mind with the body, and dualists are mistaken to identify the mind with the soul.

The medium through which this interaction can occur needs to be discussed. As already mentioned, Descartes failed to provide a plausible explanation in this respect, which is not surprising considering that at that time certain phenomena such as waves and fields were unknown. A better grounded account is possible if these concepts are utilised.

The starting premise is that the medium of interaction must be something that has a dual nature. The phenomenon that fits this requirement is the wave. Waves sometimes behave like particles, but not always (for example, they can propagate through a vacuum – no particles are involved). That waves transcend matter is transparent even in its mathematical expression. $\sqrt{-1}$ that is necessary to describe a wave does not correspond to anything material. Heisenberg, one of the founders of quantum physics, wrote that if particles are *not* seen as material bodies, then they show 'a distinct formal similarity to the $\sqrt{-1}$ in mathematics' (1952, p.62). Much earlier, philosopher Leibniz would say that 'the imaginary number is a fine and wonderful recourse to define spirit, almost an amphibian between being and non-being'. Waves too can be seen as an amphibian between two realities[1]. The waves travelling at the speed of light can be considered the top limit of the material world and the bottom limit of the non-material one. They connect these two worlds and at the same time separate, set the boundaries, to them. The renowned psychologist, Carl Gustav Jung writes:

> the psyche... robs bodies of their reality when the psychic intensity transcends the speed of light. Our brain might be the place of transformation, where the relatively infinite tensions or intensities of the psyche are tuned down to perceptible frequencies and extensions. But in itself the psyche would have no dimension in space and time at all. (in Laszlo, 1993, p.191)

The importance of the wave patterns in brain activity is well recognised:

> Just how the neurotransmitters affect the mind itself is unknown. But everything indicates that they affect the *rhythms* of the brain and the rest of the body. Molecules of dopamine and other neurotransmitters in the brain do only one thing: they excite or inhibit nerve cells, and thus they control the 'firing pattern' of nervous tissue. There are thousands of different patterns of such firings within the brain and elsewhere. Everywhere there are patterns and rhythms of activity... More obviously, the firing patterns within the brain can be driven by sensations coming from the 'outside'. Flashes of light or

---

[1] It is tempting to think that imaginary numbers and the wave function are just a mathematical convenience, but this is not he case. As Nunn puts it, 'the wave function is nearly as real as anything else that passes for reality. And the implications of complex numbers have to be taken seriously' (1996, p.46).

pulses of sound, touch, odours, or taste are well known for their ability to capture and 'drive', or 'entrain', rhythmic neural activity. For instance, repetitive drumming, known as 'trance drumming' - performed in great variety in every corner of the world - is ritually used to implant new rhythms, by subduing and 'taking over' personal rhythms. It does not take long in listening to classical Indian music to realise that such music - through intricate and interlocking beats, tones, and rhythms - actually operates on our neural codes and thereby works on our emotions. Literally hundreds of different vocal practices of chanting, singing, and recitation have been discovered to affect different regions of the body and to musically excite or calm the mind through harmonic manipulations and resonances. (Podvoll, 1990, p.184)

Any image, thought, or word can be expressed as a wave function. The Gabor-transforms that limit the infinite Fourier-transforms (the ways of converting complex patterns into component waves) enable a precise match between any brain activity or cerebral network and the corresponding waveform. Waves, therefore, could indeed be the medium through which the brain interacts with a non-material aspect (and *vice versa*). Cortical regions responsible for visual perception, for example, can decode incoming light signals into waveforms of specific frequency and amplitude. So, rather than assuming that the brain constructs information from the input of a sensory nerve it is more accurate to suppose that the centres of the nervous system resonate to this input (see Gibson, 1980). Of course, only waves of a particular frequency serve as the medium of communication between the two aspects. Relatively recent research indicates that the synchronisation of neuronal activity at about 40Hz can be linked to consciousness (Crick and Koch, 1990; Llinas and Ribary, 1993).

Phenomena that can be associated with the non-material part are obviously those that cannot be explained in terms of brain processes (those that do not have neuro-correlates). There are three candidates: the self, awareness and intent (they cannot be illusions because they are the essence of our phenomenological experiences). Not surprisingly, considering the overall purpose, they coincide with the properties of the One (see p.66). The following model is a simplified representation of this interaction:

$$\text{The self} \xrightarrow[\text{awareness}]{\text{intent}} \text{Mind} \xleftarrow[\text{sensations}]{\text{neuro-physiological reactions}} \text{Brain}$$

What these properties are and their characteristics will be discussed later, for the time being only the support for their existence and non-material nature will be presented.

Awareness

There are several reasons why awareness is unlikely to be the result of brain activity.

You can be aware of different external and internal phenomena, but awareness is the property of none of them. For example, you can become aware of a chair, but the chair does not possess awareness. By the same token, you can become aware of your body, thoughts or emotions, but your emotions, for instance, are neither aware of themselves nor of any other part of you. So, if awareness cannot be identified with any mental process, it either resides in a discrete part of the brain or it is not in the brain at all. A part of the brain that is responsible for awareness (not sensations that provide the materials of awareness) has not been located. Considering the prominence of awareness, if it is not located by now, it is not likely to be located ever. True, waves of a certain frequency are present when we are aware, but they cannot be the source of awareness, otherwise a machine producing these waves should be aware too.

This, of course, poses a problem for materialists, so awareness is sometimes considered an emerging property of brain activity that is evenly distributed, and therefore cannot be distinguished from the 'noise' (unspecified neuronal activity). However, if this is the case, awareness should be far less discriminatory. Yet, most of the processes in the brain do not trigger awareness, and there are no processes that we necessarily have to be aware of (including sensory, motor, cognitive and affective ones). You can have a sensation, but not be aware of it until you pay attention. For example, if you focus on your sitting in a chair, you will suddenly become aware of the sensations associated with sitting. Your nervous system has been processing these sensations all the time, but you have not been aware of them until you have turned attention to the sitting. This indicates that awareness does not automatically emerge from neuronal activity. On the basis of his own experiments, Libet concludes that awareness cannot be simply the result of brain complexity (as emergentists would like to believe):

> Many, if not most, mental functions or events proceed without any reportable awareness… even complex functions, as in problem solving or intuitive and creative thinking. On the other hand, the simplest kind of mental functions can be accompanied by awareness/subjective experience, like awareness of a tap on the skin… It is not, then, simply the complexity or creativeness of a mental function that imparts to it the quality of subjective awareness of what is going on. The cerebral code for the distinction between the appearance or absence of awareness in any mental operation would seem to require a mediating neuronal mechanism uniquely related to awareness *per se* rather than to complexity, etc. (in Nunn, 1996, p.40)

The last sentence seems to suggest that a specific brain mechanism should be associated with awareness, but Libet was not able to identify any (besides duration of the stimuli). In fact, even duration and intensity do not always correspond to awareness. One can become aware of the sensations transmitted through the nervous system or not, without any qualitative or quantitative changes in the activity of the nervous system (unless awareness triggers an intention or some other reaction). Moreover, experiments show that the threshold of awareness is lower after one has become aware of a sensation. If awareness and the brain process are identical, the relation between the intensity (or duration) of the stimuli and experience of a sensation should be fixed, and this does not seem to be the case.

Some empirical data also support the view that awareness is not a brain function.
Electrical stimulation of the cortex can initiate memory flashbacks so realistic that they are perceived as real experiences. This is sometimes taken as evidence in support of the materialistic view. However, the very neurosurgeon who conducted these experiments, Wilder Penfield, drew a very different conclusion. Patients are aware of both, being on an operating table and the triggered memories at the same time. Penfield reasons:

> The fact that there should be no confusion in the conscious state suggests that although the content of consciousness depends in large measure on neural activity, awareness itself does not... If the brain mechanism is busy creating the mind by its own action, one might expect mental confusion when the neuronal record is activated by an electrode. (1975, p.55)

Transpersonal experiences (e.g. dislocated or expanded awareness occurring sometimes in meditation) and some experiments in *para-psychology* that have produced small but statistically significant positive results under unusually stringent conditions[1], also point in the same direction - namely that awareness can exist beyond or independent of brain processes. To quote Penfield again:

> After years of striving to explain the mind on the basis of brain-action alone, I have come to the conclusion that it is simpler (and far easier to be logical) if one adopts the hypothesis that our being does consist of two fundamental elements. (*ibid.*, p.80)

If one of these two fundamental elements is not in the brain, it must be non-material.

---

[1] For relatively recent reviews see Bem and Honorton (1994) and Schlitz and May (1998).

Intent

Despite the opposition of materialistically orientated scientists[1], common experience provides overwhelming support for the existence of intentional, self-initiated activity (the nature of intent as its irreducible source will be discussed later). Libet writes:

> ... that mental processes can influence or control neuronal ones, has been generally unacceptable to many scientists on (often unexpressed) philosophical grounds. Yet, our own feelings of conscious control of at least some of our behavioural actions and mental operations would seem to provide *prima facie* evidence for such a reverse interaction, unless one assumes that these feelings are illusory. (1994, p.120)

Empirical findings are actually congruent with common sense. Libet's experiments showing that an action can start *before* the conscious decision to act may be an interesting case. The conclusion is that a decision does not always initiate action, so it is sometimes inferred that action itself triggers neural activity, reducing consciousness to its interpretative or inhibitive role at most. Yet, it is established that a brain module can be activated *without* corresponding action, which goes against this possibility:

> ...neural activity (as indicated by measurements of regional blood flow or metabolic rate) has been shown to increase selectively in the supplementary motor area (SMA) when the subject is asked to imagine moving his fingers without actually moving them. (*ibid.*, p.124)

Thus, a more plausible explanation is that a pre-verbal and even pre-thought energy impulse (an intent) initiates an action that is, in turn, faster than formulating the impulse (which is a cognitive process known as decision).

The reason why materialists try to deny intent is not only their affinity for physical determinism but also the fact that the seat of intent cannot be found in the brain. There are modules of the brain that are associated with vision, movement or language, however, these modules are not responsible for intending to move, speak or perceive. Of course, there are some other factors that can activate these brain regions, but it is universal experience that people often move, speak or even perceive because they intend to do so. Yet, no source of intent itself has been located in the cortex. One part of the brain can effect another (e.g. chemicals produced in the amygdala can affect electrical activity in the frontal lobe). However, these are invariably non-

---

[1] Willis Harman, who was a distinguished scientist himself, points out that '"downward causation", causation-from-consciousness, is for the most part considered unacceptable as a scientific concept in spite of the fact that it is one of the most impressive facts in our practical experience' (1994, p. 141).

intentional effects - any part of the body, including the brain, if left to itself, should operate on the basis of physiochemical laws – it does not have intent. Nor can the source of intent be identified with the whole. This would contradict the *principle of causal grounding* stating that 'the causal efficacy of any complex... is entirely dependent upon the causal efficacy of the basic constituents of its physical instantiation' (see Seager, 1995, p.276). To use an example, one part of a car or computer can affect another, but a car or computer as a whole does not affect its constituent parts. Analogously, mental causation cannot be explained by overall activity of the brain. Therefore, if the notion of intent (leading to a self-generated action) is accepted, it makes sense to conclude that it is a property of a non-material component of the human being.

The objection is sometimes raised that non-material intent would break the law of conservation of energy or the first law of thermodynamics (stating that the total energy in a closed system remains constant). But, there are several ways to account for this. The physical world generally and the brain specifically are better perceived as open systems. Any energy gain or loss in one place could easily be stabilised by gains or losses elsewhere, and even if any deviation from the first law existed, it could never be ascertained by measurements. This is especially the case considering that the mass of the deflected electrical current is almost equal to zero so that there is no problem in compensating for a switch which changes the direction of the current in the brain. Furthermore, as Schrödinger states, energy is equal hv, where h is a constant, a v is frequency. So, energy is proportional to the frequency, and frequencies have statistical averages. This is very much relevant for neuronal activity, because the statistical element in the frequencies of the waves would allow for intent without breaking the first law. Even if this is not taken aboard, the low of preservation of energy may not play a role in this case, on the first place. Scott writes:

> The Hodgkin-Huxley equations, which describe the dynamics of the nerve impulse on an axonal tree, are not after all, constrained by the conservation of energy. Instead this is a system of nonlinear diffusion equations which – like a lighted candle – balances the rate of electrostatic energy release from the membrane to the power that is consumed by circulating ionic currents. Since the electrodynamics of an individual neuron is not constrained by the First Law of thermodynamics, there is little reason to expect this law to constrain a system at a higher level of organization. (1994, p.156)

The self

There are two interrelated issues that need to be examined in connection with the self. Firstly, whether the self exists and secondly if it does, whether it is in the brain.

All the materialists (e.g. Crick, Dennett and others) argue correctly that there is no audience, no *homunculus* (an 'observer') within the brain. There has been a consensus that no single cell or group of cells is likely to be the site of conscious experience. So, in order to remain faithful to their ideology, they must reject that the one who is aware, who is experiencing, exists at all, despite the fact that it contradicts common sense. Note that there is not either empirical or rational support for such an assertion - it is purely ideological. In fact, there is much support that the self that is experiencing does exist (although not necessarily within the brain or body).

The *sense* of self is universal to all human beings and possibly other life forms. A unique (subjective, first person) perspective that we all have and machines do not, however 'clever' they are, indicates its existence. The self is sometimes dismissed as an illusion and compared to perceptual illusions. However, as already pointed out, there is a fundamental difference between these two. The sense of self is not based on perception, and therefore cannot be an illusion. It is a phenomenological experience not mediated by the senses that can trick us. Dismissing such experience as an illusion is on the same level as dismissing that reality exists ('maybe we are all dreaming…')[1]. Hume declared that the self does not exist because he could not find it anywhere. However, this conclusion does not necessarily follow from the premise. Self cannot be directly aware of itself because it is the source of awareness, like a torch that can illuminate everything except itself, or an eye pupil that can enable seeing many things, but not itself. The self cannot be 'found', but it can be recognised as a source – something that is not in the mind, and yet is necessary in order to have the first person perspective. It can be compared with the conductor of an orchestra (although, admittedly 'the orchestra' in this case is often ruled by other factors rather than the self). When listening to an orchestra the conductor cannot be heard, yet shis role is indispensable. Hume is mistaken to regard the self as 'nothing but a bundle of different perceptions'. Perceptions – that is, thoughts, sensations and so on, is what the self is aware of (they are the materials of awareness), so it

---

[1] Nagel writes: 'It is impossible to exclude the phenomenological features of experience from a reduction in the same way that one excludes the phenomenal features of an ordinary substance from a physical or chemical reduction of it – namely, by explaining them as effects on the minds of human observers… The reason is that every subjective phenomenon is essentially connected with a single point of view, and it seems inevitable that an objective, physical theory will abandon that point of view' (1981, p.393).

cannot be reduced to them. Popper, writes:

> One might be tempted, under the indirect influence of Hume, to think of the self as the sum total of its experiences… But it seems to me that this theory is directly refuted by the memory experiences… At the actual moment at which the memory delivers something to us, neither the delivering memory nor the object that it delivers to us is part of our selves; rather, they are outside of our selves, and we look at them as spectators (thought we may be active immediately before and after the delivery) and, as it were, watch the delivery with astonishment. We can therefore separate our conscious experiences as such from our selves. (Popper and Eccles, 1977, p.488)

Some scholars (e.g. Susan Greenfield) consider the self an emergent property of the whole brain, but this does not seem to work either. If the brain and the mind are the same, and the self is distributed in the brain, it should be distributed in the mind too. However, this does not correspond to the common experience. Take, for example, an ordinary dream. In a dream there are usually many characters that, from this position, should be all the result of neural activity. Yet the self identifies with only one character (you know in a dream who is yourself and who are others). If the self is the sum of all the processes, it should equally identify with all the characters which is clearly not the case – a single point of view is always present. Moreover, as already discussed above (p.108-109) if the self is identified with a whole (rather than being a distinct element) it would be reduced to a passive 'observer', an epiphenomenon.

Empirical evidence also supports the idea of the self. For example, *split brain surgery* (the removal of the corpus callosum that links the brain hemispheres) conducted by Sperry in the 1970s and followed up by Victor Mark and others, show that even when the two sides of the brain are separated, the person is not usually aware of it and acts normally. There is a sense that the two hemispheres still form an integrated entity, although the information they share is minimal. Brain stem and cross-perception (perceptual stimulation of both hemispheres at the same time) may play a role, but they are not sufficient. It is observed that split-brain patients can perform complex activities such as playing the piano that require a high level of synchronisation between left and right hands (and therefore two hemispheres). This integration must happen somewhere else. Only sometimes or under experimental circumstances does it become transparent that the hemispheres do not communicate directly and may even conflict each other. It would be premature, however, to draw a conclusion from such instances that split brain leads to split self, especially if it is taken into account that these experiments rely on short term memory and verbal reports that heavily depend on the brain (in the latter case, mostly on one hemisphere). Even ordinary people often have internal conflicts (one part of the person wants to go out while the other wants to stay in), but this is not to say that a single perspective, from which a whole conflict can be experienced is not retained. Quite the opposite, that the self can be aware of the processes in both hemispheres (although not necessarily able to formulate them), identify with one, or shift between them, indicates its relative independence from the brain.

Blind sight experiments point in the same direction. It is observed (in animal and human subjects) that if a segment of the occipital cortex is damaged or surgically removed, the subject is not aware of a part of shis visual field (although shis visual apparatus work properly). However, if asked to guess what is in that part of visual field, they guess correctly in a number of cases far above the statistical average. This means that neuronal processes cannot be identified with awareness. It is more likely that the occipital lobe plays the role of a relay station, producing waves accessible to awareness. Scott, a scientist with a special interest in consciousness, concludes:

> ...the split-brain and blind sight experiments, among others, provide objective evidence for the existence of a mental monitor that might or might not be in operation during a particular act of visual response. (1995, p. 162)

After all, if it is accepted that we can be aware and act intentionally, it must be somebody or something that is aware and intends (and if these are the properties of a non-material aspect, the self too is not likely to be material).

The so-called *binding problem* is also relevant in this case. Everyday experience and experiments on seeing and hearing demonstrate that there is a unifying quality to consciousness. In other words, perceptions, beliefs and attitudes 'hang together'. All our experiences are closely related and integrated not only with past experiences but also with our actions, expectations, theories, evaluations. However, the brain contains no corresponding kind of unity. Binding or the unitary character of the experience, is not reflected in its structure or functions. Constitutive parts that make up the form of an experience (a movement, colour, shape, sound, smell, texture etc.) are processed in different parts of the brain. Considering this segregated nature of the brain and the relative absence of multi-modal association areas in the cortex, the question is how neuronal inputs are synchronised and overlaid to form a single unified and meaningful perception. A simple example: the image on the retina is processed in over twenty different areas of the cortex, each of them dealing separately with specific features of the image. Neural machinery that could recombine the output of these specialised visual feature detectors is not found in the brain. So, it is unlikely that these 'point-events' are fully integrated again by purely physiological activity. Eccles writes:

> ...all the time we are learning more and more about feature extraction neurones and how they come to make more and more complex patterns but never does it get beyond the stage of showing us more than little flashes of simple geometrical fragments to which each cell is responding specifically. (Popper and Eccles, 1977, p.533-534)

Of course, there are several levels of integration: the integration of a simple image such as the shape of an object; the integration of the shape with colour and movement; the integration of a complex image (such as scenery); integration with abstract elements (e.g. a name). Indeed some binding that is dependent on intrinsic properties of the stimuli (such as direction of movement, time, edges, intensity, etc.) may occur even on a sub-neuronal level, on the level of neurons, and some binding probably also occurs on the higher level of neural organisation (cortical regions). But this is not enough:

> All we were working with there are patterns of impulses signalling progressively more complex features. There has to be an interpretational read-out. This is what we believe to give us a unified picture and it is a picture involving all kinds of features such as light and colour and depth and form. (*ibid.*, p.534)

This integration is, therefore, not an 'objective' (as, for example, the integrative character of a computer programme), but 'subjective' one that can only derive from the focal point that keeps it all together – the self[1]. In order to preserve materialistic dogma and avoid this simple common-sensical explanation, a number of complicated theories are employed to explain the binding problem (Chaos theory, Quantum theory, Object Template Constrained Feature Processing theory, etc.). Yet, with all that armoury none of them can account for all the cases of everyday visual perception, let alone other types of binding commonly experienced. Most of these theories boil down to variations of Hume's claim that the elements of perception are bound by spatiotemporal association. However, Kant already pointed out the shortcomings of associationism. We must actively bind the various features of objects together, so that what we see are the synthesised constructions of our world. Therefore, intentionality (to use Brentano's term) must be involved. The relatively recent empirical research, such as the work of Ann Treisman (1986, 114-125) on illusory conjunctions ('mistakes' in binding), also indicates that attention, which can be defined as intentional awareness, is essential to binding.

---

[1] This applies even in the extreme cases of so-called split personality, which are most likely the result of an impermeable segmentation of that with which the self identifies. Sufferers of this disorder still maintain a unique, first-person perspective that enables them to become aware of or dis-identify with some personalities.

In any case, on the level of brain processing, waves or oscillations that are a product of neural activity are likely to play a role. Indeed, research suggests that assemblies relatively far from one another synchronise their activities at a frequency between 40 and 80 Hz (the gamma range). They become phase-locked oscillations. However, this does not solve the binding problem as some scientists are tempted to declare. Nunn (a neuroscientist himself) writes:

> ...all that has been achieved is to show that temporally determined groupings are important to brain activity as well as spatially related groupings... This is an important step forward but it does not obviously get us any nearer towards accounting for awareness. (1996, p. 35)

Commenting on Libet's experiments on temporal discrepancy (that we live up to half a second behind the times) Nunn concludes that 'the main casualty of accepting the obvious interpretation is any hope that coherent EEG activity on its own can account for the binding problem in relation to awareness since epochs of coherent activity are reaching their end before awareness occurs' (*ibid*, p.42). Furthermore, the discharges were also found in a wide range of states not connected to stimulus interpretation, so synchronous oscillations may be necessary, but cannot be sufficient for feature binding. For the final level of binding these phase-locked oscillations need to be selected and 'picked up', for which awareness and intent are essential, and consequently the self - as their source. Only then they can be connected in a meaningful whole:

> This read-out by the self-conscious mind involves the integration into a unified experience of the specific activities of many modules, an integration that gives the pictured uniqueness to the experience. (Popper and Eccles, 1977, p.388)

This can also explain why it is possible to use the same group of neuro-connections in presentation of different objects. Many other phenomena point in the same direction. For instance, a changing brain would not be able to perceive a change without a non-changing element and yet, there is not an unchanging part of the brain. Thus, it is proposed that awareness, intent and the self enable particular connections out of endless possibilities (even within the restrictions of time-space associationism). Some neuroscientists, such as Sperry and Doty, who are not dualists, also acknowledge that integration seems to be best accounted for in the mental sphere. Eccles concludes:

> ...it has been impossible to develop any neuropsychological theory that explains how a diversity of brain events comes to be synthesized so that there is a unified conscious experience of a global or gestalt character. The brain events remain disparate, being essentially the individual actions of countless

neurones that are built into complex circuits and so participate in the spatiotemporal patterns of activity... *the experienced unity comes, not from a neuropsychological synthesis, but from the proposed integrating character of the self-conscious mind.* (*ibid.*, 362)

This sort of binding is not only necessary for perception but also for a meaningful, intentional action. At least some actions must be the result of an interaction with something outside the system producing these actions (i.e. you cannot move a boat by blowing into its sails if you are in the boat). Admittedly, this interaction could be between the brain and the environment, which is why behaviourists adopted the belief that we are completely socially determined. Yet, this is not the case. Every person is (to a degree) an agent. The movements of physical objects may not involve purpose (as Aristotle thought), but purposeful, teleological causation is common to human beings. We are often motivated by the future, an end result. In other words, many actions are meaningful - and such a teleological pull is different from a conditioned push. However, any purposeful activity requires something that can grasp the causal relationship between an activity and its results. Such an element needs to be, as it were, outside any specific process that contributes to the action. An analogy with a factory as a complex system may be appropriate here. The production of the factory may consist of many relatively discrete and specialised processes. Each of them is part of the whole, but none of them determines the whole. Only something that can grasp the whole and its relation to the external world can determine a meaningful direction. This, of course, does not require interfering with or being aware of all the individual processes. Particular units of the body, such as the digestive system, can act independently, but those actions are only re-actions, rather than a directed activity that involves the whole body. The same applies to the brain with its modules that have specific functions – in most cases these modules will carry on unabated by the choices a person makes, and yet they serve them.

All the above suggests that the existence of the self makes more sense than otherwise, and that this universal human experience can be vindicated by empirical findings and reason. However, as already mentioned, everybody agrees that the self cannot be found in the brain. And if it is not in the brain, it must be elsewhere. That the self is located in other parts of the body is even less likely (which is apparent from spinal cord injuries that lead to paralysis but not a loss of self). So, concluding that it is an element of non-material reality seems inevitable. An attempt can be made now to conceptualise that to which the self, awareness and intent belong to.

THE SOUL

The self, awareness and intent cannot exist in a void. It makes sense that they are the properties of a relatively discrete (non-material) energy field. Despite its baggage, the traditional name for this part of a living organism, the soul, still seems to be the most convenient. To ease possible discomfort from certain associations that the usage of this word may evoke, a brief historical perspective will be presented first.

The notion of soul (interpreted in various ways) appears in practically every culture: the Egyptian term was *ba*, the Hindu *atman*, the Jewish *neshamah*, the medieval Christian *anima divina*. Popper writes:

> There is an abundance of important evidence that supports the hypothesis that dualistic and interactionist beliefs concerning body and mind are very old – prehistoric and of course historic. Apart from folklore and fairy tales, it is supported by all we know about primitive religion, myth, and magical beliefs. (Popper and Eccles, 1977, p.157)

Greek philosophers identified the soul with the life principle itself and also the source of inner movement. Plato considered the self (soul) distinct from the body and capable of living without it. Aristotle also acknowledged a non-material aspect of a human being (although he interpreted it in a different way from Plato). A Roman biographer Plutarch speaks about *nous,* uncorrupted soul that survives death. Cicero too was a dualist. Soul, as a breath of life, appears in Egyptian Gnostic Myths, the book of Genesis and the Arabian Creation Myth. Not all religions however, support this notion. Mainstream Buddhism rejects the idea of the eternal non-material soul that is taught in Hinduism (*anatta* doctrine), which is consistent with its creed of impermanency and makes its essentially idealistic position closer to materialist views. However, this creates a number of other inconsistencies (in relation to the concepts of the self, reincarnation and Nirvana). The Old Testament seems ambiguous about whether humans are purely physical beings or not. In the earlier period, the emphasis is very much on this world (as, for example, in the Book of Job). Later, though, the soul becomes more independent from the body. In Christianity, it is considered an eternal, divine, perfect and beautiful aspect of the human, which nevertheless resembles the physical body and can suffer an equivalent of physical pains and pleasures. Some modern theologicians (such as Teilhard de Chardin) rejected these naïve notions of the soul and developed much more sophisticated interpretations. So the idea of the soul has a long tradition, and should not be identified with any particular religious framework.

THE PERCEPTION OF THE SOUL (EPISTEMOLOGICAL ISSUES)

The soul is not material, so it cannot be detected indirectly through the physical senses or mechanical instruments[1]. It can be, however, directly felt, experienced. Most people are vaguely aware of these experiences (although they are often ascribed to the body or mind). For example, it is common to describe individuals in terms of energy properties, such as 'warm or cold', 'open or closed', 'deep or shallow', 'cracking', 'being on the same wave length', etc. They may be the descriptions of some processes at the non-physical level, rather than just metaphors. Yet, the understanding of the soul has remained rudimentary even for those who believe in it, for several reasons:

• Such experiences are unstable, fleeting, vague, unstructured and difficult to classify, so they are usually consciously ignored as a background noise.

• Perception of the soul is easily overrun by more intense and concrete physical and mind processes, such as inputs from the environment and more tangible mental states (e.g. imagination or thinking).

• They are not based on sensory perception, so it is extremely difficult to conceptualise and objectify these experiences within a socially shared framework.

A fuller comprehension of the soul requires the combining of several methods: transpersonal perception, phenomenological reduction and deductive inferences.

• Transpersonal experiences are of course essential, but they involve shifting the focus of awareness. Considering that the soul is non-material, using a visual apparatus, of course, is not necessary. However, maintaining the attention (e.g. on a person) and stabilising fleeting impressions are.

• An accurate perception (that may or may not produce a mental image) requires separating that which comes from the observed soul and that which belongs to the observer. So, phenomenological reduction, concentrating on the experience of phenomena related to the soul without social and personal interpretations, is essential. In other words, the accuracy depends on the extent to which a person is capable of bracketing and going 'below' the constructs through which reality is normally perceived and other projections.

• Deductive conclusions (following the criteria of reasoning p.42) can also contribute to a better understanding by bridging the existing gaps.

---

[1] Whatever instruments can find could only be properties of the matter, because they are based on such properties. This limitation of instruments should not be a reason to dismiss other phenomena out-of-hand.

THE DESCRIPTION

An objection may be raised that any attempt to describe the soul may ruin the magic and mystery associated with this subject. However, although the soul is very special (being different from anything else) there is no reason to mystify it. Reality is mysterious enough (not only in relation to the soul), so there is no need to worry about attempts to understand and describe what can be understood and described.

The first challenge that such an endeavour faces is that the soul is not a kind of substance or 'stuff' (as assumed in the so-called 'ectoplasm' account). It is more accurate to think about it as focused fluctuations of pure energy (meaning without 'stuff' that fluctuates). However, for any intelligible account it is practically impossible to imagine or speak about the soul and avoid completely the terms usually associated with substance (i.e. shapes or colours). In a similar vein physicists represent light, for example, as a wavy line with peaks and troughs although, in fact, light is not like that. So for the sake of better understanding, these familiar terms will be used in the description of the soul, fully acknowledging that any conceptualisation is not only limiting, but crude too.

On the basis of the above methods, several inferences can be drawn. The soul, first of all, does not resemble the physical body. It would not be functional for the soul of a rabbit, for example, to have the shape of a rabbit. This shape is adapted to life in the physical environment and would not be of much use in non-material reality (what would be the purpose of legs, for example?) The difference between the body and the soul, despite their resonance, is possible because the experiences (that may be mediated through neuronal activity) are not organised in the same way as the nervous system. This is not unlike various parts of the body being disproportionally represented in the neocortex. It is already put forward that such an energy has to be focused (crate loops). So, it is suggested that the basic 'shape' of the soul can be conceived as spherical, although its better topological representation would be torus[1] (a doughnut shape) with an infinitely small point in the middle (known as 'umbilicoid') and an infinitely large field:

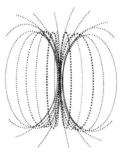

---

[1] A torus is different from a sphere – one cannot be reshaped into the other.

The soul, therefore, can be considered a field that consists of energy loops and two major vortexes. This resembles an electro-magnetic field, except that the latter does not have the centre. Transpersonal experiences indicate, however, that the soul is not a uniform lump of energy. It seems that the soul has a complex structure, with various components and their specific functions. In a way, such an energy field is better compared to a single-cell organism, with its centre, inner space and the membrane. These components are not sharply demarcated though, there is a much greater fluidity between them than between biological components. Different layers of the soul can also have a different density. For example, in the part of the soul where the processes associated with physical life occur[1], the layers towards the surface are comparatively less dense but faster. A diagram below is a simplified representation of the basic (but not exhaustive) movements of the soul; it is not, by any means, a picture of the soul, but only a highly schematised diagram of energy trajectories in relation to the central point.

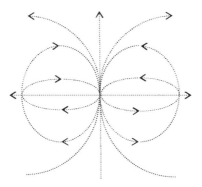

It is not controversial that energy does not need to be corpuscular (material). What makes the soul non-physical is that it exists in a non-material realm where only some known laws are relevant (e.g. the effect of a variance in energy potential). Thus, the soul is not in the body, nor does it leave the body after death. The soul is a low density and high speed energy that is all the time in non-material reality and only resonates for a while with the body.

The soul defines how one is, rather than who one is. So, various descriptions such as physical appearance, name, role, gender, race, nationality or religious affiliation have nothing to do with the soul, although they may affect it indirectly, to the extent to which these descriptions are allowed to influence one's experience and actions.

---

[1] This part is so distinct from the rest of the soul that it can be practically seen as a separate unit.

Because they are often associated with an ideal image, the common assumption is that souls are perfect and beautiful. However, some transpersonal experiences suggest that this is not always the case. For example, a soul can be so 'soft' that it loses its shape, or so solidified that it loses its fluidity. Some impulsive and uncontrollable desires (when the energy of the soul stretches out before an action) may look like protrusions from the main 'body'. Also, the surface of a soul may have 'cracks' that interrupt the flow of energy, darkened areas (that can be the result of inner conflicts or traumatic experiences) and depressions. Moreover, the movement of energy may not always be pleasant: a soul normally pulsates, but sometimes this pulsating can be erratic or resemble trembling (like in fever). Nevertheless, every soul possesses an element of infinity, which without doubt has an aesthetic quality (even if the individual shapes may not be particularly appealing).

THE DYNAMIC OF THE SOUL

Contrary to popular belief, souls are not perfect (the idea of perfect souls is incompatible with interactionism and the purpose - what would be the point of physical life if souls were perfect and unchanging?). In fact, souls are initially latent, little aware, and with minimal internal control (akin to children). They need to develop in order to become independent and capable of self-determination. In a way, souls can be seen as a raw material that have to undergo various processes (experiences) and the treatment of tools (the body and mind). In other words, they are the units of volatile energy that require a form to give them stability. To maintain a soul's coherence, its energy is first limited by the body and then by the mind, until the self is capable of controlling it. So, although the soul should not be identified with the mind, the mind (as well as the body) affects the soul. Plutarch (among many others in the Ancient world for whom the perception of the soul was a matter of fact) thought that the variations and movement of colours could reveal the passions and vices of the soul. So, the energy of the soul gradually grows and gets harmonised through the evolution and development of the mind.

The soul is shaped through life experiences, in other words, through an interaction with the internal and external environment. Every experience affects its shape – redistributes energy (which we may be aware of as a feeling, the recognition of the effects that an experience has on us). This, however, does not mean that the soul is directly involved. As in a dream, the dreamer is not really in that realm, but s/he still experiences, and these experiences can have an effect even after waking up. To follow this analogy further, like a dreamer while dreaming, the soul is, in a way, suspended during the life-time. It could be said that the soul sleeps (meaning that the self is not normally aware of non-material reality). This is why the soul does not exist for most of people, as the one who dreams usually does not exist for the one in the dream. In terms of quantum physics, the soul is suspended in a state of uncertainty until the function that is physical life, collapses (at the moment of death). Sometimes the soul can become aware of a larger reality (lucid dreams – when the person realises that s/he is dreaming without actually waking up, would be an equivalent), but such events are arguably rare. This is not to say that the soul is completely passive. The soul affects the brain (body) by intent and energy shifts, but its influence is not very strong, although it can increase in time (the more effects the self can have, the more developed life is). So, differences between souls are the result of having different experiences and making different choices.

The overall dynamic of the soul can be also considered in terms of the balance (or imbalance) between the two basic principles, static and dynamic:
• The stronger static principle is manifested as the slackness of the soul and a longing for security and predictability, which can lead to inertia and stagnation. If this principle is balanced, it can contribute to internal and external harmonisation. Balance is achieved by developing agency (which includes curiosity, courage, creativity, and also personal responsibility).
• The dominant dynamic principle can be recognised as the restlessness of the soul, a longing for freedom from the constrains of the physical environment, body and mind, which can lead to chaos and even madness. If balanced, it can contribute to self-actualisation and development. The balance is achieved by nurturing self-discipline.

The most important characteristic of the soul is that it is a focused energy. This focal point that enables awareness and intent can be called the self. However, the self needs to be distinguished from I (personality); awareness needs to be distinguished from the materials of awareness (such as thoughts, images, feelings etc.); intent also needs to be distinguished from other possible causes of activity (reflexes, urges, desires, will). To make this clearer, these three properties and how they relate to the material aspect of the human being are discussed next.

THE SELF

WHAT THE SELF IS NOT

The self is different from 'I' (or personality), which can be considered the sum of its identifications. The self (as the source of awareness and intent) already exists when an infant is born, while most of aspects of 'I' do not, but are slowly formed. The self initially identifies with that which enables the materials of awareness and can be influenced directly by intent. This is normally a physical body. That the self identifies with the body rather than being the body is implied by the fact that in dreams the self can dis-identify from the body and identify with an image (without even noticing the difference). The same applies to one's thoughts, behaviour, name, various roles, etc. They all constitute what is commonly referred to as 'I', but they are not part of the self, nor is the self part of them:

> The self itself, the necessity – as Kant put it – of the 'I think' being able to accompany all of my representations, a transcendental ego which is quite different to, and independent of, the empirical self that in the natural standpoint each of us identifies as 'me'. (Solomon, 1988, p.136)

So, any part of oneself that the person can observe, imagine or think of, is a part of 'I' not the self. For example, you can observe your thoughts, but this requires distancing from them, indicating that your self is different from your thoughts. If you have an image of the one who observes, this also can only be just another identification, not the self. Michael Daniels, a psychologist with a special interest in transpersonal psychology, explains this in the following way:

> This *mental-intellectual* realisation of our own subjectivity occurs at the moment when I have the *thought* that I exist as an experiencing and active centre. It is, therefore, based on the simple ideas that *'I experience this'* and *'I do this'*. Such thinking immediately sets up a dualism between subject and object. Since I also realise that any *ideas* about myself are themselves *objects* to experience then 'I' cannot be any *thing* I think I am. The real 'I' must, therefore, be the *subject* – the witness or agent who is distinct from any mental contents such as perceptions, thoughts, intentions or self-concepts. (2005, p.168)

In theory, the self can identify with an infinite number of forms. These identifications do not require a special type of connection, they are based on already existing connections. This is similar to a driver, for example, who identifies with the car s/he is driving (it often feels like a body extension while driving) or a person who identifies with a pair of glasses as long as s/he is wearing them.

WHAT THE SELF IS

The self is a different kind of entity from anything physical. This becomes apparent if the *argument from personal identity* is considered. Philosopher Geoffrey Madell writes: '...while my present body can thus have its partial counterpart in some possible world, my present consciousness cannot. Any present state of consciousness that I can imagine either is or is not mine. There is no question of degree here' (1981, p.91). In other words, if your parents conceived your body a day earlier or later it may have been to a degree different; but *you*, as a subject, would either exist or not (it would be you or somebody else – no degree). This makes the self unique, and unlike physical bodies, it cannot be described (or imagined), except perhaps as being an infinitely small, indivisible point. A developmental psychologist with a transpersonal bent, Jenny Wade, writes:

> Everyday consciousness contains a transcendent element that we seldom notice because that element is the very ground of our experience. The word transcendent is justified because if the subjective consciousness – the Observing Self – cannot itself be observed but remains forever apart from the contents of consciousness, it is likely to be a different order from everything else. Its different nature becomes evident when we realize the observing self is featureless, cannot be affected by the world any more than a mirror can be affected by the images it reflects. (1996, p.56)

This 'true' self is recognised and variously described by different traditions as the Atman, spark, centre, apex of the soul, or ground of the spirit. However, sometimes the self is taken as something above and superior, implying that individuals should strive to 'connect' with it[1]. Such interpretations can be misleading (especially if it is attempted to imagine that 'higher self'). Considering that the self enables experience, and we are experiencing most of the time, the self must already be 'connected'. This relationship can be compared to the relationship between somebody who is playing a computer game and the character in the game with whom the player identifies. The player can be so engrossed in the game that s/he may forget shimself and the real world, but nevertheless the one who is experiencing and is the source of any action within the game is the player shimself not the character in the game.

The self can be considered the focal point of a relatively discrete energy field, and is a property of all life forms. From this perspective, it is universal. Everybody is different, but this has nothing to do with the self. Individual differences are the result of qualitative and quantitative differences in the focused energy and mediums with which the self identifies.

---

[1] One example of this view can be found in Assagioli's 'Psychosynthesis' model.

THE PURPOSE OF THE SELF

The most important function of the self, as the focusing point, is to enable awareness and intent. Without the self, nobody would be there to be aware. As Chandler puts it,

> Both understanding and consciousness depend on something outside, i.e. transcending the computational system, something which knows and relates them. (1995, p.360).

Awareness is intimately related to experience, so it can be said that the self makes experience possible. But, what sort of experience one will have and its quality depends on what a self identifies with. Physical pain, for example, will affect the person to the extent to which the self identifies with the body at that moment[1]. The intensity of an experience can make, in turn, this identification stronger (up to a point). Without the self, intent (self-initiated action) could not exist either. Awareness and intent can be considered other forces (besides the four recognised in the material world). Certain scholars reject this possibility on the basis that in this case we would all be telepathic or telekinetic. But this does not follow. The effects of awareness and intent come about only in particular circumstances and on a subtle level (the same applies to the physical forces - electro-magnetism, for example, was not even discovered until relatively recently). Intent can directly affect only the matter that its source (the self-soul) is engaged with, which is usually the brain, and awareness is even more specific. It affects its source, rather than its object (some quantum physicists would claim that it can also affect its object, but this is debatable). This is not to say that the self exists only when the person is aware and intends (just as the eye pupil does not disappear when the eye is shut). The continuity is preserved despite unconscious episodes, because at least some soul waves remain focused even when awareness and intent are not obviously involved.

The self is also necessary for binding, so that a person can be and can act as a whole. It has a unitary or integrative function not only in relation to our past experiences but also our present evaluations and constructs, and our future expectations or predictions. Eccles writes that 'the self has the drive or the need or the tendency to unify and bring together the various activities of the brain.' (Popper and Eccles, 1977, p.498)

---

[1] A character in Charles Dickens's *Hard Times*, when asked on her sick-bed whether she was in pain, answers: 'I think there's a pain somewhere in the room, but I couldn't positively say that I have got it.' Anecdotal evidence suggests that many people have had a similar experience when their association with the body (or a part of the body) is weakened.

All this enables a degree of auto-control. Although many processes in the body and brain are not under the direct influence of the self, self can still have (through its identifications) an overall control, a function similar to an operator. The importance of this function can be recognised if the experience of those who have lost it is observed:

> ...without the everyday orientation of being the one who controls, the 'operator' who directs the mind, he realizes that he must function without a sense of self... the person entering psychosis creates limitless confusion by trying to reinforce his personal identity, in an attempt to catch his bearings by trying to build himself up. (Podvoll, 1990, p.145)

The comparison with an operator should not be pushed too far, though. In most cases the self is only a potential operator. Other stronger factors (such as physical and environmental conditioning) may have a greater influence. Usually the self can have an effect only when these factors are in a relative equilibrium. Through the processes of evolution and development they gradually lose their dominance and the role of the self increases. In other worlds, through life experiences the self-soul is learning to master its energy.

The self is the equivalent of the One on the level of individual life forms. It relates (potentially) to one's inner word as the One relates to Reality. The self intends, but does not perform. The self also does not think in a conceptual way, but it enables a person to be aware of shis thoughts (as well as everything else) and form proactive, creative ones. That the self is the source of awareness and intent, but not the source of conceptual thinking is not a contradiction. It is like a user-computer system. The computer has its own language that the user does not need to understand in order to interact with the computer and be aware of what is on the screen; which is in the case of the self, the end result of mental process. To think in terms of images, words and other representations, some hardware is also necessary – the brain. The self is, in fact, rarely aware of the routes that lead to formed thoughts and conversely, our thoughts are not always intentional.

THE DYNAMICS OF THE SELF

The self does not change, it simply is. What brings the dynamic principle is the energy that the self focuses, which is why its relative position within the energy field is not fixed. Metaphorically speaking, the self is like an antenna, that collects, connects and focuses the waves on a particular frequency and in that way transforms them into information or experience. Factors that can affect these changes (starting from the most intense one) are: the processes in the body, in the mind and in the soul.

The self can change 'size', direction and position.

• The 'size' regulates the focus (attention). Note that the self, in fact, does not have size, the term refers to the volume of information that is in the focus at any particular point (in theory, an infinite number of lines can intersect at one point).

• Direction enables identification with different sides of one's personality (which can be compared to changing radio stations). This is not to say that when a direction of the self is changed the self really moves. Rather, the energy configurations with which the self is associated shift. Such a shift is experienced as being in different states of mind or different mind-frames.

• A change of the relative position within its energy field is commonly recognised as being in depth or near the 'surface', for example. It depends on the energy redistribution (or a change of the 'shape' of the soul). This move depends on the qualities of interaction with the environment (i.e. intensity and attachment). For instance, increased intensity (excitement), usually draws the self towards the surface (while calming down leads to depth). A degree of involvement or attachment to external events can have even more lasting and profound effects in the same way. This move towards the 'surface' is usually perceived as pleasant, because it enables a quantitative increase in experience and information. However, self-control is more difficult on that level, and the quality of experience may be reduced.

• A change of the absolute position can be compared with moving from radio frequencies to, for example, mobile phone frequencies. The intensity of and engagement with the material world usually fix the self in one position. When the absolute position is changed, what is perceived may change too, because different waves are focused. Such a change can be induced deliberately (through some esoteric practices or the use of psychotropic drugs), but sometimes it can happen spontaneously. Exhaustion, for example, can affect the brain is such a way that the habituated structure of reality that keeps the self in a particular position loosens up. This may lead to a spontaneous shift of awareness, and hence altered perception (although ordinary hallucinations, that are just projections, are far more common).

AWARENESS

WHAT AWARENESS IS NOT

To clarify what awareness is, first a distinction has to be made between awareness and other phenomena that are easily confused with it.

Awareness is different from mental processes such as thoughts, images, sensations, emotional reactions etc. The Ancient Greeks had separate terms for awareness (psyche) and mental activity (pneuma), yet this difference is obscured nowadays. Some philosophers and neuro-scientists (e.g. G. E. Moore, Baars) have recognised though, that they cannot be treated as the same thing. Grossman, for example, writes: 'We can introspectively discriminate between the contents of consciousness and the quality of being conscious' (in Bogen, 1998, p.237). Libet makes the same point: 'The *content* of an awareness can be anything. But being aware is a unique phenomenon in itself, independent of the nature of the particular content in awareness' (2004, p.188). To preserve this distinction, the term consciousness is used throughout the text for all the mind activities (of which some comprise the materials of awareness). Awareness, on the other hand, does not refer to any specific mental processes, but to that which enables the self to relate to them. An analogy can be made with a movie projection: everything that is on the screen can be considered consciousness, while awareness would be the equivalent of the projector light that is not a part of the movie, but enables whatever is on the screen to be visible. Another parallel can be made with a torch that casts light on various objects. If what is lit by the torch comprises consciousness, awareness is the light from the torch (and like a torch, it cannot illuminate all the objects at the same time).

Awareness cannot be identified with sensory perception either. Rather, it refers to the effects that perception has on that which is aware, establishing the relation between the subject and the perceptual representations. In fact, we do not need to perceive to be aware (as, for example, in dreams)[1]. Awareness of our thoughts, emotions, feelings and other mental states is also a direct experience not mediated by the senses. By the same token, some perceptual sensations can escape awareness (e.g. we may not be aware of all the details in a picture we are looking at, although our brain receives them).

---

[1] This was recognised a long time ago. For example, the following rhetorical question can be found in Vedanta: 'Impressions arise from light, but during a dream no light from outside enters the body. So, what is that light that creates images that we see in dreams?'

WHAT AWARENESS IS

Awareness is the crucial concept for a proper understanding of reality, because the only certainty is that one is aware (it does not matter of what: sensations, thoughts, external reality, feelings, or anything else). The usual translation of Descartes' famous dictum '*Cogito ergo sum*', as 'I think, therefore I am' is somewhat off the mark. Being aware (of my mental processes among other things) rather than thinking, is the evidence that I exist. It seems that Descartes' himself recognised the importance of awareness, given his definition in the *Principles of Philosophy*: 'By the term "thought" I understand everything which we are aware of as happening within us, in so far as we have awareness of it' (in Güzeldere, 1995, p.45). So, the claim 'I am aware, therefore I am' may be more appropriate[1]. This puts awareness in its proper place, as being one of the two fundamental properties (the other being intent) of the focused energy. As the gravitational field is a property of matter, awareness can be considered a property of life. Being a fundamental property, awareness cannot be defined by using other, more basic terms. For all practical purposes, however, awareness can be described as an ability to illuminate to the self some of the materials that comprise consciousness[2].

THE PURPOSE OF AWARENESS

Awareness is necessary for life. The soul feeds on information and experience, which is what we are aware of, and the function of awareness is to enable this process of subjectivisation (or appropriation). In other words, the energy is assimilated through the process of transforming it into information and experience. Moreover, agency, or voluntary action, would not be possible without awareness, every action would only be a reflex re-action (which would make human beings and other life forms automata). The self can affect only what it is (or has been) aware of. So, as awareness grows, the amount of energy that is under the influence and control of the self grows too.

---

[1] The state of deep sleep or unconsciousness does not count in this case, because one cannot make any judgements when in these states. True, they can be confirmed by somebody else, but the person involved can legitimately doubt that the other person really exists ('perhaps I am only dreaming shim'), while s/he cannot reasonably doubt that s/he is aware, when s/he is aware.

[2] The above refers to the usual use of this ability. It is possible in some instances to become aware of reality directly rather then mediated by mental constructs (such as images and thoughts), but these can be considered as exceptional cases.

THE FUNCTIONING OF AWARENESS

Direct awareness of reality may be possible, but it is impractical (for the reasons described below) and short lived. Normally, the materials of awareness are first mediated by the senses, nervous system and the brain, and then by mental constructs. Electro-chemical processes in the brain create waves or oscillations on a particular frequency. These carrier waves provide most of the content of awareness. There are strong indications that synchronisation of neuronal activity at the frequency range of 35–70 Hz can be associated with awareness[1]. When in a deep sleep, for example, these waves are not present. The body can react to changes in the surroundings (e.g. temperature variations), without any awareness. However, when the brain starts producing these waves the self becomes aware - with a sensory input (when awake) or without (in dreams[2]). So, awareness depends, first of all, on the frequency, although, of course, other factors, such as the recurrence of a particular neural activity, also play a role.

Even the awareness of processes in one's own soul is normally linked to the same band of frequencies that are produced in the brain. Hence, such awareness is usually limited to phenomena that are associated with experiences in physical life, rather than to the rest of the soul or non-material reality. The focus is maintained within a certain range by the intensity of physical stimuli and habituation (in other words, it is largely biologically and to some extent socially conditioned). This is not to say that awareness can function only within the above range, but that the perception of reality is fixed because the range of frequencies within which awareness operates is fixed by these factors. Therefore, transpersonal experiences that require expanding awareness beyond usual perception, can be facilitated by reducing the input from the senses and the brain (without losing awareness). So, sensory deprivation, the hypnagogic state (between being awake and falling asleep), or meditation, can all be conducive in this respect.

---

[1] Relating these synchronous oscillations in the brain to conscious experience (the temporal binding of various sensory features) is attributed to Koch and Crick. More than a hundred years earlier though, Payton Spence came to the same conclusion based on purely theoretical work. A neurophysiologist from that period, M. M. Graver, followed it up experimentally and found that mental activity is sub-served by a cerebral oscillatory mechanism with the frequency of 36-60Hz. Their work passed almost unnoticed. It seems typical that Crick is accredited for the work already initiated by somebody else (the other case is the largely unacknowledged contribution of Rosalind Franklin to the discovery of the DNA structure).

[2] It is interesting that these episodes of awareness occur, as a rule, several times during sleep, as if it is not desirable to suspend awareness for prolonged periods. Why they seem to happen in regular time intervals is not clear.

THE DIRECTION OF AWARENESS

Broadly speaking, there are three common domains of awareness[1]:

The physical domain: awareness of the physical phenomena, including one's own body.

The mental domain: awareness of mental states and processes (e.g. thoughts, images and other constructs, related to oneself and external reality).

The non-physical domain: awareness of some processes in one's own soul (e.g. being open, being in one's depth) or in the souls of others that are usually experienced as a feeling, but can also be perceived as a shape, colour, or movement.

The self can be aware of information from all these domains, but the signals coming through the brain (the physical domain) are on the whole the strongest. The intensity of the information from this domain screens out, to some extent, potential information from the other domains. Furthermore, the mental processes (e.g. thoughts, images) are also more intense than the processes in the soul, so the latter are often concealed by both, sensory perception and mental activity. Hence, even though they are more direct, sensations from the non-physical domain are normally recognised only if those mediated by the brain and mind are not prominent, because they are not as strong and clear as the other ones. Nevertheless, despite being usually clogged up by the stronger stimuli, some materials from this domain are attainable. Intending to become aware of them and bracketing information coming from the other domains (see p.37), maximise the chance of this happening. These two (intending and bracketing) are also sufficient, no special techniques are required.

In addition, awareness can be directed towards external reality or internal reality. The latter can be called *self-awareness*, which is awareness of the system with which the self identifies, commonly referred to as 'I'. It includes awareness of some processes in one's body, mind and soul (the effects of experiences on its dynamics). Self-awareness is sometimes taken to be a uniquely human ability, but this claim is dubious. Animals can also be aware of themselves (that they are in pain or hungry, for instance). They, however, are not capable of *reflection* and *self-reflection*, which requires not only self-awareness, but also mental distance. What enables this distancing and why it is uniquely human, will be discussed later in the text (p.162-167).

---

[1] The transpersonal domain (awareness via non-material reality including so called mystical experiences or shamanic journeys) is not included because it is rather exceptional.

RESTRICTING AWARENESS

When not restricted by the body and mind, the soul potentially has a wider awareness, but such a wide awareness is difficult to organise and contain. Awareness of all the potential information in each of the above domains would not be practical. Too many stimuli may, in fact, decrease awareness. Making sense out of disparate pieces of information would be harder without some restrictions. So, to minimise confusion and overload, there are mechanisms that limit the quality and quantity of experience and information accessible to awareness. In other words, potential information passes through several filters before it becomes actual information. This narrowing enables paying attention to details and organisation, which in turn allows gradual development. Awareness can be restricted in the following ways:

Limiting potential materials

First of all, materials that are accessible to awareness are limited depending on their source. These limitations can be grouped in three categories:

Limits of perception - potential information about physical reality and the body are restricted by the limitations of the sensory apparatus and nervous system. The 19th century philosopher and psychologist Henri Bergson was not much off the mark when he suggested that 'perhaps our senses are intended to keep things out, rather than to let them in'. Indeed, they do not register at all many signals (for instance, those on the frequency of infra-red light). Also, some signals are not intense enough, and some are overrun by stronger stimuli.

Limits of the mind - the mind is not only narrower than the brain (there are processes in the brain that never become a part of consciousness), but it imposes its own limitations. The main purpose of the mind is to construct reality out of experiences and available information, which implies selectivity. Also, in time, many pieces of information become inaccessible (because they are blocked or because an associative path is lost).

Limits of the soul - only a part of the soul is related, at any point, to a physical or mental life. We are normally aware of experiences connected just to this part. Furthermore, awareness of the processes in the soul depends on their intensity and their relative position within the energy field. For example, awareness seems to increase with a decrease of density (that allows a greater momentum), which is why becoming aware of something is generally associated with bringing it to the 'surface'. In other words, the deeper processes are, the harder it is to become aware of them.

Limiting awareness itself

Awareness is characterised by selectivity which is demonstrated by the fact that only a few of the myriad of neural events are illuminated, and these few are arranged hierarchically. Eccles writes:

> The self-conscious mind has to select. We'd be overloaded by information if at any moment we had to take notice of everything that was poured into all our senses. This is perhaps one of the very important reasons for the operation of the self-conscious mind and its evolution... It gives a selection or a preference from the total operative performance of the neural machinery. (Popper and Eccles, 1977, p.475)

This selection is achieved by amplifying some signals at the expense of others, possibly through the process of positive feedback (see, for example, Harth, 1993).

Awareness is a complex phenomenon, closely related to short and long term memory, which makes the matter even more complicated. Three distinct states (but with fuzzy boundaries between them) can be distinguished in relation to the focus of awareness: being unaware of what is received; being aware only superficially (floating awareness that scans incoming stimuli without ascribing meaning to them); and being fully aware (focused), which enables constructing and memorising the available materials.

Non-awareness - we are not aware of everything we receive. One simple example has already been mentioned. If you are sitting right now, you are most likely oblivious to the sensations that are the result of your body being in contact with the chair until you turn attention to them, yet they are always present. Similarly, you are usually aware of only a few elements that are in your visual field at any time. Filtering or ignoring some potential information is necessary, so that awareness can be freed to focus on what is new, important or interesting. For this selection procedure, the existing constructs (based on previous experiences and other forms of knowledge) are normally used as a template with which the immediate experience is compared. Information congruent with what is expected can be ignored. These corresponding constructs are brought up automatically (on the basis of expectation and recognition). On the level of mind, some potential pieces of information are accessible, but awareness is simply not focused on them. Structured activities such as writing or driving, for example, are usually automatic and ignored by awareness (unless a novel element is introduced). Awareness is, therefore, narrower than both, perception and consciousness. By the same token, certain available processes in the soul may be ignored too (we may not feel them).

Divergent awareness (sometimes called *peripheral awareness*) - awareness often 'floats' loosely, which is why we can become aware of unexpected information. Those materials that are insignificant or match what is already structured or expected are filtered, so we are only superficially aware of them (meaning that we do not pay attention, do not focus on them). As above, this comparing and filtering is mostly an automatic process, the parameters, 'commands' are pre-defined. However, it is important to bear in mind that the template (to take the case of visual perception) does not consist of the exact images of objects or movements but of the *ideas* of objects and movements. For example, if we walk down a familiar street we normally ignore most of the information. This is possible not because we have ever seen exactly the same scene before; cars and pedestrians change all the time. Nevertheless, we can ignore most of them because we are familiar with that scene on the basis of an heuristically formed idea of what to expect. Only orientation pointers (necessary to direct an activity such as walking) are briefly in focus, while the rest remain on the periphery.

Convergent awareness involves attention and concentration. Attention is an ability to focus on a particular object, while concentration is the ability to maintain awareness on the object of attention. Therefore, attention is essentially a type of intention. An intent directs awareness by creating tension that is resolved by a matching set of information (a corresponding form). Elements that are similar to the pieces of information contained in what is looked for will enter our awareness. For example, if we are trying to find the keys with a yellow key-ring, any small yellow piece will attract our attention. Of course, other factors, besides our intentions, can influence this focusing and directing of awareness. Here are the most important ones:

Intensity: its influence is determined by a variable threshold that depends on a general degree of sensitivity, tension or competing stimuli.

Novelty, unexpectedness (e.g. appearance of an unusual colour, movement, shape, sound, smell etc., or recognition that something familiar is missing): information that does not match expectations and requires re-structuring or expanding of the existing constructs.

Interestingness is another (subjectively determined) attractor. The element involved may not be necessarily novel, as in the case of when something is perceived from a different perspective.

Importance ascribed in advance to a potential piece of information. One familiar situation in which this factor plays a role is so-called 'cocktail party' phenomenon: you are attending to a conversation at a party, but suddenly become aware that your name is mention somewhere else in what was just a background noise a moment earlier.

EXPANDING AWARENESS

The expansion of awareness means an increase of either the variety (quality) or the amount of information and experience, and the ability of the self to hold them together. This is achieved by grouping (organising, structuring) existing materials, which enables adding new ones. The main function of consciousness is connecting various pieces of information and creating such a network of energy configurations. The brain and mental constructs play an important role in this respect. So, the expansion of awareness depends on the ability of the mind to receive, organise and store information, and on the amount of neuro-connections established in the brain, which is enhanced through their use.

THE DEVELOPMENT OF AWARENESS

Awareness is first restricted by the body to the point at which the energy can be organised and managed. It only slowly expands through biological evolution, and later on social and individual development. Thus, at the beginning awareness is narrow, and then it gradually increases. Animals are generally more aware than plants, and humans are more aware than animals. The flip side, however, is that awareness of the non-material domain normally decreases throughout this process. This is because the better constructed reality is, the more difficult it is to perceive beyond the constructs.

Some possible questions

What is the difference between focusing waves with the pupil of the eye for example (which does not produce awareness), and with the self?

The eye is a part of the material world, while the self is not, so it is not surprising that they function differently. Awareness is a property of focused energy that enables the formation of loops with which new pieces of information interact, leading sometimes to their integration. On the other hand, an eye pupil is a mechanical instrument, acting like a window that enables some light waves to pass through.

Is that what enables awareness the same as that what is aware (these two may be different, the eyes enable us to see, but they do not see)?

The soul and self can be only in theory considered as separate entities. In reality they are not. So, what enables awareness and what is aware is the soul-self system.

If awareness is linked to a particular frequency, how are its materials differentiated?

As the individual instruments of an orchestra are differentiated in a radio transmission, although they all arrive in a 'parcel' of the same frequency (a carrier wave).

What happens when we are unconscious?

As long as a soul is connected to the body, awareness responds to the brain waves and depends on the brain for its content. In a similar vein, as long as we look at the screen we depend on the film in the projector for the content. The self is in a position that focuses waves of a particular frequency, produced by neuronal activity. In other words, a self focuses pieces of information that are on the frequency it is tuned to. If there is no information on that frequency, if the brain is inactive in this respect, but the self remains in the same position (e.g. deep sleep without dreams), it does not have anything to focus on and is aware of nothing which, for all practical purposes, cannot be distinguished from not being aware[1]. If the receiving frequency is changed, it is possible to become aware independently from the brain, but, in most cases, we do not remember such experiences when we wake up, because there is no associative chain.

Why do we sleep (why do awareness and intent need to be regularly switched off)?

The brain has a natural tendency to return to an inert state. The neurotransmitter *arexin* activates arousal, the wake-promoting systems in the brain, otherwise we would always be asleep. On the other hand, awareness and intent are anti-entropic (they are associated with synchronised wave patterns) so they require an effort. This effort (focusing) is difficult to sustain, which is why falling asleep regularly occurs. Deep sleep involves a shift of the dominant frequency of the brain below the threshold of awareness.

---

[1] Some practitioners of meditation claim that they can maintain 'pure' awareness – without being aware of anything, but this can be considered an exception and is also debatable. For example, the very knowing that one is aware can be regarded as a material of awareness.

INTENT

WHAT INTENT IS NOT

Intent is different from other possible causes of activity (such as instincts and urges, reflexes, desires, aims, or will). The distinction between will and intent may need to be clarified because it is not self-evident. Intent is a pre-thought, pre-language (in other words pre-construct) phenomenon, while will has a cognitive basis, closely related to decisions. Animals and young children do not show much will (they may exhibit the peculiarities of their character, but this is not will). They do not have an overall conscious control of their actions. Intent, on the other hand, is present in all life forms from the start, although it may not be strong and is often muted by more intense determinants. Will can be triggered by intent but also by other factors (e.g. social pressure, rational principles etc.).

The already mentioned Libet's experiments (p.108) provide experimental support for the difference between will and intent. In the case of a voluntary action, such as moving a finger, for example, a pre-verbal and pre-thought energy impulse (intent) fist initiates a neuronal activity. This is called *readiness potential* (a tension before an action, detected by EEG as a voltage change in a brain region associated with such action). Formulating the impulse (a cognitive process known as decision and normally associated with will) comes later. It is like a driver who first starts the engine, and only after a few moments moves the car. So, in a way, the engine is prepared for the action before the driver decided to move the car (but after s/he had intended to do so). Congruent with Libet's own conclusions, will (decision) has a purpose either to veto or proceed further with the act (see Libet, 2004).

To summarise, the main difference between intent and other phenomena related to action is that the former is not structured (so it can never be precisely formulated) while the latter are. Roughly speaking, will is based on decisions, desires on imagination, and aims on thinking. Of course, these processes are often intertwined. For instance, intent can underlie an aim (that, as a rule, has a convergent role). The aim can provide a form for intent, but intent is still necessary to sustain the act. Other processes in the body and mind can also trigger, modify, contribute or block an intent, but they do not have intent. Such activities are reflexive or conditioned responses. Only the self-soul intends.

WHAT INTENT IS

Intent is the ability of the self to affect and utilise its energy field directly (rather than through constructs). Intent does not act, but creates and maintains tension (creates potential), so that the energy itself spontaneously tends towards a resolution. In a way, intent can be seen as content in a search of a corresponding form. A simple activity such as looking for a word may illustrate this. A person knows *what* s/he wants to express, but s/he is searching for the way (form) to express it. The tension so created is the result of one's intent. Once the word is found, it is experienced as a release (as if a light was turned on or a dam opened). Polanyi and Prosch summarise this process:

> Heuristic tension in a mind seems therefore to be generated much as kinetic energy in physics is generated by the accessibility of stabler configurations. The tension in a mind, however, seems by contrast to be deliberate. A mind responds in a *striving* manner to comprehend that which it believes to be comprehendible but which it does not yet comprehend. Its choices in these efforts are therefore hazardous, not "determined". Nevertheless they are not made at random. They are controlled (as they are evoked) by the pursuit of their intention. These choices resemble quantum-mechanical events in that they are guided by a field which nevertheless leaves them indeterminate. They are therefore also "uncaused", in the sense that there is nothing within the possible range of our knowledge that determines or necessitates that they become precisely what they do become. (1975, p.176)

The wave energy from the soul can produce manifest effects due to the receptivity of the brain to scalar wave-propagations[1] and the sensitivity of the neural network to the chaos dynamics. The latter means that vast collections of neurons can shift abruptly and simultaneously from one complex activity pattern to another in response to extremely fine variations. In other words, neural activity is susceptible to so-called chaotic attractors that can amplify the minute fluctuations and affect an overall process although no exact neural path is determined. This is why intent cannot be specific and yet it can influence a general trend.

It is suggested that the effects of intent can be detected in experimental settings as the above mentioned readiness potential. Readiness potential is linked only to intentional movements, and not to reflex actions such as a scratching or pulling away from something painful. Libet also noticed that if his subjects had chosen not to actively participate in his experiments, readiness potential was very different, which is another indication that it is related to agency and intent (even if the decision to act comes later).

---

[1] Scalar waves have magnitude, but unlike vector waves they do not have a specific direction.

THE FUNCTIONING OF INTENT

The effects of intent on the brain is relatively slow and weak:

> The self-conscious mind does not effect a direct action on these motor pyramidal cells. Instead, the self-conscious mind works remotely and slowly over a wide range of the cortex so that there is a time delay for the surprisingly long duration of 0.8s... It is a sign that the action of the self-conscious mind on the brain is not of demanding strength. (Popper and Eccles, 1977, p.365)

This is not surprising if the intensity of the material world is taken into account. Intent can be and often is, in fact, muted by stronger influences: physical or social conditioning and the individual will. It is possible to pay no attention to or to override intent. Thus, in many cases it does not make a significant difference. However, if maintained, intent can have an accumulative effect (like drops of water that individually produce negligible results, but their prolonged action can break a rock). This can lead to a more fulfilling outcome, but is not easy because it requires abstaining from immediate gratifications (e.g. fantasies or other substitutes) and sustaining the state of suspension, which is not always comfortable. On rare occasions though, intent can take over. It is felt most intensely in so-called flow experiences that occur when the waves produced in the brain become synchronised. Many engaging activities such as writing, playing sport or an instrument or discussing an interesting subject can produce this effect (after the skills have been acquired). Such an event, compared to the usual brain activity, is the equivalent of laser light in comparison to normal diffused light. It is experienced as an effortless but highly focused state, like being in a tunnel or on rails (in the words of the late Formula One champion, Senna). It also includes an ambiguous sensation of not being aware of oneself and still being in control at the same time. This is because the ego personality, that we normally identify with, remains in the background. Intent initiates brain activity directly, rather then through its constructs which is usually the case (although, of course, the awareness of constructs is still preserved). So, performance can be faster and less energy consuming than when consciously controlled. Being in such a state is not always an advantage though, since it can lead to losing sight of a larger perspective. A highly focused state normally narrows the scope of awareness[1].

---

[1] Moreover, these states may be pleasant and conducive to achievement, but they rarely contribute to development. The circumstances need to be favourable too, in terms of not producing an unpredictable resistance, and overcoming resistance is what leads to a constructive change. Similar to so-called 'peak experiences', these ones provide a glimpse of possibilities, but are not fully integrated in most cases.

THE RELATIONSHIP BETWEEN AWARENESS AND INTENT

The energy of the soul can be shaped unintentionally. In fact, every experience and information restructures the energy, which happens all the time and does not have to involve intent. Intent depends on awareness, because without awareness it cannot be directed. This means that one has to be aware in order to intend, but this is not to say that one has to be aware of shis intent permanently. Some intents and their context may be forgotten (the person is not aware of them any more) and yet they can still have an effect. With increased awareness (as in lucid dreams, for example) the potential for intentional control grows as well. Conversely, intent can direct awareness, too. Not by guiding, for instance, our sensory apparatus, but by creating tension that spontaneously turns awareness in a direction that would lead to a release. Moreover, besides affecting direction, intent may also play a role in the process of selecting and extracting pieces of information.

THE DEVELOPMENT OF INTENT

Although it may be very weak, intent is present from the start, and like awareness it also grows through evolution and development. Intent is a delicate force, so the less a soul is developed, the smaller its role is. With an increase in the complexity of the nervous system it is much easier to balance stronger factors and be more frequently responsive to the minute influences of intent. This means that humans have a greater potential in this respect than animals. The souls of animals are mostly shaped through an interaction of bodily instincts and their surroundings, while the self, although indispensable, has little direct effect. As already mentioned, intent does not seem to be strong even in humans, but there is still substantial scope for growth within the existing boundaries. These boundaries, or the physical aspects of life and how they relate to the above elements, are worth considering, so they will be addressed next.

THE NATURE OF LIFE

The materialistic interpretation

Materialistic doctrine is based on the belief that the functioning of living organisms can be reduced entirely to physical and chemical processes[1]. Some of the propagators of materialism, zealous to associate life with inanimate matter, even use machine-like terminology. For example, biologist Richard Dawkins describes living organisms in terms of mechanisms, replicators and robots. Ironically, this, in fact, contradicts materialism:

> It has for some time been generally supposed that organisms are mechanisms and that, since mechanisms work in accordance with physical and chemical laws, organisms must also do so... Unfortunately this assumption has been misconceived to mean that organisms must be wholly explicable as the resultants of physical and chemical laws because mechanisms are. Actually it means exactly the opposite. For mechanisms are *not* wholly explicable as the resultants of the operation of physical and chemical laws. (Polanyi and Prosch, 1975, p.168)

Machines are purposely built and they can be fully understood only in that context. So, if life forms are machines, the same should apply[2].

Leaving this philosophical point aside, explaining life in terms of the physical and chemical properties of its components is not straightforward. Although science has identified most of the necessary chemicals and can describe fairly well many processes in a cell, why a living cell functions at all remains a mystery. It says nothing, for example, on why cells replicate (especially when the process goes from a simple to a more complex structure). The replication mechanism may be encoded in the DNA, but this does not explain why and how it is encoded in the first place:

> Whatever the origin of a DNA configuration may have been, it can function as a code only if its order is not due to the forces of potential energy. Just as the arrangement of a printed page is and must be extraneous to the chemistry of the printed page, so the base sequence in a DNA molecule is and must be extraneous to the chemical forces at work in the DNA molecule. (*ibid.* p.172)

---

[1] Consequently as biologist Morowitz puts it 'the study of life at all levels, from social to molecular behaviour, has in modern times relied on reductionism as the chief explanatory concept' (1981, p.34-35).

[2] Polanyi concludes: 'Biologists will tell you that they are explaining living beings by the laws of inanimate nature, but what they actually do, and do triumphantly well, is to explain certain aspects of life by machine-like principles. This postulates a level of reality that operates on the boundaries left open by the laws of physics and chemistry' (1969, p.154).

Thus, the boundary conditions that determine the structure and organisation, 'must consist of principles other than those of the material they bound' (*ibid.*, p.177). This, of course, does not apply only to replication, but also metabolism, growth, cell cooperation, etc.

There are a number of other issues worth mentioning. While alive, an organism maintains a highly ordered, low-entropy state. Silver writes:

> The fact that the contents of the cell include very large (highly improbable) molecules, and that the cell is a highly ordered (highly improbable) structure, implies that living matter is in a state of comparatively *low entropy* as compared with the disorganized mess of small molecules into which it disintegrates when it dies. (1998, p.323)

This is contrary to the second law of thermodynamics. Although it does not break this law because it is an open system, the question remains why it persistently acts against it[1]. If life is nothing more than chemistry and physics, why does a living cell behave so differently than a cell that has all its components intact, but is not alive?

Explaining ontogeny (the sequence of events involved in the development of an individual organism) is also a problem. Laszlo states that 'the principles of the regulatory circuits involved in embryonic development are not known... almost nothing is known about how the human organism instructs itself to build, for example, a human hand' (1993, 101). The development of the embryo requires the ordered unfolding and coordinated interaction of billions of dividing cells (e.g. some cells become a liver and some a thumb at a precise time and place). If this process were entirely coded by genes, the genetic program would have to be complete and detailed and yet flexible enough to ensure the differentiation and organisation of a large number of dynamic pathways under a potentially wide range of conditions. Yet, the genetic code is the same for every cell in the embryo. Anticipation of embryo development is more than a technical issue:

> Since the chemical compound DNA is assumed to act only chemically, it cannot vary its actions in the way a builder with a mind can. Therefore, there must either be another element in the organism that can function as a builder, merely using the DNA compound as its blueprint, or, as the theory supposes, the DNA must merely be responding chemically to chemical compounds. In the latter case, if it acts differently at different times, there must be different chemical compounds for it to react with at different stages of embryonic development. But these compounds must be called into existence only *at the end* of the embryo's previous stage. Timing is therefore most important. No theory yet exists to explain how this can be done in a strictly chemical way.

---

[1] Entropy can also decrease in some inanimate open systems (sometimes called *dissipative structures*) but not with an increase of functionally different dynamic processes and non-uniformed (but not random) complexity at the same time, as in the case of life.

The development of such a theory is rendered more difficult because, as Driesch first showed in his work with sea-urchin embryos, there seems to be some resilience possible in the development of tissues. Some tissues can sometimes seemingly be "pressed into" undergoing changes they do not normally undergo, because some part of the embryo has been prevented from developing in its usual way. It is almost, in these cases, as if there *were* a builder who has had to use some ingenuity because of shortages of one material or another or because something has previously been built erroneously and he must now build upon and around this. (Polanyi and Prosch, 1975, p.166)

This is reinforced by the findings that some organisms 'possess programs of repair that could not have been naturally selected: the kind of damage which they repair is not likely to have befallen their progenitors in the entire history of a species' (Laszlo, 1993, p.102).

The problems that the materialistic framework faces are not limited to the internal workings of living beings, but extend to some widespread behavioural aspects of complex organisms. One among many examples highlighted by biologist Rupert Sheldrake is the European cuckoo that lays its eggs in the nests of birds of other species. The young never see their real parents. Towards the end of the summer the adult cuckoos migrate. About a month later, the young cuckoos congregate and also migrate to the same region. They instinctively know that they should migrate, when to migrate, in which direction they should fly and what their destination is. Materialists believe that this is all somehow programmed by their genes, but this is far too complex behaviour to make this explanation likely.

The results of a series of experiments meant to test whether learned behaviour patterns are inherited are equally puzzling. Behavioural psychologist William McDougall in the early 1920s trained some rats to perform a simple task. The experiment involved 32 generations of rats and took 15 years. Later generations of rats (separated from the previous generations) consistently learned more rapidly than the previous ones, the last over ten times faster than the first one. More significantly, when separate experiments in other parts of the world replicated the original one, the first generation of rats learned almost as rapidly as McDougall's last generation. A number of them even performed the task correctly immediately, without making a single error.

The above suggests that not all biological functions cannot be comfortably explained within the materialistic paradigm. Life seems to be more than just molecular reactions. Polanyi and Prosch conclude:

We must admit that we do not yet have the reduction of living processes to physical and chemical laws that modern biologists seem to think we can have. We not only *have not proved* that these adaptive aspects of the DNA's building capacity can be reduced wholly to physical and chemical operations, *but we never can do so.* (1975, p.167)

Religious interpretations

Most religions accept a dualistic nature of life, meaning that it cannot be cut down to the physical or chemical properties of the organism. A non-material component is, in fact, considered essential for life. Almost every spiritual tradition recognises the existence of soul, spirit or atman, which is one of the main differences between them and the materialistic perspective. However, it is unclear how this component interacts with the body and to what extent it can exist independently from the body (before birth or after death). Moreover, it is also uncertain which organisms have this non-material component. Philosopher Descartes, for example, who attempted to provide rational foundations for dualism, reserved it only for human beings, but this seems arbitrary.

The contribution of philosophy

Vitalism is a major contribution of philosophy to the debate about the nature of life (Henri Bergson being its best known exponent). Its main input was to point out the incompleteness of reductionist and mechanistic interpretations. Like the ancient Greek philosophers, including even Aristotle, Vitalism argues that the difference between living organisms and inanimate bodies cannot be explained solely in material or physicochemical terms. Living forms, it is claimed, have an additional, non-material, vital element - a universal life force, which may or may not be capable of existing apart from its hosts. The nature of the life force was debated even earlier by numerous philosophers of which some (e.g. Paracelsus) believed that it is an external property and others that it is an internal, spontaneous, event. Life as an explanatory and evaluative concept appealed to many philosophers in the 19th century as a reaction to scientific materialism, although the success of synthesising an organic compound artificially in the first half of the same century weakened dramatically the Vitalist position. Failed attempts to find *vital élan* in the body which, in fact, would have reduced it (if they were successful) to another type of physical force similar, for example, to the electro-magnetic force, confused the matter further. Vitalism resurfaced in the 20th century in the work of the already mentioned Hans Driesch, when he discovered that despite extreme interference in the early stages of embryological development, some organisms nevertheless develop into perfectly formed adults. He proposed the existence of a soul-like force which guides the development of an embryo (in his later writings, Driesch argued that all life culminates ultimately in a 'supra-personal whole'). Such conclusions are, of course, only interpretations of data available at that time. However, there are further reasons why prevailingly dismissive attitude at present towards similar ideas may be inadequate. They will be considered below.

THE SYNTHESIS PERSPECTIVE

Life is usually defined as an entity that has the capacity to perform certain functional activities including metabolism, growth, reproduction, responsiveness and adaptation to stimuli such as light, heat and sound. It is further characterised by the presence of complex transformations of organic molecules and by the organisation of such molecules into the successively larger units of protoplasm, cells, organs, and organisms.

Although the above mentioned abilities are obviously a very important part of the life process, it is questionable if they really define life. An organism that does not reproduce (e.g. mules that are born sterile) or has stopped reproducing or growing is still alive, thermometers can respond to heat yet they are not alive. These examples are brought up not to point out that such a definition is imprecise (after all, most definitions have fuzzy boundaries) but that something essential may be missing. What common-sensically seems fundamental to life are the abilities to experience and to be pro-active, and consequently, having a *unique* centre of experience and pro-activity (meaning that my experience cannot be your experience). In other words, awareness, intent and the self. A computer, for example, can perform certain operations that can be paralleled to mental processes. Yet, a computer has nothing that can be paralleled to awareness. A computer can perhaps simulate thinking, but it is not aware, it does not experience. It can beat a human being in chess, but it is not aware that it has won and it cannot feel happy about it.

There is, however, an epistemological problem with the above proposition. An ability to be aware may be a necessary characteristic of life, but due to the inherent limitations of observation, it cannot be easily verified. We phenomenologically know that we are aware. It can be also extrapolated from verbal reports and the behaviour of others that they also experience. Animals react in a similar way to situations that cause pain, pleasure or fear, so it is plausible that they have a similar capacity. But what about plants or bacteria or even individual cells in one's body? Do they experience at all? They may have some rudimentary experiences that are so different (e.g. temporally) that it is impossible to make any conclusions on the basis of observations, including transpersonal ones[1]. The self is also non-observable. However, something that separates an organism from inanimate matter can be observed, and this is self-generated movement. Some believe that this will

---

[1] The concern here is not with the nature of such experiences (which is the subject of Nagel's classic paper 'What is it like to be a bat?'), but whether they experience anything at all.

also eventually be traced back to physical causes, but nobody has ever managed to come close to proving it. Philosopher Teichman writes: 'A human being is in a way a self-caused cause so far as his actions are concerned, unlike a stone' (1974, p.33). There is no reason why this should not be expanded to other living organisms. That innate activity is an important difference between the animate and inanimate has already been pointed out by Cicero, Thomas Aquinas and many others. While one of the main characteristics of the matter is inertia, agency is one of the main characteristics of life. Inanimate objects can undergo certain processes or be moved under the influence of various forces, but are not active. They are passive, acted upon. A stone does not fall, it is fallen by the combination of gravitational force and other physical factors. On the other hand, life can be proactive, as well as reactive. Many internal processes are the result of an organism's chemistry and some of its activities can be reduced to reflexes, but not all. Similarly, many processes in the car and its movement are the result of the car machinery and its interaction with the environment, but a driver is necessary to start and direct it. This distinction is quite clear in practice. The limbs of dead frogs can be made to twitch by applying an electric current, but nobody in shis right mind would confuse this with life. What is recognised as self-initiated movement is associated with life and only with life. As discussed earlier (and as is also evident from any introspective analysis), intent seems to be its most plausible source. Considering that intent is impossible without the self and awareness, they too can be linked to life. To put it simply, energy is alive if it is focused.

The self, awareness and intent are attributes of the One. If life forms are in the process of becoming the counterpart to the One, they must also have self and at least rudimentary intent and awareness, and consequently a non-material aspect – the soul[1]. So, energy is alive if it has the self and the abilities of awareness and intent (they, of course, do not need to be always active - an unconscious person is not dead, just as a switched off radio is not broken[2]). This is what distinguishes the animate from the inanimate. The soul brings the dynamic principle (inner movement) into that interaction,

---

[1] If referring to these elements rather than to the physical body, humans and, in fact, all life forms reflect indeed 'God's image' (in the case of the latter, of course, God merely reflects the human image).

[2] These inactive states are temporary, so the above argument regarding reproduction, for example, does not apply. A permanent cessation of awareness and intent, for all practical purposes, indicates cessation of life (there are border cases though, when a person is artificially kept alive, but if there is no hope that such a person will regain at least some awareness, life support machines are usually turned off). Permanent cessation of reproductive ability, on the other hand, does not indicate cessation of life.

which enables life, development and evolution. This view was commonly held since antiquity. Thomas Aquinas wrote (using the Latin term *anima* for the soul):

> Animate means living and inanimate non-living, so soul means that which first animates or makes alive the living things with which we are familiar. (in Thompson, 1997, p.120)

What does not have the self, awareness and intent does not have its own life. Only humans can conceptualise their intentions and what they are aware of, but it has been observed that even simple organisms possess a certain level of awareness and intent[1]. This implies (contrary to what Descartes thought) that soul can be associated with all living organisms not only humans. Which is not to say that an individual soul always corresponds to an individual biological form. Almost certainly not every fruit-fly or ant has its own soul and self. Considering the highly synchronised nature of their societies it is more likely that most of the related non-material energy of single-cell organisms, some insects and plants is focused collectively, while individual selves constantly appear and disappear depending on the extent of separation from the collective that is happening at any point. Evidence for this is that an insect such as ant, for example, cannot learn from experience, but insect colonies can. Even in higher organisms some energy fibres may still be attached to a collective energy field, which could account for the cumulative learning of species mentioned earlier on (p.142)[2].

Thus, the basic premise here is that life is a result of an interaction between two distinct types of energy (material and non-material) and therefore cannot be reduced only to the physical and chemical properties of the body. Reductionist attempts run into numerous difficulties, and also certain phenomena can be better explained otherwise. So, although the claim that all life forms (including one-cell organisms, plants, animals and humans) have a non-material aspect cannot be materially verified, it is not less rational than the belief that one day everything will be possible to understand in terms of physical and chemical properties. Such reasoning is not foreign to science. Gravitational fields, for example, (not to mention super-strings and other esoteria) cannot be detected directly either, but are postulated from their effects or the requirements for a coherent model of reality. It should be also taken into account that the above inference is supported by common sense (e.g. the notion of self) and cross-cultural transpersonal experiences.

---

[1] Polanyi and Prosch maintain that '...even paramecium is an individual that quite apparently strives... to adapt itself to its conditions and to stay alive and to reproduce' (1975, p.170).

[2] Rather than bubbles, souls can be imagined as the crests of waves that are connected underneath.

The connection

It is already suggested that the waves produced in the brain are instrumental for mental processes, but they are not sufficient to maintain the relationship between the material and non-material aspects of a living system (otherwise the connection would be broken in a deep sleep or when unconscious). The body, however, produces other wave patterns. The body can be indeed considered 'a complex network of resonance and frequency' (McTaggart, 2000, p.53). All the organelles (cell's 'organs') are rotating and vibrating. Each of them is involved in this 'musical' activity of creating rhythmic waves of energy. Some of these vibrations are innate to chemical components, but some of them are genetically programmed. It is known that DNA produces a wide range of frequencies, so genes can be understood as 'notes' in a composition that is unique for each person. Of course, functional genes are not the candidates for the connection. However, the wave patterns produced by some of the DNA sequences that present scientists call 'genetic garbage' (because they do not contribute to protein production) may be responsible. One curious characteristic of life is that, unlike machines, life cannot be interrupted. For example, a car can be switched off and turned on again much later. Life cannot. A living organism needs constant activity. In principle, this should not be necessary in order to preserve body functioning, and is ineffective from the energy consumption point of view. It is more likely that the constant working of the body is needed to maintain the vibrations that connect the body to the soul[1].

Non-material energy consists of wave patterns too, so there are reasonable grounds to believe that, at least in some cases, they can resonate with the waves produced by heavy and slow matter (or its constituent parts on the border with non-material reality). The soul and the body can therefore be considered different forms of energy that are linked via waves[2]. Thus, the soul is not in the body or attached to the body, but body and soul resonate with each other. This process goes in both directions, but the material aspect is normally more intense. The likely way that this connection happens is that each body and soul has a specific wave pattern, a unique signature. When a new organism is created, if those signatures are compatible, the waves of the soul harmonise with the waves of the body and in that way the body gets connected to the soul. When the body ceases to function (and produce waves), that connection is broken. This means that the body is a replaceable part of that system.

---

[1] Plant seeds and some simple organisms can be dormant for a long time, which seemingly contradicts the above. However, they can be considered not a life but a potential life, similar to frozen sperm.

[2] It should be pointed out though, that not the whole soul, but only a part of it is associated at any point with physical (or mental) life.

Although the connection between the body and soul may be attributed to the waves produced on the molecular level, the question may be raised whether there is a 'relay station', a crucial part of the body in this respect. Historically, several 'seats of the soul' have been suggested (liver, heart, brain, pineal gland), but the only part of the body that could really be a candidate for this role is the brain stem (the area at the base of the brain that includes the midbrain, the pons, and the medulla). The brain stem contains the ascending reticular activating system, which plays a crucial role in enabling and maintaining alertness. Even small lesions in some parts of the midbrain and the pons cause permanent coma. The brainstem also contains the respiratory centre that is responsible for breathing (so it can be associated with the 'breath of life'). Moreover, all of the motor outputs from the cerebral hemispheres (e.g. those that mediate movement or speech) are routed through the brainstem, as are the efferent fibres of Autonomous Nervous System responsible for the integrated functioning of the organism as a whole. Most sensory inputs also travel through the brainstem. Consequently, if there is no functioning brainstem, there can be no integrated activity of the cerebral hemispheres, no thoughts or sensations, no interaction with the environment.

All this, of course, does not amount to a proof and is no more than suggestive. Because of its anatomical position and other factors brainstem is notoriously difficult to study. Nevertheless, if there is a crucial part of the body responsible for a stable connection with the non-material aspect, brainstem seems the safest bet. This is not to say that the brainstem is an 'organ of connection' (otherwise organisms that did not develop a brainstem would not be really alive). It is the only probable place though, where there could be a necessary and sufficient concentration of wave patterns to maintain the permanent resonance in higher organisms. Possibly all body parts have weak connections, but they most likely cannot be maintained if not linked to this centre[1]. It is interesting that an interference with the wave patterns of an organ can cause disassociation even if it is still attached to the body. For example, when one's arm is exposed to a strong electric current, it is not experienced as one's own, but as a foreign attachment.

---

[1] 'Most likely' is added because of strange recent claims that patients with transplanted organs can apparently pick up some experiences that belonged to their donors. More research is required for all these issues, but in the present climate, this is something that one can only hope for.

The beginning

An answer to the question how life started can now be attempted. As discussed earlier (p78-80), it is likely that the necessary conditions and an initial push are the result of the Intent, but then the process could unravel in a more spontaneous way. It can be speculated that non-material energy separated from the rest by the material world (see p.70-71) was at the beginning amorphous – a sort of energy soup. Some energy or, to continue with the above metaphor, some drops from the energy soup at the edges (of speed and density) may have developed a 'resonance attraction' to the heavy matter. But not any matter would do for life. Being movement, the energy has an affinity towards a form of matter that gives least resistance to movement. The specific features of carbon based matter (e.g. amino acids that can be spontaneously formed) make it perfectly suited to attract energy: plasticity (e.g. water is too fluid to allow formation of discrete structures, while crystals are too solid to allow the necessary dynamics); the capacity to form multiple bonds and a vast numbers of diverse compounds; relative stability (the inertness of carbon in its molecules) and yet propensity for chemical reactions; possibility to grow in complexity (the forming of long chains of atoms).

The above characteristics enable the segments of undifferentiated non-material energy on the boundaries with the matter to resonate with and get attached to it. This process does two things: it separates (at least partially) these segments from the rest, which enables differentiation, and at the same time keeps them coherent. Such 'enclosing'[1] leads to energy loops that make possible the focusing of energy into one point. Thus, separation and focusing are the result of an interaction between non-material and material forms of energy. However, separation alone is not enough to keep energy focused. A certain degree of integrated complexity that minimises permeability, a plasticity that allows activity, and reproductive potential are also needed. The molecular structure of RNA/DNA and the resonance it produces fulfil these criteria. The pro-activity of the energy, in turn, separates a particular form of organic matter from the rest, reflecting the separation on a non-material level. This is possible because organic matter is sufficiently flexible to enable the expression of self-generated movement. So, the first cell membranes that can keep the intricate chemistry inside can be formed and maintained long enough to start the whole process.

---

[1] This, of course, is not a physical enclosure, but the resonance field enclosure. A crude analogy can be made with the gravitational field of the Earth that captures the Moon, yet the Moon is not inside the Earth and its own field also subtly influences the Earth.

THE BODY

The Synthesis perspective concurs with the view that physical bodies are extremely complex organic instruments. Materialists make a similar claim, but it is inconsistent within their framework. They seem to neglect the facts that instruments are always built with a purpose and their working has to be externally initiated (at least the working of the first one that may create and initiate the working of other machines). This inconsistency is avoided here since the Intent and purpose are acknowledged. 'Instrument' does not imply though, that the body is simply a mechanical thing. Its enormous complexity and organisation is unparalleled, so a real comparison with machines is admittedly a gross simplification. In any case, the body is considered the material aspect of a living system that consists of comparatively slow but very dense energy. This is why physical sensations (e.g. pain, hunger) can have such a strong effect. The body is the intermediary through which the interaction between the non-material and material, the soul and the environment, occurs. The body enables physical life, but itself is not alive. It is a part of a living system for as long as it is coupled with the soul. To say that the body dies feels counter-intuitive because it has never lived.

The relation between the body and the soul

Asking where the soul is in relation to the body (e.g. whether it is in the body) does not make sense, since they do not share the same 'space'. It could be said, though, that the soul encompasses the body it is connected to, because it belongs to the realty within which the physical domain is situated, and because it has potentially a wider scope than the body (as the one who dreams includes the one in the dream). On the other hand, the body is largely a boundary at least for the part of the soul during the life-time. So, depending on the perspective, the soul 'encloses' the body and the body 'encloses' the soul[1]. An urge to see the soul as being somewhere else in space (usually above as if it was a satellite) should also be resisted. This is as misleading as imaging that the soul dwells in the body. One metaphor, however crude, may, perhaps, help to avoid these temptations: the soul and the body can be compared to a wind and a sail. A sail captures some wind, and the wind blows into the sail, so they interact for a while. But, where does the wind dwell? Not in a particular place, it is a moving mass of air, in which the sail, boat and everything else is submerged.

---

[1] As already mentioned (p.149) this is not a physical enclosure, but the resonance field enclosure.

The purpose of the body

The function of the body is to hold the soul grounded (to slow down the energy), which enables its rudimentary shaping. The body allows dynamism, but a limited one. So besides enabling communication with the environment, it also creates the boundaries that are needed until the non-material aspect is capable of self-control. In other words, the body has a role to stabilise and protect (primarily from the volatile exercise of agency and an excessive amount of input)[1]. As already mentioned, the senses are the first instance of selecting that of which we are going to be aware. This narrowing of the soul is necessary to allow a gradual development. Without these restrictions, it would be like a radio or TV receiver that picks up all the available transmitting signals; they would not produce potential information, but a meaningless noise.

The contribution to development

An interesting fact is that the brain is allowed to use an extraordinary amount of energy relative to its size. In humans, as much as 30% of the body's resting energy expenditure (oxygen and glucose) is due to the brain, while its mass accounts for around 3% of one's weight - ten times more than its share. No other part of the body by far is in such a privileged position, which strongly indicates that biological evolution is geared towards the development of the brain. It seems that the body exists to support the brain, not the other way around. This is congruent with common sense: if you had to choose, would you rather be without the body and retain the brain, or without the brain and retain the body?

Some possible questions

Why does the soul not separate from the body during a lifetime (or join another body)?
For the same reason why people do not jump out of cars at full speed. A car must stop or substantially slow down so that the person who is in it can get out safely. Similarly, the body and the brain must stop or at least substantially slow down and the corresponding soul must dis-identify in order to separate. Connecting to another body is practically impossible, not only because every body has its own unique code, but also because it would have to be 'vacant', not already resonating with another soul. In such a case it would not be a functional body any way (although purely physico-chemical processes in some parts of the body can continue even without the connection).

---

[1] In the later stages of development additional factors are involved too, which will be elaborated later.

THE AURA

There is a long and widespread tradition of belief that the body extends beyond its physical boundaries, in other words, that it has its own energy field. In Christianity, the term aureole is used for such a field surrounding the whole body and halo for the part of it around the head. Bio-energy fields are also commonly recognised in the East (e.g. Kundalini, chi, or energy flows that are associated with chakras and treated in acupuncture). In modern times, a morphogenetic (form-generating) field was postulated as early as the 1920s by biologist Alexander Gurwitsch, who claimed that the generation and regeneration of organisms is guided by it. In the 1930s, as a result of experimental work[1], a professor of anatomy Harold Burr and a professor at Yale at that time F. S. C. Northrop, proposed the existence of a life-field that shapes the organism. Experiments at Lanzhou University and at the Atomic Nuclear Institute in Shanghai seem to confirm the existence of an energy field generated by the human body; moreover, it appears to be affected by the mental power of the subjects. Scientists at the A. S. Popov Bio-information Institute in Russia reported that the field consists of frequencies within the range of 300 to 2 000 nanometres. All this indicates that the existence of such a field, for which a common term in the West is the *aura,* should not be dismissed.

The body, as any other physical object, ultimately consists of subatomic entities that have a dual nature. So, while the physical body, as normally perceived, can be identified with its corpuscular form, what is commonly called the aura could reflect its wave (or field) nature. This is not to say that there is an exact correspondence between those two (just as the two sides of the same coin can have different engravings). The body perceived as a field may have some properties that the body perceived as a conglomeration of particles does not, and the other way around.

In any case, such a field seems necessary. About 100 000 chemical reactions per second occur in each cell of the human body, so billions of chemical reactions happen at every moment. They all have to be synchronised for an organism to function. Chemical processes throughout the body are simply not fast enough to achieve this. It was already suggested (by physicist Hebert Fröhlich, for example) that some sort of collective vibration was responsible for getting proteins to cooperate with each other and carry out DNA instructions. As early as the 1960s, a Nobel laureate for Medicine Albert Szent-Györgyi proposed that protein molecules can function as

---

[1] It consisted of separating and mixing up the cells of a salamander embryo. If that mixture was then put in a slightly acid solution they would re-form into an embryo.

semiconductors, meaning that they can conserve and pass along the energy of electrons as information over relatively long distances (Becker and Selden, 1985, p.93-94). Both, molecules and intermolecular bonds, emit unique frequencies, so it is possible that they interact with other molecules through a resonating wave, creating a cascade of electromagnetic impulses.

This 'morphogenetic field' may also account for some phenomena that remain a mystery for modern science, for example, how the one-dimensional sequence of bases in the genes determines three-dimensional tissues and organs that give the organism its shape and properties. The extremely complex and intricate processes of embryogenesis (the development of an embryo) are most unlikely to be mapped by stable attractors[1] and governed alone by genetic information. It is more probable that such a chaotic (meaning ultra sensitive) system results from an interaction between DNA, environment, and the organisation of the morphogenetic field – or the aura. According to biologist Brian Goodwin, bio-fields are the basic unit of organic form and organisation; molecules and cells are merely 'units of composition'. Life evolves in the interaction between organisms and the field in which they are embedded. Polanyi and Prosch write:

> A considerable amount of experimental work, done by such biologists as H. Spemann, Paul Weiss, and C. H. Waddington, has shown that some of the development that takes place in embryos is controlled by fields, although exactly how this occurs is still uncertain. (1975, p.176)

Guiding the development of each organism by its own species-specific morphic resonance can also explain why species always breed true (the morphology of the offspring becomes similar to the morphology of its progenitors). The aura is already three-dimensional and contains complete information, so it can form a mould before the cells form a body. In other words, it is possible that when an egg is fertilised, a three dimensional blueprint (as a potential) is formed, which governs the activation of different sets of genes in different cells[2]. It 'envelops' embryonic cells which allows some genes to be expressed while others are suppressed. So, the dual nature of organic matter enables the whole to act upon the parts.

This concept may also account for an extraordinary re-generation ability of some simple organisms. It appears that the cells are guided by an orientation

---

[1] Equilibrium states or end points into which these process would settle.

[2] This coincides with transpersonal insights. The spiritual philosopher (with a Christian bent), Rudolf Steiner, described the etheric body, another name for aura, as 'the principle which calls inorganic matter into life'. For this reason it is sometimes also called 'formative-force-body'.

system that functions even when they are separated from one another. Such a capability diminishes though in higher organisms. This is probably the case because the processes in their organs are less chaotic and seem to lose their sensitivity to the feedback from the field fluctuations. With greater organ specialisation the intensity and power of the aura to act as a blue-print for the body is decreased and the regeneration capacity is largely lost. Such an explanation is in line with the experimental research done by biophysicist Fritz-Albert Popp showing that the more complex the organism, the fewer photons are emitted (McTaggart, 2001, p.50).

The aura, however, should not be mistaken for the soul for several reasons. If the above mentioned pieces of research are credible, the aura has to be a part of the material world (situated within the space-time framework) while the soul is not. The aura cannot be separated from the body (chakras for example, roughly correspond to bodily glands, and the meridians of chi energy partly to the nervous system) and it dissolves after death. The soul, on the other hand, does not correlate to the body so closely. For example, the aura of a new born baby reflects its relative structural simplicity, while the associated soul is, according to Jenny Wade who researched pre-natal consciousness, more complex (1996, chapter 2). Moreover, it seems that only highly sensitive individuals may be able to perceive this field, while to perceive a soul (or more accurately, the soul processes associated with an immediate experience), extraordinary abilities are not necessary[1].

There are some indications though, that the aura can reflect the state of the soul. It is well known, for example, that attention (which is linked to awareness and intent) can have an effect on the aura. So, it is likely that the non-material aspect of a living organism communicates with this field rather than the corpuscular body, and such *interference*[2] may be reflected in the aura. This mutual interaction can be accounted for by the findings of physicist Renato Nobili, showing that the fluid in cells promotes wave patterns that correspond with wave patterns in the brain cortex and scalp. If this is correct, the aura cannot be reduced only to an electro-magnetic field that *the body* produces (as some investigators believe). Thus, the characteristics of the field depend first of all on the body and environmental factors, but also the mind and the soul itself, which is why it is apparently possible to distinguish different layers of the aura.

---

[1] Tuning in beyond the constructs of reality and stabilising perception is sufficient in this case (see p.117).

[2] Interference is the mutual action of two or more waves that results in a new wave pattern.

THE BRAIN

The brain does not have a uniform structure. It is neurologically organised into three distinct parts that reflect the evolutionary development of species. The part of the brain that is developed (*in utero*) and starts functioning first, is dominant during early life; it is also the most primitive, corresponding to the reptilian brain (hence, the name The R-Complex), and is chiefly responsible for physical preservation through instinctive behaviour. The second one built on top or rather surrounding the first one, is called limbic system; it corresponds to the brain of early mammals and is involved in emotional reactions. The last one, the neocortex, that is developed in primates but is especially enlarged in humans, is related to cognitive functioning. The neocortex is also divided into two hemispheres that have somewhat different functions (for example, the region associated with language is situated in the left one). On the cellular level, the sheer complexity of the human brain is hard to grasp. It is estimated that it contains approximately thirty billion neurons (3×10^{10}), and each neuron can have as many as ten thousand synaptic connections. These give an unimaginably high number of possible combinations. Any detailed description of the brain structure and its functioning is far beyond the scope of this book, so the focus will be only on those aspects that are relevant to the relation between the brain and the non-material side of the living organism. In a nutshell, neurons, via synaptic links, enable electro-chemical processes that provide the material basis for consciousness. They create waves that through awareness become information or experience, and in this way affect the soul.

The brain's contribution to consciousness

There is no doubt that the brain is instrumental for consciousness, especially for the formation of specific patterns (images, words) that correspond to, or are associated with, the phenomena and events of physical life. In a way, the brain helps in forming scaffoldings to support more fluid energy configurations. The likely mechanism that enables this process is the interference of coherent electromagnetic fields at the point of dendritic interactions[1]. This interference can (at least in theory) produce holographic-like representations. It also allows memory to be recalled by a 'reference' signal (any associated element can be a trigger, 'reminder' for the activation of the pattern), and enables the storing of potential information in a distributed rather than localised manner. On the basic level, though, a very complex structure of the brain does not seem to be necessary. A cytoskeleton

---

[1] Dendrites are numerous branches from the main body of a neuron that connect it with other neurons.

consisting of micro-tubules could play a similar role to the nervous system in cells with a nucleus. Pribram, Hameroff, Schempp and many others have applied quantum physics to analysing the relation between consciousness and neuronal functioning. They claim that quantum coherence (which means that when two quantum systems interact, their wave functions become 'phase entangled') can occur in micro-tubules and provide a mechanism for intracellular quantum holography. If this is correct, it is possible that all living organisms (even very primitive ones), have at least a very rudimentary consciousness. Of course, this is not to say that the activity of neurons and their simpler equivalents is sufficient. A global, synchronised production of waves of a particular intensity and frequency is necessary to enable the 'read-out' by awareness. Like any other matter-energy systems, the brain continually interacts with a non-material energy field of a specific sort - in other words, with a part of the soul.

Brain Functions

The brain has several essential roles regarding the mind.
Perceiving - one of the main functions of the brain is to be the intermediary between the soul and the environment, translating signals into the wave patterns that awareness can pick up. In other words, the brain provides the materials by transforming sensations into potential information or experience. The already mentioned 'blind sight' experiments (p.112), for example, indicate that the major function of a particular brain region is to enable the link with awareness, rather than perception as such [1].

Selecting within an accessible range of signals, happens on several levels, but first of all in the brain. Bergson regarded the brain as a filter whose purpose is to reduce the amount of data which would otherwise invade our consciousness, and to eliminate what is superfluous. This view is experimentally vindicated:

> Much of neural activity is known to be inhibitory... There is ... evidence that selective attention operates, in part, by the inhibition of nonattended stimuli (cf. Arbuthnott, 1995). This is consistent with the view that the brain may act as a filter (as well as an organizer) of information. (Velmans, 1995, p.261)

The importance of this selection becomes clear considering that 75% of neurons in the human brain are inhibitory, compared with 45% in the monkey brain and even less in rabbits or cats. A *release* from inhibition

---

[1] This may also explain the paradox of the primary visual brain area (V1): it is claimed that 'V1 does not 'explicitly' represent colour and form because it has no cells that are sensitive to colour, and so on. And yet conscious appreciation of colour and form is destroyed by damage to V1' (Baars, *at al.*, 1998, p.275).

though, could explain certain phenomena such as the sudden improvement in short-term memory performance, if after a series of trials with similar stimuli, the features of the stimuli to be remembered are changed (see Wickers, 1972). Alleged extra-sensory perception might also be a result of bypassing this filter.

Constructing - another important function of the brain is structuring and organising. Neurons and synapses create a network that is strengthened by repetition. The brain is not aware, but it can perform complicated operations and preserve connections without awareness (similar to a computer). *Corpus callosum* (the structure that bond the two hemispheres), for example, is necessary to maintain the link between the image of an object and the corresponding word. However, it is important to remember that different brain modules process different types of signals (shape, colour, movement etc.) They do not form meaningful representations (which is why it is possible to use the same group of neuro-connections to form images of different objects). So, awareness is still necessary as a field within which these connections are established and reinforced (therefore, the claim that one can learn a foreign language while sleeping is largely unfounded). Although awareness is required for the process of connecting and separating, to what extent and what can be connected or separated depends on the complexity of the brain organisation. Psychologist Rock writes:

> ... it would seem that the world we perceive is the end result of events that occur in the nervous system and in this sense is a construction. It bears a certain kind of similarity to the realm of the material world, but is also very different from it.' (1975, p.4)

Storing - the brain also has an essential function in storing information in a specific form. Neuronal connections enable particular structures (e.g. images and words) to be permanently preserved. Without the brain, experiences and information are not lost, but the form they have taken can be. This is because the brain configuration is more solid than its non-material equivalent, and because a form can be reinforced by sensations from the material world, dialogue and internal monologue (language structures). It is still possible to create and preserve mental constructs without the brain, but in such cases they are much more fluid, so normally, the brain is necessary to consolidate, stabilise and maintain them.

Movement - the brain also plays an intermediary role for both, voluntary and automatic movements, in terms of coordination of its sequences. Furthermore, it can amplify a weak intent signal and initiate the mobilisation of physical energy for an activity.

The contribution of the brain to development

The increase of brain complexity enables the development of the mind which, in turn, can enhance the complexity of energy configurations in the soul. In other words, the growth of consciousness (that depends, to a large extent, on the growth of the brain) enables expansion of awareness and a greater influence of intent. A larger number and variety of neural connections also facilitate the further separation of the soul from the rest of non-material energy, leading to self-reflection and internal feedback. This not only enables individualisation, but also the intentional shaping of the soul. So another factor, besides the body, that contributes (with the help of the brain) to the forming of the soul is the mind - the subject of the following part in the book.

Some possible questions

Does every (intentional) thought trigger brain activity?

Every thought carries some energy (because it is essentially made of waves), so it should have an effect on brain activity. This energy, however, can be so small that it is practically undetectable. The important point to be made in this respect is that the mind affects the brain field, so there is no one to one correlation with brain processes. This enables the mind to utilise the plasticity of the brain. For example, having an active mind can slow down the progress of Alzheimer's disease because unaffected areas of the brain can be used (however, when they become affected too, the deterioration becomes rapid).

Is there any symmetry between the material and non-material aspects?

If the soul is considered parallel to the body, its 'surface' can be paralleled to the brain. So, in a way, there is an inverse symmetry: the body is the cover of the brain and the nervous system, while this surface is the cover of the soul.

Why this exceptional increase in complexity does not happen in the kidney, for example, but in the brain?

One of the conditions for evolution is an exposure to a variety of external stimuli or an adaptation to environmental changes. All the senses are connected to the brain. So while kidney cells are exposed to a relatively narrow range of stimuli, brain cells are frequently brought into contact with new ones, which is conducive to learning and ongoing development. In other words, the kidney can 'afford' its relative simplicity.

THE MIND

In the study of the mind there is a popular distinction between the 'hard' problem (the mind-body problem, qualia) and 'easy' problems (perception, memory, sensory-motor control etc.). However, even 'easy' problems do not seem to be fully understood with the methodology that psychology and neuroscience use at present. As Barbara Churchland (herself holding strictly materialistic views) puts it:

> It is important to acknowledge that for none of the so-called "easy" problems, do we have an understanding of their solution… It is just false that we have anything approximating a comprehensive theory of sensorimotor control or attention or short-term memory or long-term memory. Consider one example. My signature is recognizably mine whether signed with the dominant or nondominant hand, with the foot, with the mouth, with the pen strapped to my shoulder, or written in half-inch script or in 2-ft. graffiti. How is "my signature" represented in the nervous system? How can completely different muscle sets be invoked to do the task, even when the skill was not acquired using those muscles? We still do not understand the general nature of sensorimotor representation. (1998, p.112)

The above example has been touched upon earlier (p.174), but it may be worthwhile to reconsider some major faculties of the mind in more depth. A dominant approach at the moment, cognitive psychology, has been a huge improvement to its predecessor, behaviourism, but still does not go far enough. Firmly embedded in a materialistic paradigm, cognitive psychology has been enthusiastic about modelling the mind on the principles that govern computers (assuming that the brain is a very complex computer). Serial and parallel processing in such models can account for some brain events, but this does not say much about experience (e.g. of pain or colour), affect, humour, creativity, insights, understanding etc. The philosopher of the mind Ronald Puccetti and neurophysiologist Robert Dykes write:

> …it appears that the more we learn about details of brain function, the greater the difference between these and the known qualities of sensory experience. (1978, p.337)

Furthermore, processes in a computer are of a mechanical nature, so a computer is completely passive. In other words, it is not aware, and does not have the self and agency. Excluding these essential factors from the study of mind can provide at best an impoverished picture, so a broader approach is needed. In this part, several subjects will be discussed: the role of mental constructs; experience, information and meaning; and some sources of experience and information (perception, memory and auto-generating processes such as dreaming).

CONSTRUCTS

We can relate to the world directly or indirectly, through mental constructs. Both ways can affect the soul, but they are different. The direct interaction is more penetrating and fluid, while the indirect one is more concrete and easier to control. Direct perception is difficult to conceptualise but is not that uncommon. For example, it can explain greater speed of reaction in emergencies or in sports than the speed at which information can normally be processed[1]. It may also be involved in implicit awareness and even antedating as documented in experimental settings. In principle, considering that everything is essentially a set of vibrations, a direct receptivity to these energy fluctuations is always possible. However, most of the time we relate to reality indirectly, via our mental constructs, thus special attention will be paid to them. One clarification is, however, needed first. Although it is tempting, for the sake of simplicity, to identify indirect perception with constructs, they are not the same. The constructs are *the result* of perception (direct or indirect). Direct experiences can also be structured, without the help of mental representations (analogous, perhaps, to music). After all, avoiding chaos or harmonisation is one of the main aims. However, there is a difference between structuring the content of the mind and energy. The latter is not governed by the same principles, it is less stable and fixed, and consequently, its deliberate control is harder.

One of the main functions of the mind is to construct reality (which does not mean, of course, that there is no correspondence with what is 'out there'). This process consists of first fragmenting, and then connecting so created elements again, using various principles (e.g. generalisation based on similarities and differences, association etc.). The mind not only creates constructs but also maintains them. Constructs need to be supported all the time, or otherwise they can easily break down, as evident in situations of sensory deprivation and social isolation. They are kept together by exposure to physical sensations and use of language (dialogue and inner monologue). Therefore, we are not only aware of the world indirectly through the 'glasses' of the brain and body, but also through the 'glasses' of various mental systems.

---

[1] Libet concludes that these experiences are unconscious (without awareness), but this is not plausible – we do not draw a blank in this situations. However, we may not *know* what we are aware of. This requires at least a rudimentary level or reflection, which may not be present indeed.

THE RINGS

Mental categories do not exist independently, our 'thoughts, beliefs, attitudes, and behaviour tend to organize themselves in meaningful and sensible ways' (Zajonc, 1960, p.261). In other words, the constructs are connected in a system, an 'inner structure' that can be loosely defined as a network of prior knowledge, or a set of memory schemas that support each other. Processing new information means fitting it into this overall structure that is created through interaction between the person and the world. Everybody starts building shis inner structure from the beginning, and continues to do so throughout shis life. Some parts are adopted and some are the result of personal experience. As sociologist Peter Marris points out, 'in part, these mature structures of meaning can be represented as the common knowledge into which the members of a society are inducted by the language they learn, the principles of classification and causality they are taught - its science, cosmology, ideology, and cultural assumptions. But they also interpret the unique experience of each personal history' (1982, p.192). So, the structure is not only physically and socially determined, but also depends on the individual.

There are indications that the inner structure is organised into several layers or rings. Although the content of the rings can be extrapolated through introspection, verbal reports or behavioural clues, perception of the rings is prevented by our own rings[1]. Thus, while the body can be perceived indirectly (through the senses) and some processes in the soul directly, the rings cannot be. Their existence and organisation is postulated here on the basis of two revelatory experiences and deductive inferences. Considering that it is difficult to validate revelatory insights, the rings do not need to be accepted literally. They can be taken as a conceptual device that is conducive to providing a fuller account of mental operations. Such tools have been used in other disciplines. Science, for example, has created several models of the atom, of which some appeared later not to be entirely accurate, but nevertheless have served a purpose at a certain stage of understanding.

It is suggested that human beings can have up to four rings (while animals have only one). Any mental event can, of course, cut across the rings as brain modules cut across several layers of neuro cells. Each ring has two aspects: one forms the self-concept (personality, or 'I'), while the other forms the world concept. Every further ring is less conditioned and rigid, and therefore more susceptible to the influence of intent.

---

[1] If an attempt is made to bracket our own rings, the rings of others get bracketed too, so again we cannot perceive them.

The first ring is primarily constructed through images (and other perceptions). The reference point is physical reality. As all the other rings, it has two faces: one consists of the perception of the material world, and the other of the perception of one's own body (as a primary identifier). Virtually everybody agrees that our perception of the physical world is a part of consciousness consisting of constructs that correspond (to some degree) to reality. This applies to our own bodies too. The image of the body is also a construct reinforced by physical sensations from moment to moment. Searle writes:

> Common sense tells us that our pains are located in physical space within our bodies, that for example, a pain in the foot is literally in the physical space of the foot. But we now know that is false. The brain forms a body image, and pains like all bodily sensations, are part of the body image. (1992, p.63)

But the brain constructs a 'wrong' image, very different from our perception of our bodies (e.g. the neck is *not* next to the head). We, however perceive the body correctly. It is proposed that this is due to the first ring. A so created image is, of course, a dynamic structure – as the body changes, the structure changes too (often in a subtle way).

The two sides, the perception of one's body and of the physical world, are closely related and integrated. Their de-fragmentation can have a devastating effect (as it is well documented in psychiatric literature). Although a largely spontaneous process, sustaining the ring requires some effort. As early as the 1920s, neurologist Paul Schilder wrote that 'The body-image is the result of an effort and cannot be completely maintained when the effort ceases' (1935, p.287). This effort consists of the attention to sensations received through the body from physical reality and the body itself, and of intentional control over some parts of one's body (as already mentioned, if one's limb, for example, is paralysed or cannot be controlled, it is almost immediately perceived as alien).

The second ring consists of socially determined constructs and is primarily structured through language. The reference point is social products (e.g. text-books, religious texts, instructions, rituals). These conceptual schemas create a net of information that becomes, beside the body-world image, another frame of the soul. It is more permeable and broader because it has elements that cannot be physically perceived (e.g. abstractions such as 'happiness') and because it has more flexible rules.

This ring also has two complementary sides: the one that relates to oneself (one's name, social identifications, roles and functions, etc.) and another relating to one's social world, the particular ideological framework within which a society operates - in other words, the cultural embodiment (e.g. one's religion).

The third ring also has two aspects: one relates to personal views, opinions and values about the world and others (e.g. friends). The other incorporates personality constructs (the self-image or ego). The reference point is not the physical or social world but one's own private world, which is why a sense of personal importance is one of its main characteristics. Self-creation is also an imperative. Ego, therefore, is not permanent – it is an evolving projection, a construct, an image that we have about ourselves (which does not need to correspond fully to the real person). It is largely based on impressions that we leave on ourselves, self-assessments. For example, although judgements such as 'I am old, fat, beautiful...' refer largely to the body, they belong to the third, not the first ring. This construct is another embodiment of the soul, another identity besides the body and social roles. As the other rings, self-image has a protective role – we create an ego-shell as a psychological shield to protect us when we go beyond the conventional and start developing individuality. This ring not only enables further separation of the soul from other non-material energy, but also its intentional shaping based on self-reflection (rather than just through instincts and responses to the environment) and a better control over mental processes. It is, therefore, more modifiable and permeable than the previous rings and can accelerate development.

The fourth ring has two sides as well. One consists of global ideas about oneself as a human being (e.g. perceiving oneself as an electro-chemical process, an emergent brain process, or an interaction process). The other consists of the constructs related to wider reality beyond an individual's immediate experience. In other words, a 'cosmology' that defines one's view of reality (which may involve, but does not need to, the non-material aspect). So, the reference point is the universal. All the major ways of acquiring knowledge, at their best, contribute to this ring. For example, the laws or thermodynamics in science, the dialectic principle in philosophy, common sense realism, and the notion of the purpose, meaningfulness of life in spirituality. Not all of them, of course, need to be correct, but it is notoriously difficult to prove or refute them (even the laws of thermodynamics are in fact not laws but theorems). Thus, an element of belief and choice (that is sometimes based on unadulterated intuition) may be involved. This does not mean that they are relative and subjective, only that their validation (or refutation) requires a complex or multidisciplinary process, often difficult to achieve using existing language and linear logic. For this reason, they are frequently expressed in highly symbolic ways (e.g. geometrical and mathematical representations, archetypal images, metaphors etc.). This ring has the most permeable boundaries.

The following diagram is suggested as a schematised representation of the rings:

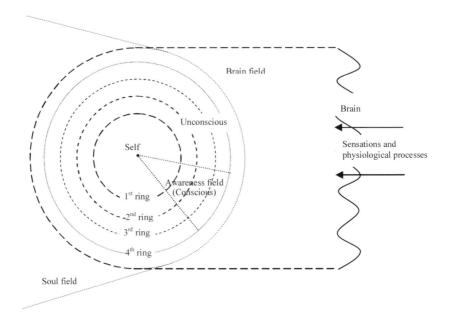

This diagram, of course, is only an abstraction. As already mentioned, the rings cannot be observed, and the part of the soul associated with physical life is perceived as a whole (like a 'person' in a dream that appears as a whole, although only the part of the one who is actually sleeping and dreaming is involved)[1]. The figure is also an idealised representation, the rings are not so clearly demarcated in reality, they may cross or overlap with each other.

In any case, this representation shows that both, the brain field (that consists of waves produced by neurons) and the soul field, go beyond rings. On the other hand, the field of awareness (marked out by the two lines coming from the self) is normally restricted to the rings. To use the above analogy again, it is like a dreamer who is usually limited by the boundaries of the dream and does not remember anything else. Moreover, at any particular moment, we are aware of only a small part of the rings (and, of course, not all four need to be included). However, awareness can move, in which case we become aware of different constructs.

---

[1] Recalling that the basic shape of the soul is a torus (see p.118), can explain how it is possible that a part of the soul that identifies with a physical body can be separated from the rest of the soul and at the same time feed the experiences into it.

It is important to clarify that although the rings are constructed with the help of images and words, they do not consist of them, but of ideas extracted from personal information and organised into schemas. They capture abstract, ideational content (similar to propositional representations in psychology but more fluid and fuzzy). Their constitutive elements are representations of conceptual objects and relations in a form that is not particular to any language or to any modality (e.g. vision, audition)[1]. So, although they may contribute to especially long term memory recall or restoration, they are likely to have a negligible role regarding specific memories. This is evident from mistakes that those who have suffered brain damage typically make (e.g. misplacing time, locations or persons). Therefore, there is no straightforward correlation between the rings and either episodic memories (experience related) or semantic memories (information related).

Some possible questions

Is walking, for example, also a construct?

Constructs do not need to be associated with symbolic representations. Walking is a type of knowledge that is based on a selection of movements, affirmed by repetition and habituated. Walking is, therefore, an action based on physical constructs.

Are animals more aware because they have only one ring to limit their awareness?

The further rings, in fact, enable an expansion of awareness (because it is possible to encompass more). For example, animals are not aware of what they know (they can use their knowledge, but cannot reflect on it). On the other hand, although the first ring may have a narrow scope and is the least permeable, it is still more so than all four rings together. This is why animals may be sensitive to some information to which humans are normally not (besides the point that their sensory apparatus may also be superior).

Does information arrive first in awareness or in the rings?

Information is not information if somebody is not aware of it. However, any new information is perceived through the 'glasses' of the existing constructs. In other words awareness is filtered, and therefore, when a sensation becomes information, awareness and the rings operate simultaneously.

---

[1] Barry Stein's laboratory at Wake Forest University found that the shape of a right angle drawn on the hand of a chimpanzee starts the visual part of the brain working, even when the shape has not been seen.

The purpose of the rings

The inner structure exerts a far-reaching influence on everyday life. It controls and guides the implementation of plans and actions. It governs the selection of what is important to remember. It enables us to supply missing information, to make inferences, to guess what we do not know and to reconstruct what we have forgotten. People tend to perceive and remember things that fit the relevant schema and forget things that do not. However, the purpose of the inner structure is not limited to its utility in daily activities. It also has several functions related to the soul.

Protection - the rings protect the soul from excessive amounts of information, and prevent an uncontrolled dispersion of the soul's energy. They create a sort of barrier - most pieces of information stop there (we are aware of them because this is where awareness remains) and also many reactions start from there.

Personal integration - the rings maintain the coherence of the soul. Without the rings, the mind would not be able to make a meaningful whole out of the various pieces of information. Fragmentation of the rings can cause intense anxiety and other problems including, in severe cases, a disintegration of personality.

Stability - the rings are more concrete (but less dynamic) than the energy of the soul. This concreteness contributes to stability and provides a sense of security, which is why it is difficult to let go of our beliefs (like inexperienced swimmers who cling to the side of the swimming pool). It is only when the energy can be internally controlled that the rings are no longer essential in this respect.

Separation - the rings do not only separate the part of the soul associated with physical life from the rest, but also keep that part separated from other non-material energy. This is necessary in order to preserve the soul as a unit and achieve independence. When awareness expands beyond the rings (through, for example, the use of psychotropic drugs, spiritual practices, or simply 'peak experiences'), a temporary sense of the unity with one's surrounding or even the whole universe can be felt.

Shaping - the rings act as a dynamic mould that reshapes the soul.

Growth - when the rings expand, the soul can grow too, because its shell or boundaries expand. This enables a gradual and controlled expansion of awareness.

The rings have drawbacks too. They may close a person down, become restrictive and decrease flexibility. They can also grow without any corresponding experiential content, creating a bubble of empty 'space' (e.g. an inflated ego).

THE OUT OF BODY EXPERIENCE

The out of body experience (OBE) deserves special attention because it indicates that mental constricts are able to serve, at least temporarily, as sole 'host' for the self. If this is correct, the rings must have an ontological status. In other words, they must be something real. An OBE can be defined as having a point of view which does not coincide with that of the physical body. Such experiences are characterised by being (at least at the beginning) in the same environment where one's body actually is, but moving away from the body, and after awhile, coming back to it. It is reported that 15-20% of people have had an OBE at least once in their lifetime (Blackmore, 2005a, p.188).

The first point that should be clarified is that an OBE is not a dream. The conclusion of the research is that 'the pattern the brain waves showed [during an OBE] is like ordinary dreaming is some ways but distinctly different in other ways' (Tart, 2005, p.105). Psychologist Susan Blackmore also points out that 'it is certainly clear that OBErs were not in REM (rapid eye movement), or dreaming, sleep. Therefore OBEs cannot be considered to be a kind of dream' (2005a, p.189). It is now known, though, that dreaming does not only happen in the REM state, so further phenomenological differences need to be considered. Unlike a dream, an OBE typically starts from the same place where the one having the experience physically is, and has a beginning and an end ('separating' from and 'reconnecting' with the body). During an OBE awareness and memory are not narrowed like in dreams, but expanded (relative to the awake state). Not only does the person have at shis disposal all the usual mental faculties, but it is also possible (presumably because there are no restrictions imposed by the senses and nervous system) to become aware and remember experiences that cannot be associated with the awake state. For example, after an initial surprise at certain 'new' abilities such as floating or flying, one is in disbelief that s/he could have ever *forgotten* them[1]. Moreover, the person recognises that some phenomena do not belong to physical reality. One of the most interesting aspects of dreaming is that a dreamer accepts even the strangest events as normal. Likewise, a person who has an hallucination believes that what s/he perceives is real. During an OBE one is immediately aware that something unusual is going on and is capable of separating and comparing this state with normal perception (s/he is conscious of what belongs to the usual description of reality and what does not). In other words, s/he is aware of a difference. Because there is no body to stabilise perception, the person in such a state may feel somewhat strange (as if mildly under the influence of drugs or alcohol) which does not happen in dreams. Yet, the experience is

---

[1] Note that in dreams that involve flying this ability is taken for granted.

more full than in a dream (this can be compared to a difference between a two-dimensional and three-dimensional image). Blackmore writes that 'Vision and hearing are said to be more powerful and clearer than normal... unlike ordinary dreams, an OBEs feel very real, consciousness is clear, and the experience is usually remembered very vividly afterwards' (*ibid.*). In addition, the events or objects do not seem to be only a result of one's inner state. Permanency is one example: if in a dream we look again at an object we have spotted previously, it will most likely be changed in some ways, while during an OBE it will not. Another example is a sensory incongruence, rare even in the most bizarre dreams. Hearing laughter, for example, would in a dream spontaneously lead to *creating* its source. This may not be the case in an OBE – the sound of laughter may come, as it were, from nowhere. The environment is also not subject to the arbitrary will of the experiencer, so an OBE cannot even be identified with so-called lucid dreams.

All the above indicates that, unlike dreams, OBEs are not an auto-generated process. Nevertheless, considering that it is difficult to verify perception that does not rely on the senses, the OBE is open to different interpretations. A materialist could say, for example, that some parts of the brain are activated during an OBE that can mimic reality better than dreams. Blackmore proposes that the OBE is only experientially real and does not involve a perceptual separation from the body. She claims that the change of perceptual perspective derives from a mixture of memories and imagination. However, this interpretation does not look plausible. A shift in perceptual perspective may happen in any case, and therefore it does not rule out the separation. An OBE does not always involve a different perspective (i.e. from 'above'). It is not clear why a change of perspective would make such an experience so different and more real than dreams. Imaginative people should be more susceptible to such experiences, which is not the case. And finally, if only a change of perceptual perspective is involved, once experienced, an OBE should be easier to repeat, but this does not seem to happen. Such a view also cannot account for many common elements of the OBE. For example, Blackmore claims that 'OBErs sometimes try to touch people they see, only to find that the people do not notice them at all' (*ibid.*). Such surprising events are to be expected if they are real experiences, but not if they are a result of imagination. Therefore, the simplest explanation congruent with the beliefs of the majority who have had an OBE, which is that the OBE is real, seems more likely[1]. In other words, it is suggested that the OBE is the perception of reality without the intermediary of the senses.

---

[1] That certain chemicals (e.g. ketamine) or allegedly even electrical stimulation of the temporal lobe may be facilitative to an occurrence of OBE is not evidence that they *cause* such experiences.

The self normally cannot perceive reality without the body because it is on the frequency of the brain, but the senses are not a necessary condition for awareness (otherwise we could not be aware even of dreams). The self can perceive reality directly if the frequency range of awareness is expanded (this can be metaphorically compared with listening to a live concert, instead of a radio emission). However, this is not to say that an OBE is a fully direct experience. To be released from the body does not mean to be released from mental constructs. Indeed, an OBE usually involves a mental projection of ourselves and the world, super-imposing constructs that we are accustomed to onto reality. In other words, the mind provides recognisable forms to familiar energy configurations. This is why what is perceived during an OBE can be almost identical to what is perceived normally. The rings can (at least for awhile) maintain these forms even without the help of the physical body. Sometimes an OBE also involves an image of the person who is experiencing (a so-called 'astral body') but not always. Therefore, an 'astral body' is also, in fact, a mental construct that corresponds to the image that one has of shimself. The perception is interpreted in a familiar way, so the astral body is similar to the physical body (usually including even one's clothes). In fact, perception during an OBE relies on constructs far more than when information is received through the senses. The interpretation is partly guess work and, therefore, more likely to be inaccurate (especially relating to symbolic representations such as words and numbers). The solidity of the imprints of the senses on the brain circuits is needed in order to interpret physical information correctly. Perception of an action during an OBE is also a mental projection. The 'astral body' is too light to tangibly affect the material world. So, moving a chair, for example, means, in fact, moving a mental construct of a chair. This does not rule out the possibility that an OBEr can influence more subtle forms of energy, but some popular accounts of OBEs, which claim actual physical effects, are probably grossly exaggerated. So, it can be concluded that although physical and OBE perceptions have the same source, they cannot be regarded as the same thing. If these projections can be bracketed, OBEs can lead to genuine transpersonal insights.

Some possible questions

How is it possible to separate from the body? What maintains the connection?

The body and soul are not connected only through the mind. An OBE leads to the separation of the body from the other identifications of the soul, not the body and soul that remain connected. So, considering that the body and 'astral body' are not linked (no so-called 'silver cords'), the distance between them is irrelevant.

What would somebody, in physical proximity to a person having an OBE, perceive?

A person in the normal state would see only the physical body of the one who is experiencing and not notice anything unusual. An OBEr could affect though, in a subtle way, the energy of the other person (if s/he can penetrate the rings). So, although it is unlikely that an observer would be aware of the 'astral body', s/he may recognise an attempt to influence shis energy field. Animals have only one ring and are more open to direct experience. Anecdotal evidence suggests that if the attention is turned towards them, they can sense the presence and the direction of its approximate location. This indicates that not only the perception during an OBE, but also the mental identification through which the self perceives correspond to something objectively real.

How is it possible to have full access to the memory during an OBE?

There are two options here. One is that the range of frequencies is widened, so awareness still has access to the brain processes. The other is that the soul and the rings can temporarily re-create memories without direct connection with the brain.

Why paralysed people, for example, do not have OBEs more frequently?

This would have been merciful, but there is no evidence in this respect. One explanation may be that paralysed people are aware that they are paralysed, and, therefore, their existing construct of reality is a further barrier to such experiences.

How is it possible to remember an OBE after returning to the usual state?

Whatever enters awareness has the potential to be in awareness again (to be remembered) regardless of the source of the original experience. In other words, 'translation' is not necessary, especially if it is taken into account that constructs are involved in the first place. However, if after the experience one falls into a deep sleep, an associative link may be difficult to establish, and s/he may not remember what happened.

THE MATERIALS OF THE MIND

THE FORM AND THE CONTENT

In order to determine which roles different aspects of a living organism have in relation to a mental event, it is necessary to make the distinction between the form of a metal event (the explicit side) and its content, its meaning (the implicit side). A simple example can be used for this purpose. The sentences 'one and one are two' and 'jedan i jedan su dva' have different forms but exactly the same meaning. If the same meaning can have different forms, the meaning cannot be identified with the form.

The form is evidently preserved in the brain, but there does not seem to be a part of the brain responsible for the meaning. This suggests that the meaning and the corresponding mental representations are stored in different aspects of the person, and that the brain plays an important role in storing these representations, but not necessarily meaning. It is indicative in this respect that the disruption of articulated language due to a brain injury is not inevitably accompanied by loss of comprehension. Sufferers of aphasia often know that the words they are uttering are wrong, but they cannot correct or alter them ('Pass me the bread – no, not the bread, the bread – no!') (in Gregory, 1987, p.31). Or, they recognise the meaning of a written word, but not the word itself and use a similar one to describe it (e.g. *sword* for *duel* or *monk* for *hermit*) (Gilling and Brightwell, 1982, p.63). As early as 1930 physician A. A. Lowe showed a patient who had suffered a stroke (that had damaged his brain) simple words such as *dad, child* or *vice.* The patient read *father, girl* and *wicked.* The patient evidently understood the meaning of words, although he could not read the printed version. There is now strong evidence that most amnesic patients are well able to process information in terms of its meaning, although their memory remains impaired. This all indicates that the comprehension of meaning does not seem to be affected even after the brain has been damaged.

On this basis it is proposed that the non-representational, implicit content of a mental event (meaning) is preserved as energy structures in the soul. This, however, is not so simple. Any particular instance of an image or word is too specific to be directly related to its meaning. When we learn a new word (e.g. *table*) we usually connect it to the idea that such a word represents. This idea is never a specific table (otherwise the word would not have acquired universality). The rings consist of these ideas that act as an intermediary between the content and the form, between the soul and the brain.

In relation to the example 'one and one are two' the above can be summarised in the following way: neuro correlates in the brain are mostly responsible for a particular form (e.g. the English language). These correlates are constructed through physical exposure to such forms. Considering that the brain acts as a relay between the soul and the material world, when the brain is damaged the content is not lost. Rather, it is like being in a prison – the transformation of sensations into perceptions is impeded, as well as the output (e.g. verbal report). What is preserved in the rings are the general ideas of oneness, plus-ness, equal-ness and their relations (so speakers of different languages have fairly similar ideas about 'one plus one are two'). Any specific instance of 'one plus one is two' requires both, the rings and their neuro-correlates. On the other hand, the non-representational content of a mental event is preserved in the soul as an imprint, or energy configuration. That tacit meaning of 'one plus one is two' consists of relations without necessitating the objects that relate[1]. This is why it is difficult to formulate them (what would be the meaning of 'one and one equals two'?). These relations represent a dynamic component. Those aspects of experience and information that are preserved in the soul are not context dependent and are timeless. They approximate universal principles[2]. So, the soul does not contain any formal representations (e.g. specific images, symbols or words), not even their generalised ideas. Its constructed energy can be intimately linked, but cannot be identified with the rings. Of course, related soul processes, mental processes and brain processes tend to reinforce each other, although the brain processes are the strongest. In other words, the brain and the mind act like scaffoldings, helping the formation and reinforcement of energy configurations in the soul, which, in turn, enables meaningful organisation of mental representations.

The above does not only refer to language structures, but to our perception of objects too. One clarification may me necessary in this respect: the form and the content are not intrinsic features of an object, but rather the result of an interplay between a subject and an object. For example, the form of a table (e.g. its solidity) is influenced by our perception (in fact, it is, as any other object, mostly empty space). The meaning of a table also depends on an observer (presumably, it has a different meaning for a human being and an ant crawling on its surface).

Not surprisingly, our mental faculties, such as cognition, affect, and volition, also have this dual aspect.

---

[1] Some quantum physicists tend to perceive reality in a comparable way, but such similarities are beside the point here.

[2] Of course, the above example *can* be formulated more universally, such as $x + x = 2x$, but this is still far too narrow. The nearest expression of its content would probably be through musical tones.

Affect - at least two components of affect can be distinguished: feeling (an experiential component) and emotional reactions (a physiological and behavioural component). It is proposed that the former is a capacity of the soul. The brain does not *feel* the pain. Neither, of course, the body does (otherwise the nerve impulse from an affected area of the body would not need to travel to the brain centres that relay the pain). On the other hand, emotional reactions normally involve certain physiological processes, and are closely related to the brain and body. This distinction applies also to Autonomous Nervous System (ANS) reactions, not only semi voluntary ones. Observations of animals and humans who have a damaged ANS show that they still *feel,* although their feelings are somewhat muted (see Dana, 1921, and Hohmann, 1966), which is to be expected. The patients' reports indicate that they experience affects even in the absence of physiological reactions. Thus, physiological and behavioural changes reflect the type and degree of a reaction, but not the quality of a feeling.

Cognition (thinking) - although computer processing is sometimes compared to cognition, computers, in fact, are not near to thinking in human terms. When we think, we constantly make choices and are creative. Computers cannot do either. Thoughts can be intentional, while computers do not have any intentions (they are programmed). This unbridgeable difference arises because thinking also involves the non-material aspect of the person, and has its formal and tacit (implicit) component. Sometimes our thoughts may be formulated but they do not need to be. We usually think too fast for any formulation, so it is likely that a pre-verbal process takes place. A cognitive event starts with intending a meaning that creates a tension in the non-material energy configurations. This, in turn, triggers corresponding activity in the rings and the brain, which can produce a sentence or an image related to this configuration.

Volition also consists of one implicit aspect and the explicit one. The tacit aspect can be associated with intent which is, as already discussed, different from will. It is observed, for example, that sufferers of Parkinson's disease can be more successful in their movements if they intend to *get* somewhere, than if they focus on the movement itself (one patient, for instance, danced to the toilet). This is because intent can exploit the plasticity of the brain, and therefore, utilise unaffected areas (intent is not very strong though, so it has limited value in this respect). On the other hand, willing the movement is an attempt to recreate the form, and therefore uses the same brain circuitry that is not working well. This can also explain how different muscle sets can be invoked to do the same task, even if the original skill was not acquired using these muscles (e.g. you can sign with your foot and the signature will still be recognisably yours, see p.161).

Spontaneous mental processes - beside the mental processes that are intentional or responses to stimuli, there are also spontaneous mental processes. They are worth a closer look too. Sometimes (in fact, very often) it seems as if our thoughts or images have come from nowhere. They often intrude, impose on us. Yet, normally we own them, we are aware that they are a part of ourselves. So, it is more appropriate to call them spontaneous, rather than unconscious or subconscious. After all, we are conscious of such mental events, although perhaps not of what has caused them.

The part of the soul associated with the rings consists of a number of fields. Each field has a certain amount of energy and is in interaction with other fields. The result of that interaction is an increase or decrease of the energy in the field and a change in its shape or volume. Energy has a natural tendency towards equilibrium if other factors are not involved. Thus, even those fields that are not in one's awareness can be active if there is some permeability between them and a non-equilibrium state. Spontaneous changes are based on mutual interaction of the fields (energy does not have its own will). They can affect the soul if they have an energy potential even when we are not aware of them, and this can trigger unintentional thoughts. This makes the notion of the unconscious more complex: it may involve automatic brain processes, energy shifts in the soul, and spontaneous realignment of the rings. The trigger for all of them may be an external stimulus (e.g. association), although this is not necessary.

The other issue is why it is notoriously difficult to stop thinking - it is observed that even in sleep mental activity does not cease completely:

> ... the impression of absolute nothingness between falling asleep and waking up is more apparent than real, facilitated by an impairment of episodic memory and by some degree of confusion upon awakening... careful studies of mental activity reported immediately after awakening have shown that some degree of consciousness is maintained during much of sleep. (Giulio, 2004, p.17)

One way of looking at this is to consider that energy is a process. Both, the brain and the part of the soul associated with mental life are not objects but processes. The brain is not the brain and the soul is not the soul unless working (the brain can get energy from the body, the potential between energy fields in the soul, or intent). To be what they are, they need constant activity. However, thankfully, this is not to say that this activity has always to involve an ordinary level of thinking, as characterised by beta-waves. The whole system has the capacity to move below ordinary clatter and chatter (which can be empirically detected by a change in dominant wave patterns). This can be beneficial in many ways and is a standard practice in spiritual traditions.

EXPERIENCE AND INFORMATION

As the body, the soul also sustains itself and grows through getting energy from the environment. There are two types of 'food' for the soul: information and experience. Information can be defined as a comprehended relation between the objects of attention. Experience[1] is a comprehended relation between the subject and the object.

Both, information and experience, can affect the soul. Information affects the surface, which allows accumulative change. Experience, on the other hand, affects a deeper or inner configuration of the soul, which brings a qualitative change. Thus, information has a horizontal trajectory, while experience has an 'in-depth' trajectory[2].

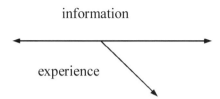

information

experience

Information involves understanding, while experience involves quale (singular of qualia, see p.84). Therefore, information is usually cognised (belongs to the cognitive domain), while experience is felt (belongs to the affective domain). Experience is more direct but less constructed and precise than information, which is why it is easier to share information than experience. This is not to say that information and experience can be strictly demarcated. Information can be transformed into experience and vice versa, but they should not be identified. Information is possible without experience, and experience is possible without information. For example, scenery may be experienced with disregard to its informational content, or the pieces of information can be gathered about the scenery without experiencing much. Nevertheless, they often go together - an event can provide an experience and information at the same time.

To summarise, the soul is either enlarged by expanding its surface through the inclusion of new information, or it is qualitatively modified by incorporating new experiences. There is also a third way of strengthening the soul, which is exercising intent, in a similar way to how physical exercises make the body stronger.

---

[1] Using the term 'subjective experience' is common, but adding *subjective* does not seem necessary. Every experience must be subjective, because it requires a subject that is experiencing.

[2] For the difference between the parts of the brain that process information and experience see, for example, Block, 1998, p.329.

Some possible questions

Is information an intrinsic property of energy?

Awareness is necessary for sensations to be transformed into experience and information. Nothing is information if it is not perceived, if somebody is not aware of it. Computers are not aware, and cannot feel or understand, so the electrical impulses passing through them really become information only when perceived by a user. This means that information can only be a potential rather than an intrinsic property of energy (which does not mean that this potential does not objectively exist, even in the absence of an observer).

What determines the quality of experience?

Experiences create energy shifts in the soul. In other words, they are vibrations or a set of vibrations that can be sensed or felt. If these vibrations are harmonious, they are perceived as agreeable, if not, they are perceived as disagreeable. An orchestra could be used as an analogy. At any point some instruments can add a new tune (perhaps due to external factors), which may or may not fit well with the rest. This is experienced (by the conductor or the self) as being in tune or not, being pleasant or not.

Are all experiences 'deep'?

Most experiences are close to the soul surface, so they are in a sense superficial. Deeper experiences (that should be distinguished from strong emotional reactions) require quieting the mind, a contemplative state. This is because such states allow more direct, and therefore more penetrating experiences.

Does every incorporated experience remains linked to information?

Experience has more energy than information, so it may remain even if the associated information is lost (which may lead to distorted or even false interpretations).

Are all information and experiences useful?

The soul is not facilitated by any information or experience. Some of them are useful, some are not (the intrinsic energy of stimuli, such as a photon emission bouncing from a printed material, for example, can be considered irrelevant in this respect). Only information that is incorporated can expand the surface of the soul, and the same applies to experiences. The factor that enables this will be discussed next.

MEANING

Information, experience and intent only potentially contribute to the soul. The common factor that is required in order to achieve this is *meaning*. New information, for example, is not attractive if not perceived as meaningful (e.g. reading a phone book). Three dimensions of meaning corresponding to information, experience and intent can be discerned.

The informational or the horizontal dimension of meaning, arises from the recognition of relations between sensations, between words (and other symbols), between sensations and words, and between the ways words or sensations are organised (e.g. the sentence 'sound is bigger than colour' is linguistically correct, but still does not make sense). Recognition, for example, requires making a connection between the immediate perception and previous experience or knowledge (that contain similarities). Sensations and words, in themselves, are meaningless. This means that the significance of any material arises not from its elements, but the way they are connected:

> When we become conscious of the meaning of a word and understand it, our understanding of the word, our subjective sense of it, is of the relations that constitute its meaning. (Rosenfield, 1992, p.99)

The experiential or 'in-depth' dimension of meaning arises from a connection between the subject and object, recognising the effects that a sensation has on oneself (what it *means* to oneself). If an experience does not mean anything to the one who is experiencing, it is not really an experience at all. Seeing a frog, for example, induces experience only if the event has any meaning for that person. This is often, although not always, based on previous experiences (the context of which may even be forgotten).

The intentional or vertical dimension is related to action that is deemed meaningful (not every intention or action is meaningful, but those that are not are usually short-lived). To be meaningful, an action has to be constructive, progressive. Destructive actions are difficult to perceive as meaningful, which is why even the most horrendous crimes in history have always been accompanied with an ideological justification (e.g. future or greater good; protecting a true faith, etc.). Therefore this dimension is essentially anti-entropic. However, considering that meaning has a subjective element, even those actions that may seem meaningful are not necessarily constructive from a larger perspective.

All these dimensions are contained in the soul, although certain mental structures that lead to them are usually constructed with the help of the brain and the rings.

Awareness plays an essential role regarding meaning. It is not enough that there is a relation, it needs to be *recognised*, which requires awareness. The constitutive elements of an image, for example, and some ways that they get linked can be a product of brain activity, but awareness is necessary to make a meaningful whole from them. Therefore, meaning always requires a subject (even if only the horizontal dimension is involved), as the following observation exemplifies:

> Considered in themselves, [words on paper], are just patches of ink. As such, they are not intrinsically meaningful, but are meaningful only in virtue of the relations in which they stand, directly or indirectly, to things that have gone on in certain conscious minds. (Lockwood, 1998, p.86).

So, conceptualisation is only contingently related to meaning. Words can be compared with a train, and the meaning with passengers. Words serve as a scaffolding for meaning, but meaning is elusive and can never be fully conceptualised. The meaning of representations rarely has precise boundaries and is implicit rather than explicit (even the meaning of a simple word such as 'table' is notoriously difficult to capture fully by a definition). Meaning is felt, sensed, intuited. In some cases conceptualisation is not present at all (e.g. of the term *space*). The meaning of a dream or story could be perhaps only felt, or the meaning of an event can be experienced without being able to put it into words. This is not to say that the meaning of a sentence, poem, dream or an event escape any formulation, but such attempts are never complete. Psychologist Macnamara (1972) points out that children have a world of meanings before words are produced or even understood. The infant has been categorising the environment and discovering the purpose of objects well before learning language. So, there is no reason why even animals cannot have an (albeit limited) sense of meaning, including all three dimensions, although they cannot formulate it.

Meaning is what bonds together the elements of mental structures. If relations are deemed meaningful, they are preserved, which enables the creation of constructs. If information is not considered meaningful, it is either rejected or an attempt is made to discover its meaning[1]. This search for meaning is an expression of the interplay between the static and dynamic principles and can contribute to both harmonisation and development of the soul.

---

[1] Sometimes it is very hard to find meaning in an event though (e.g. the accidental death of somebody close), which can result in restlessness and difficulties to come to terms with the event.

THE SOURCES OF EXPERIENCE AND INFORMATION

The three major sources of experience and information are chosen: perception, memory and learning, and dreams as an example of auto-generating processes. The intention is not to provide a comprehensive overview, but to outline an interpretation from the Synthesis perspective.

PERCEPTION

Some issues related to perception have been already addressed. The focus here will be only on one essential question: how are nerve signals turned into perception of the world? Psychology and other related disciplines have not and are unlikely to provide a satisfactory answer as long as they operate within the presently dominant paradigm. Eccles writes:

> There is a general tendency to overplay the scientific knowledge of the brain, which regretfully, also is done by many brain scientists and scientific writers. We are told that the brain "sees" lines, angles, edges, and simple geometrical forms and that therefore we will soon be able to explain how a whole picture is "seen" as a composite of this elemental "seeing". But this statement is misleading. All that is known to happen in the brain is that neurones of the visual cortex are caused to fire trains of impulses in response to some specific visual input. Neurons responding to various complications of this specific visual input are identified but there is no scientific evidence concerning how these feature-detection neurones can be subjected to the immense synthetic mechanism that leads to a brain process that is "identical" with the perceived picture. (Popper and Eccles, 1977, p.225)

It is known that retinal processing is involved in detecting intensity and wavelength contrast; early cortical areas in the brain are involved in orientation, curvature, spatial frequencies and movement; and high visual areas (in the parietal and temporal lobe) process sensations about the spatial relationships and the identity of visual objects. This, however, is not sufficient. Sherrington's comment from 1938 is still valid:

> A star we perceive. The energy scheme deals with it, describes the passing of radiation thence into the eye, the little light-image of it formed at the bottom of the eye, the ensuing photo-chemical action of the retina, the trains of action potentials travelling along the nerve to the brain, the further electrical disturbance in the brain, the action-potentials streaming thence to the muscles of eye-balls and of the pupil, the contraction of them sharpening under the light-image and placing the seeing part of the retina under it. The 'seeing'? That is where the energy-scheme forsakes us. It tell us nothing of any 'seeing'. Much, but not that. (1940, p. 248)

In order to tackle this problem the terms *sensation* and *perception* need first to be distinguished. Putting it simply, while sensation is about touch, vision and audition, perception is about feeling, seeing and hearing. Perception can be defined as the process of transforming sensations into information or experience. Although the neuronal activity without doubt contributes to perceiving, we are not even aware of such activity - we operate with words, images and feelings, not with neurons.

The first point that needs to be made is that perception ensues from the relation between the subject and the object. If this statement sounds obvious, it should not be forgotten that in the last hundred or so years everything possible has been done (without much result) to find an alternative explanation that would exclude the one who experiences and is aware. So, reinstating the subject, as an essential ingredient that transforms sensations into perception, is necessary. Perceiving sensations as meaningful images, for example, involves, besides electro-chemical processes in the brain, also awareness, intent and the self, without which meaning would not be possible. Thus, in accord with the previous posits, it is proposed that the non-material aspect plays an essential role in the transformation of sensations into perceptions and their interpretation.

It is not controversial that when we perceive something the brain is prompted to produce coherent wave patterns, which are otherwise in a chaotic state. In the 1970s neuroscientist Walter Freeman conducted research on the olfactory perception of rabbits. He established that what distinguishes the response to one smell from another does not depend on which neurons fire or what part of the olfactory bulb (the brain region associated with smell) is affected. Rather, it is determined by the relative amplitude of the response in different parts of the bulb. If no smell is introduced, an irregular, chaotic EEG (measurement of the electrical activity of the brain) through all possible frequencies and local amplitudes can be detected. When the rabbits were exposed to a familiar odour, their EEG patterns immediately move from a chaotic to a coherent state. An unknown smell causes a modification in the *collective* amplitude pattern of all neurons in the olfactory bulb. Thus, the production of a coherent wave pattern is what matters, not specific neurons. A comparable principle is likely to govern vision and it is even possible that these patterns can form something similar to holograms.

This is, however, only half of the story. As already argued, the wave oscillations produced in the brain need awareness to be perceived as meaningful images or words (a hologram too needs the interference of two light waves to be created). Moreover, perception is not passive, and therefore cannot be identified with the processes that happen in a camera, TV or computer (although there may be some resemblance on a very basic level). This is an active, creative process, involving several interrelated activities that transform sensations into information and experience:

Participating (attention, interest, curiosity, exploratory drive, seeking sensations and stimuli) is an innate drive. Its importance is highlighted by the experiments with kittens performed by Held and Hein in 1963. They created an apparatus called a 'kitten carousel', which allows two kittens to have exactly the same visual experience, but only one of them can initiate movement. When the kittens were tested, it was found that the 'active' one could see perfectly well, while the 'passive' one behaved as if it was not able to see much, although there was nothing wrong with its eyes or optic nerves. So, the passive kitten could not develop a perceptual ability without active participation.

Selecting - as already discussed, selecting from all possible stimuli is an active process, although over time it becomes mostly automatic.

Organising - the materials of perception are not just received, but they are also combined and structured. Perceptual organisation groups the smaller units into larger ones. The principal organising tendency is to identify part of the world as the target (the figure) and view the rest as the background. Other organising tendencies include 'the law of Prägnanz' (the law of simplicity), good continuation, closure, and the laws of grouping, such as proximity and similarity.

Interpreting - the sensory input is not perceived mechanically, but it is continually interpreted. One piece of evidence for this is *perceptual constancy*, related to size, shape and brightness. It refers to a phenomenon that the perception of invariant object properties remains constant despite changes in proximal stimulation (e.g. we always tend to perceive grass as green, although with decreased brightness it becomes, in fact, brown – which can be easily checked at dusk). Brightness constancy appears to be innate, whereas size and shape constancy are largely influenced by experience. So, the interpretation of reality is mostly achieved over time, and it takes over almost completely from un-constructed perception. This does not mean that what is perceived through our senses is not related to reality. Our perception normally corresponds (in some measure) to something real 'out there'. After all a fly, cat or human being may perceive a table leg in different ways, but they all try to avoid bumping into it. Actually, although our interpretations may be wrong, they often reflect reality better than sensations themselves, as exemplified by *shape constancy*, a subcategory of the above mentioned perceptual constancy: the shape of an object such as a door, for instance, is perceived as constant, even though the retinal image changes with its movement (a rectangular shape becomes trapezoid).

Perception therefore, is not a passive process, the perceived is evaluated, modified to some extent, and interpreted on the basis of previous experience and expectations. This indicates that not only awareness, but also an active involvement (hence intent and the self) are necessary in order to perceive.

Some possible questions

Why are we aware of the external reality rather than processes in the brain?

To function efficiently, it is necessary to be aware of the outside world, rather than an intermediary. If we were aware of receiving impulses from the brain, we could not identify with the body. This identification is important because it enables correlating the materials of perception to its real source – the world outside, which makes distinguishing between the external and the internal possible.

Why do we see images, rather than energy configurations?

For the reason of simplification. We perceive a table, for example, as solid and constant, because we have learned to disregard any fluctuations that are unimportant. Narrower perception is more condensed and therefore more stable. Mystical experience, for example, can be wider, but it is hard to make sense out of it.

How do we separate what comes from the outside and what comes from the inside?

As already mentioned, identifying with the body is a necessary condition to separate the internal and external, but it is not sufficient. Distinguishing whether the waves are triggered by nerves or our own constructs (e.g. dreams) is not straightforward. In fact, what is the internal and what is the external is gradually learned, and this process relies on many factors (an ability to exercise intentional control, continuity, relative stability, confirmation by other senses, shared experiences, etc.). Without them external reality could be perceived as internal, or more often, the internal is perceived as the external.

How do we choose what is the figure and what is the background?

This depends on the characteristics of the information (e.g. the spatial unity that tells us what is in front), the habituated selection procedures that may be biologically or socially conditioned, and intent (as when we are looking for somebody, for example).

What is the difference between transpersonal experiences and seeing things as they are (behind their physical and social constructs)?

These experiences are different - the first one requires going beyond the constructs, while the second one requires going 'below' them. Consequently, they require different methods: the first one is the result of applying transpersonal methods, the second one may be achieved by using phenomenological reduction (see p.36).

MEMORY

Memory is also a very complex phenomenon. Although psychology has made substantial progress, it is still poorly understood and some fundamental questions remain unanswered. Three processes related to memory will be addressed: encoding (memorising), storing, and retrieval (recalling, remembering).

Encoding

There is no doubt that the brain plays a crucial role in the encoding process. A still quite popular view is that each encoded information or experience creates a specific 'groove' along neuronal paths, implying that every new piece of information is encoded locally. There is, however, ample evidence against this possibility (see, for example, John, 1972). It is more likely that encoding is an analogue, a distributed but integrated process, akin to a field modifying activity (which fits well with the corresponding interpretation of perception). Such an encoding may be more conducive to an interface with awareness, but intentional awareness does not seem to be always essential. Encoding can be automatic - we remember many things that we have never attempted to remember. Such an encoding (which, perhaps, can be paralleled to the 'memory' of the immune system, for example) is likely to rely mostly on the brain. To be encoded, a stimulus needs to reach a memory threshold, which can be achieved by sufficient intensity or repetition.

Deliberate encoding, on the other hand, is qualitatively different. While the automatic one is difficult to influence, deliberate encoding is controlled to some extent by the learner. Attention (which cannot be simply reduced to brain functioning) plays a significant role in this case. Not only can convergent awareness reinforce an encoding pattern, but it can also involve remembering relations or principles (understanding), besides isolated pieces of information, so it has a greater degree of generality. The contributing factors include interest, effort and meaning. Meaningful features lead to an easier organisation – and hence a better memory. Intent seems to be important too. For example, an infant can make many unsuccessful attempts to catch a ball, but remembers the successful one. This is because such an attempt leads to a decrease of the tension created by intent, so it is repeated and retained[1]. Therefore, at least in some cases, encoding involves more that just mechanical brain activity.

---

[1] Later in life though, it is quite common that a failure is subjectively perceived as more important (and therefore more intense), so it is remembered better and is likely to recur.

Storing

Despite extensive research, the issue of where memories are stored is still surrounded with uncertainty. In order to address this question, it is necessary to postulate the two aspects of memory: implicit[1] and contextual, that can be paralleled to the previously discussed content and form. This can be justified even in relation to simple, conditioned memories. Based on his experiments with rats, Karl Lashley established two principles: memories are non-locally distributed (there is no memory storage in the brain)[2] and cortical regions are interchangeable in respect to memory. If different parts of the brain can be used to execute a learned activity, a 'blueprint' for that activity is unlikely to be in the brain, although the brain can be used to situate and exercise it within a particular context. Thus, it is proposed that implicit memory is stored as energy structures in the non-material aspect associated with mental life, while contextual memories rely on their neuro-correlates. This could explain how the same neurons can be used for different memories (despite their huge number, there are not enough neurons to individually store all the bits of information throughout a life-span), and why they do not get mixed up. It can also account for re-creating memories after brain injures (although, of course, association plays a role too). A weak and unstable memory blueprint that is in the soul can activate open modules in the brain.

The above does not mean that the brain is not very important, especially regarding short term and contextual memory. Through synaptic connections neurons can establish configurations and create a network that reinforces energy patterns. Non-material energy is more fluid, so although a form, such as an image, can be (re)created, stabilising it is difficult. Thus, the soul has only a limited ability to maintain the form without the support of the brain. Brain injuries and amnesia indicate that especially those elements of the mind that relate to interaction with material reality (language ability, face recognition etc.) are heavily dependent on the brain, which is to be expected. Many pieces of information do not have a lasting value - there is no need for the soul to remember the names of streets or politicians, for example. This bifurcation of the two above mentioned aspects of memory happens spontaneously, because the form (a material aspect) of information or experience is too 'heavy' to be preserved as such in the soul.

Some empirical support and the further details of storing process (that include the role of the rings, for example) can be found in the chapter 'The form and the content' (p. 173-174).

---

[1] The term implicit memory is sometimes used in psychological literature differently, to refer to alleged unconscious, non-deliberate memory. For the reasons why it is inadequate see Butler & Berry, 2001.

[2] This does not mean only that different memories are stored in different parts of the brain, but more strongly, that neuronal correlates of every memory are distributed.

Retrieval

Retrieval can be understood as the process of reconstructing a mental configurations that have already existed. This process also depends on the subject:

> The very essence of memory is subjective, not mechanical reproduction; and essential to that subjective psychology is that every remembered image of a person, place, idea, or object inevitably contains, whether explicitly or implicitly, a basic reference to the person who is remembering. (Rosenfield, 1995, p.42)

If the non-material aspect (that is associated with subjectivity) plays a role in retrieval, it can be expected that the formation of specific wave patterns is crucial, rather than the activity of individual neurons. This is supported by empirical research.:

> ...when a specific memory is retrieved, a temporal pattern of electrical activity peculiar to that memory is released in numerous regions of the brain. To that released set of wave-shapes corresponds the average firing pattern of ensembles of neurons diffusely distributed throughtout these widespread anatomical domains. Individual neurons within these ensembles display different momentary discharge patterns but the individual average firing patterns converge to the ensemble mean. (John, 1972, p.862)

It is true that, as perception is not always deliberate, some events from memory can appear in awareness spontaneously. When the connection is established in awareness, various elements, an image, sentence, thought or feeling, remain 'entangled' and one can recall the others (the strength of these connections depends on the underlying principles that govern in a particular situation). A recall may be based on an association that can be between images, words, or feelings, so an initial trigger can be sensory, abstract, and affective. For instance, an energy configuration (that can be felt) or the activation of a particular brain region can recall an image, and conversely an image can recall a feeling or activate a brain region. Any cue can trigger one of these elements, which in turn can bring about the others (it happens more often as a burst rather than a chain). Here is one familiar example: we may not remember a dream we had until we hear or see one detail that is connected to that dream, and then the whole dream suddenly comes back. These cues can enter our awareness accidentally as a part of a different context (like two train-tracks that cross at a certain point, which enables a train to pass from one track to another). The context, therefore, can affect a recall positively (association) and inhibitively (it is difficult to remember a dream when awake because it is out of context). This is why it is easier to remember something if we are in the same environment, mood or mental state as when we learnt it. Body imbalance or energy imbalance in the soul can also trigger memories, as well as habit (repetition).

It is now accepted that the brain does not work linearly and it is suggested that parallel processes take place, forming neural networks. Even this, however, is limiting. It may be more accurate to suppose that the brain works in a systemic way, following the principles of fields (created by impulses travelling through synaptic connections). This could account for the plasticity of the brain and why remembering one element illuminates surrounding elements. It can also explain flash-bulb memory – one strong stimulus increasing the clarity of a memory and of all other elements present at that moment. Eccles postulates that

> ...the self-conscious mind scans this modular array, being able to receive from and give to only those modules that have some degree of openness. However by this action on open modules, it can influence closed modules by means of impulse discharges along the association fibres from the open modules... and may in this manner cause the opening of closed modules. (Popper and Eccles, 1977, p.367)

The hippocampus (a part of the limbic system) clearly has a significant role in learning and memory – especially regarding transition from short term to long term memory. Patients with a removed hippocampus find it difficult to recall events after the removal (*ibid.*, p.391). This does not mean that they cannot have experiences, but they cannot put them in a spacio-temporal context (time for them does not exist, and also relating the experience to a specific spatial framework is hard). Apparently, amnesiacs can have dreams that refer to events or persons forgotten in the awake state and some of them have galvanic skin reactions when shown photographs of people that they had known but cannot remember. So, the hippocampus seems to be merely an instrument (a relay station) responsible for the laying down of the memory trace or engram, which is presumably largely located in the appropriate areas of the cerebral cortex (*ibid.*, p.392). This means that in the case of a brain injury, the experience is not lost, but a reference, an ability to recall, verbalise or recognise the experience. In other words, connectivity (between the content and form) is missing, which typically causes frustration in people whose brain is not fully-functional[1].

The same is evident in ordinary retrievals, as for example, when we search for a word. We have the pre-verbal sense of meaning (the content), but we are looking for an expression (a form). When found, the word is immediately recognised as the correct one. Eccles writes:

> We have a kind of diagrammatic representation of the thing we wish to find before we try to find it... when we really find it, we are usually quite certain that we have reached what we were looking for. (*ibid.*, p.505)

---

[1] See Rosenfield (quoting Kurt Goldstein), 1995, p.26

It is proposed that we have the sense of what we are looking for because the content, as a particular vibration without a form, already exists in the soul. Intent leads to a match between the meaning of what we want to say and a corresponding word that requires a neuro-correlate. This notion is further supported by the *feeling-of-knowing* phenomenon: even when we fail to recall the actual memory, we still may have a 'feeling' about it (e.g. we can predict accurately whether we will be able to recognise this information). Recognition, therefore, is not based on image matching, but matching the content and the form. This is why, even if we cannot describe or imagine a person that we have met before, if s/he appears, we immediately recognise shim. Experimental work that analysed the wave patterns produced by the brain seems to concur on the importance of meaning:

> ...the differences in readout wave-shapes seem to depend upon... the specific meaning of the signal. (John, 1972, p.859)

To summarise, remembering involves a three stage process, although not all of them are always present (recognition, for example, does not always require the first stage): a search or generation process (utilising intent), followed by identification[1] (that is a mind process) and finally, situating the memory in context (for which a functioning brain is necessary).

Memories are not only retrieved but also created to some extent, by filling in the existing gaps. New experiences, changing perspective or different moods can modify some elements of a memory or even create new ones. Obviously, the self and intent play an important proactive role in retrieval (possibly to avoid the taboo term *self*, cognitive psychology coined the phrase *central executive*). Eccles writes:

> In retrieving the self-conscious mind is continuously searching to recover memories of words, phrases, pictures by an action which is not just a mere scanning over the modular array, but it is probing into the modular array in order to evoke responses from it and in order to try to discover the preferred modules, the ones which are related to the memory by their patterned organisation. In that way the self-conscious mind is, as it were, taking a very active role in recovering memories which it regards as being desirable at that time. (Popper and Eccles, 1977, p. 504)

It is interesting, in this respect, that the electrical stimulation of brain regions of patients under local anaesthesia can trigger only 'passive' memories, in which the patient is an observer not a participator (e.g. watching or hearing the action or speech of others). The memories that would require an active or intimately experiential involvement of the self (making decisions, carrying out skilled acts, speaking, writing, tasting food, sexual or painful experiences) are conspicuously absent (Penfield and Perot, 1963).

---

[1] For the further clarification of these two stages see Zechmeister & Nyberg, 1982.

LEARNING AND KNOWLEDGE

Learning is an essential mental process (not only for human beings) and deserves a special attention. Psychology has extensively studied this subject and made a significant contributions to its understanding. In fact, several 'gradients' of learning can be distinguished.

1. The simplest form of learning, but by no means simple, is often referred to as *reflex conditioning* (or its variant *instrumental conditioning)*. For example, if you ring a bell every time when a dog gets food, eventually it will start salivating on hearing a bell even in the absence of food. The term reflex conditioning, though, has somewhat misleading connotation. Animals or humans are not completely passive in this process, as these words suggest. It is experimentally proven that at least the initial stages of conditioning involve cortical activity, indicating that any response is a purposeful act motivated by goal attainment. Penfield points out that 'every learned reaction that becomes automatic was first carried out within the light of conscious attention and in accordance with understanding of the mind' (Penfield, 1975, p.59). Thus, it is more plausible to assume, in line with Popper and Eccles' reasoning (1977, 503), that the stimuli incite particular expectations (perhaps in the form of an image such as food) that then trigger a certain response. Of course, if such a response produces desirable results, in time it will become automatic. This is concurrent with the notion that a reward contributes to motivation rather than learning, as 'latent learning' experiments confirm. Animals (and humans) learn even if they do not have any incentive to do so, probably as a result of innate drives to explore and form cognitive maps.

2. A more complex form is *cognitive learning*. There are a number of learning types in this category.
• The basic one is *memorising*. As already discussed, although we may spontaneously remember some isolated pieces of information, memorising usually requires active participation (investing an effort, concentration).
• *Observational learning* (imitating or mimicking others) belongs to this category too. This learning is not straightforward either. It is a sort of experimentation or a role-play, testing what outcomes particular behaviour produces.
• *Insight learning* is yet another type. Sometimes, the solution to a problem for example, is found in an instant, with a sudden grasp of the concept. Something clicks when we discover a new, central connection that reveals a larger picture or other possibilities and connections, like a piece of a jigsaw that reveals where the other parts fit. These insights enable the integration of new information in a meaningful way. They can be understood as a product

of the accumulative pressure that a sustained intent creates, which usually requires a period of incubation (seeming passivity). Certain techniques or faculties (e.g. intuition) may facilitate this process, but this does not mean that such insights are reserved for humans. It is observed that some primates are also capable of learning in this way (see, for example, Köhler, 1925).

3. The most interesting and complex type of learning is learning that besides memorising also involves *understanding* (that can be tacit, as in the process of learning new skills). The term learning, in fact, commonly refers to this type. We learn meanings, or the relations of one stimulus to another, which is what makes it different from just memorising. Such learning involves extrapolations - awareness of principles behind the specific events, procedures or tasks, and thus requires an active self. As any good teacher knows, proper learning needs understanding, and understanding implies attention. If no active effort is made, no learning of this type occurs. Experiments with animals (e.g. the 'kitten carousel' mentioned earlier, p183) and some educational methods (e.g. learning though discovery) show that the more proactive learning is, the better it is. Real learning, therefore, is a dynamic process that cannot be reduced to conditioned responses or training. For example, an infant puts shis hand in a fire, gets burned and 'learns' not to do it any more. Scientists at the beginning of the 20th century carry pieces of radioactive material in their pockets because they glow, get leukaemia, and 'learn' not to do it anymore. However, this is very different from *understanding* why fire burns skin, and why a radioactive material kills. Hence, this type of learning deserves a category of its own.

The result of learning is knowledge. Learning creates a network, it is a process of constructing information and experience (the materials of awareness) by selecting, separating, linking, sorting, generalising and storing information on the basis of formal or tacit principles. Knowledge is this network. Knowledge acquisition starts from setting boundaries to possibilities in order to open new ones on a different level. So, learning at first limits, but then expands one's freedom. For instance, learning to ride a bike narrows the possible ways of riding a bike (excluding all the 'bad' ones), but knowing how to do it well enables a greater freedom of movement. Learning and accepting chess rules limits the number of possible moves, but it allows the freedom to play chess in a meaningful way and endless combinations within the given boundaries. This of course does not refer only to practical skills, but to empirical and theoretical knowledge too. Learning and understanding how physical forces work, for example, limits the number of possible interpretations, but then using that knowledge allows operating within a larger perspective, which opens further possibilities.

The relationship between awareness and learning

Awareness and learning are closely related, but they are not the same (they are qualitatively different mediums). Unlike awareness, learning constructs the materials, but it does not have a focus (constructs have no focus). Moreover, although awareness can be, it is not necessarily accumulative, while learning always is (characterised by 'becoming' rather then 'being').

How awareness and intent affect the learning process
Nowadays, it is common to say that machines or computers learn, but this is a misuse of language. Computers are not aware and are completely passive (meta-algorithms may be used to streamline their output, which may resemble conditioning in appearance, but is certainly not learning). Learning is not possible without awareness. We can know only what we have been aware of. Awareness, however, is not enough. Learning, being essentially an active process, requires intent too. This is not to say that all types of learning necessarily require intent, but understanding certainly does.

How learning affects awareness and intent
Learning, that involves understanding, does not have a significant survival value in evolutionary terms. All other species on this planet have survived without it, so early humans would probably have survived too. However, learning is indispensable for the development of the mind[1]. It enables much faster social and individual processes to take over biological evolution. Learning is not possible without awareness, but knowledge affects awareness too. Without connecting information in a network (or larger units) only an awareness of confusion and noise would increase. In addition to this organising quality, the capacity of knowledge to make a whole also contributes to the expansion of awareness. Polanyi points out that 'when we recognize a whole, we see its parts differently from the way we see them in isolation' (1969, p.140). Besides awareness, knowledge influences intent as well, by providing routes to its realisation, for example. Thus, through awareness and intent, learning affects existence and agency and therefore, it can influence both, the dynamic and static principles.

---

[1] Consequently, if understanding is epiphenomenal to survival, it is more likely that biological survival serves the development of mind, rather than the other way around.

DREAMING

Dreaming is chosen to represent auto-generating processes because it is a fundamental faculty common to humans and most animals, and because it can provide both experience and information. Dreaming is also so unusual that its better understanding can provide insights about reality itself.

The difference between a dream and the awake state

In a dream everything seems real, so the question may be raised what the difference between a dream and the awake state is and how we know that the awake state is not just another dream. Some thinkers have concluded that we cannot know, but this seems premature. The basic difference is, of course, that the self identifies with the physical body when awake, while in a dream it identifies only with an image (motor, perceptive and the volitional functions are partly inhibited). This has several consequences.

Exclusiveness - the images in dreams mostly originate from or are related to the experiences of the awake state. Yet, in dreams we are normally not aware of daily life (not only do we not experience it, but it does not exist for us), while when awake we are aware that dreaming exists. Even if a dreamer remembers the awake state while dreaming (as in lucid dreams, see below) it is never perceived as a subset of the dream. This indicates that the awake state includes dreams and therefore is more fundamental.

Inconsistency - although the perception of the world is to some extent a construct, it is more objectively consistent than a dream. A dream environment cannot prove us wrong, while waking reality can (if we believe that we can walk through the wall, we will, but only in a dream). Also, in the awake state there is a sense of continuity that is lacking in dreams, even after interruptions such as sleep.

Diminished self-control - with some exceptions, volition is also usually weaker in dreams. We are inertive and reactive rather than proactive. Although we can potentially use all the mental abilities as when awake, we usually behave instinctively ('here and now' reactions are far more common than elaborate decisions). As Eccles writes:

> A characteristic feature of most dreams is that the subject of the dream feels a most disturbing impotence. He is immersed in the dream experience, but feels a frustrating inability to take any desired action. Of course he is acting in the dream, but with the experience that in doing so he is a puppet. (Popper and Eccles, 1977, p.374)

Instability - the awake state is more stable and consequently more predictable than a dream (it is governed by fixed, unchangeable laws – no miracles). On the other hand, dreams are not anchored by perception and constrained by physical laws. As a consequence, experiences are less filtered, range more widely, and are more direct and engaging. Dreams are richer, but also highly unstable and fluid (in this way they resemble non-material reality). Without an external support we rely on ourselves more, so it could be said that in dreams we are really what we are.

Attachment - when awake, the support of stable external structures makes distancing from the immediate experience easier (if we stop to think, the world is not going to change or disappear). The self has a chance to detach, which allows a person to become aware of the past, reflect, think about the future and remember dreams too. In a dream such a distance does not exist, which is why we do not remember awake reality while dreaming. This is similar to watching a programme that can be so engaging that we forget the world around us. Dreams are characterised by motion rather than rest, events are too flitting to give us time to reflect. They don't have pauses, and we are never bored. When nothing happens, we sleep. The dream state is akin to flow, being fully emerged in an immediate experience. This attracts the self and narrows awareness to the extent that we take it all for real (as long as it lasts). In other words, we are hypnotised by the inner reality.

Selective cognition - what is really puzzling is not that strange things happen in dreams, but how easily they are accepted as something normal. This indicates that not only the physical level is removed but also, at least partly, the other ways we construct reality. In dreams we do not have a sense of time, do not normally operate with abstract concepts and systems, and are less self-reflective. Memory in a dream is not suspended, but is highly selective, we remember only information that is relevant to the dream. We are also unable to sustain attention. In other words, we are more aware when awake than in dreams (from this perspective, dreams are a step backward, rather than forward). This, of course, is not to say that dreams are not an extremely valuable source of experience and information. To highlight this point, the purpose of dreams will be discussed next.

The purpose of dreams

Experiential - dreams are usually the result of re-balancing energy, so they can be understood as a complement to reality. While in reality our experiences affect our states of mind, in dreams a state of mind creates an experience. This interplay can be understood in the following way: our daily experiences sometimes create energy imbalances. They are not always dealt with or processed immediately, but placed in a 'buffer' and left for later, when the input decreases. However, the conscious mind often forgets or is not inclined to recall them from the buffer, so they return into awareness when the control of the mind is not so strong and when the bombardment of external information is drastically reduced. In other words, either pleasant (e.g. sexual desire) or unpleasant (e.g. fear) internal experiences that have not been fully acknowledged and assimilated and need to be addressed, are brought to awareness. They produce images and can generate brain activity, as sensations do while awake (in fact, the same brain regions are activated by external stimuli and corresponding mental events in dreams). Considering, though, that an energy imbalance that triggers a dream is not attached to a specific form any more, the dream content does not necessarily corresponds to whatever has caused this imbalance. Dream images and events are usually chosen because they are readily available (from memory) and do not cause much resistance. In any case, dreaming enables us to safely deal with and integrate an experience and in that way achieve better balance. Although our agency may be somewhat limited, this process requires active responses (otherwise we would not need to be aware of our dreams). Resolution, therefore, happens in a dream, rather than in its interpretation.

Informational (or *interpretative*) - there is much disagreement about the meaning of dreams. On the one side of the spectrum is the view that dreams are meaningless images generated by random activity of neurons in the brain[1]. This is unlikely to be the case: however bizarre, a dream is rarely totally fragmented (which is what can be expected if the above explanation is correct); they have a linked if not always coherent narrative, and even more importantly, a unifying perspective – the self (as in the awake state). On the other side of the spectrum is the view that dreams are messages from some hidden part of ourselves with universal symbols and syntax (found in psychodynamic approaches, and also in many popular books on dream interpretations). This is also not very plausible. Even Freud acknowledged that 'a cigar in a dream is sometimes just a cigar'. It is more likely that dreams are idiosyncratic expressions of our states of mind (emotions, desires, worries, and other drives). They can be meaningful, but their meaning is specific to the person involved, rather than universal. Dreams do not follow a fixed logical structure though, but a chain of associations, which is why they are often confusing and difficult to interpret. In any case, a dream is an experience, not just a surrogate for life. Therefore, dreams are not necessarily meaningful, just as events in an awake state do not seem always to have an underlying meaning. This is not to say that the content of

---

[1] *Activation-synthesis hypothesis*, for example, leans in this direction (see Hobson & McCarley, 1977).

dreams is irrelevant. After all, they are products of one's own mind. However, the ways the person relates and reacts to dream events and the ways s/he connects them to other experiences is what provides valuable insights. If a dream is triggered by day-time experiences but can create a different scenario, a dream's actual content is clearly not intrinsically related to these experiences. So, we again have here an explicit side of a dream (images and events) and its implicit side (relations and ideas that they represent): the latter contributes to the understanding of meaning more.

Types of dreams

The above mainly relates to balancing dreams that are the most frequent. However, there are other types of dreams. Inertive dreams are a prolongation of the awake state (for example, if one plays chess all day, s/he may dream chequered surfaces). They are caused by the continuous firing of neurons that were already active and have not calmed down yet. There are also inspirational dreams in which an intent generated while awake is manifested (e.g. the dreams that have led to some scientific discoveries mentioned in the first part). Revelatory dreams involve tapping into or receiving information from external sources (strictly speaking, these experiences are not dreams at all, but they usually, although not always, happen while asleep because it is easier to get through then). It is also possible to become fully aware and take control over one's dream. This happens when the dreamer realises that s/he is dreaming (the self becomes aware that it is identifying only with an image). These are called lucid dreams. Lucid dreams can be very beneficial. They are, in a way, a training in direct self-control, without the reliance on the outside structures. On the other hand, they may prevent spontaneous experiences that are also important. Day dreaming or fantasising is another type of auto-generating process that creates images and experiences. They are similar to dreams, except that they happen while awake and are, therefore, much weaker (intense fantasies or hallucinations usually indicate a mental disorder). Fantasies create images that correspond to an internal state (e.g. the feeling of longing may trigger an image of home). These images make internal states more concrete and are a pre-verbal way to direct one's actions, but they may decrease motivation.

All the elements described in this part (*The Mind*) and in the previous part (*The Being*) are, of course, subject to dynamic processes. The most important ones are biological evolution, individual development, and social development. No account can be complete without addressing them, so the final part will focus on these subjects.

THE PROCESS

EVOLUTION

NEO-DARWINISM

Evolution undoubtedly happens, however, it is far from clear how and why it happens. Neo-Darwinism, the dominant interpretation at present, attempts to operate within a strictly materialistic framework. Evolution is regarded as a gradual process that comes about through the interplay of two factors: *random mutations* (accidental changes of genetic material) and *natural selection* that enables some of these changes to take over on the basis of their adaptive and reproductive advantages. The dynamic of evolution is based on the struggle and competition within and between species for limited resources. Although this process is considered directionless, it is apparently responsible for bringing forth the successive forms of life from single cell organisms to human beings. This interpretation of evolution has its merits, but also has some flaws. It was widely accepted in the 20th century not because it explained everything perfectly, but because it accounted for the facts better than any alternative and because it fitted well with the prevailing ideology of materialism. The purpose of what follows is not an attempt to prove Neo-Darwinism wrong, but to show that it is incomplete, which is why it cannot provide plausible explanations for all the characteristics of evolution (e.g. the increase of complexity) and for all the paleontological and biological facts. Actually, almost every key term associated with this view: chance, natural selection, competition, and gradualism, raise some doubts, especially if taken dogmatically as it is often the case at present[1].

Chance

The materialist view is that all the changes in living organisms from the original single cell to a great variety of species that have existed and exist nowadays are the result of accidental genetic mutations[2]. Sure enough, some

---

[1] The phrase 'survival of the fittest', which is also linked to this model is not considered, because, as biologist Waddington already pointed out a long time ago, it is just a tautology: the existing species have survived because they have been the fittest, and they are the fittest because they have survived.

[2] It may be worth mentioning that Darwin is not responsible for this but his followers, who are trying, as any other ideologists or religious people, to be more Darwinian that Darwin himself. He allegedly wrote: 'I cannot, anyhow, be contented to view this wonderful universe, and especially the nature of man, and conclude that everything is the result of brute force. I am inclined to look at everything as resulting from designed laws, with the details, whether good or bad, left to the working out of what we may call chance' (in Fontana, D. 2003. p.73).

mutations may be accidental, but the claim that all the mutations in all the organisms have been, seems improbable for several reasons.

The effects of random mutations are almost always harmful and incur a loss, not a gain of information and complexity. Only in extremely rare cases may they be harmless. As Denton points out, 'the fact that the vast majority of all mutations which have some detectable influence on the functioning of the organism are deleterious suggests that each functional living system is indeed enormously constrained to adaptive changes along only a tiny fraction of all the possible evolutionary trajectories available to it' (1998, p.341).

Even if an advantageous mutation occurs, the chances of it spreading throughout the population are very small and the chances against are extremely large. Taking into account the number of mutations that should have taken place, it is highly improbable that they would randomly lead from a single cell organism to human beings. The above quoted biologist states that '...evidence for the doctrine of the spontaneity of mutation is hardly ever presented. Its truth is nearly always assumed' (*ibid.*, p.286). Chance mutations acted on by natural selection could scarcely account for variations *within* species (microevolution) let alone for successive variations *among* them (macroevolution). A blind process on an erratic trial-and-error basis is not impossible, but is incredible. Laszlo concludes:

> ...A random process could not have produced the kind of order that we meet with in our experience; it could not even have produced the kind of chaos that surrounds us at times. The fact is that pure, unadulterated chance could not have existed in the universe even if it coexisted with strands of order. If a series of chance events had punctuated the developmental process, the things that would have emerged out of that process would have randomly diverged among themselves... Given a process that is subject to pure chance, even previously ordered things would each grow their own way... Evidently, mere chance did not dominate the evolutionary process: there must also have been a significant degree of binding and coordination. (1993, p.18)

A usual response by neo-Darwinists to these challenges to chance as an explanation for the evolutionary process is that given enough time, random mutations would eventually lead to the complex life forms that exist today. However, this does not hold water, especially if long periods of stagnation are taken into account. The rates of mutation necessary are staggering, even within billions of years, considering the cost involved in disposing of the predominant bad mutations. Also, for a good mutation to become fixed in a population, all those individuals which do not have the new trait must die. When these considerations are combined with the low rates of reproduction of many animals, there has hardly been enough time for the present species to have evolved. To quote Laszlo again, 'it is highly unlikely that random processes could have constructed an evolutionary sequence of which even a basic element, such as a protein or a gene, is complex beyond human capacities'. (*ibid.*, p.91)

Environmental changes - another reason that makes evolution by chance implausible is adaptation to environmental changes. A suitable habitat may become less suitable in a relatively short time, which may threaten the survival of some species. In order to carry on, they have to adapt to new conditions. But, if species changed only by random and gradual mutations, they could not adapt fast enough. Yet, many somehow have managed to do so, by producing numerous and complex mutations that were just right.

Specific mutations - chance may play a part in mutations, but there are many instances indicating that genetic mutations are not always random and that specific genomic changes can take place under certain conditions. For example, both plants and insects can mutate so as to decontaminate the chemicals that enter their environment and develop a resistance to toxic substances. Some experiments (carried out independently by John Cairns and Barry Hall) also show that bacteria seem to be able to mutate solely their defective genes. Purely random mutations could never be so specific.

Inter-species consistency (*evolutionary convergence*) - despite the staggering variety of organisms brought forth during the Cambrian period (about 500 million years ago), the species that now populate the Earth exhibit striking regularities both within and among themselves. Some highly specific anatomical features show remarkable consistency among species with very different evolutionary histories. For example, the wings of birds and bats have similarly positioned bones as the flippers of seals and the forelimbs of equally unrelated amphibians, reptiles and vertebrates. Diverse species also exhibit common orders with regard to the position of the heart and the nervous system: in endoskeletal species the nervous system is in the back and the heart in the front position, while in exoskeletal species these positions are reversed. Another example is the eye: its basic structure appears to have been invented independently by about forty unrelated species. Organisms faced with the same challenge repeatedly arrive at the same solutions. Even if chance is streamlined through natural selection, the convergence of many highly 'creative' solutions beggars belief.

Natural selection

Natural selection is also a problem. Although it can weed out the misfits, natural selection cannot make new things (*selection* means choosing a few from a greater number). It does not create features but merely selects those that provide a greater survival value, and by doing so only narrows the width of the evolutionary process. Although Neo-Darwinists usually claim that the growth in complexity is the result of adaptation to environment, the appearance of increasingly complex organisms cannot be predicted solely from the work of natural selection upon random mutations.

The classical Darwinian mechanism works mainly to adapt individuals to their existing niches; individual variations do not contribute significantly to the emergence of new, more complex species. Even more importantly, many simple organisms are equally or better adapted to environmental variations than complex ones. Only they can be found in extreme conditions. Some unicellular life forms are spread across different environments much more than complex organisms (with the exception of humans). Evolutionist Gould states that '...without question, these earliest and simplest cells, the bacteria and their allies, remain the most abundant, widespread, and successful of all living things' (1988, p.44). If only adaptation directs evolution, evolution should not have moved from one cell organisms. This reasoning can be pushed even further:

> If mere survival is the sole desideratum, then it would seem that some rudimentary type of organism would be all that is needed. And there would seem no reason why even a rudimentary type of organism should appear, since it could not hope to rival in longevity the everlasting rocks – but unstable DNA? (Edmunds, 1997, p.159)

Natural selection also cannot adequately explain long term adaptive changes. Some changes have immense consequences, and yet they could not have had adaptive advantages when they happened. One example is bisexual reproduction that increases diversity at great cost. Laszlo points out that 'such a mechanism, while offering an obvious long-term advantage (the more rapid spread of advantageous mutations) does involve an equally obvious short-term disadvantage (the reduced average number of descendants due to males failing to produce offspring)' (1993, p.169).

Finally, natural selection seems to be based on a circular argument (everything that survives is adaptive and therefore selected, and everything that is selected is adaptive and survives) so it cannot be refuted, which does not make good science. When natural selection is used to explain everything, even mutually contradictory adaptations (e.g. the indistinctive colours of some insects, as well as very distinctive colours of others), in fact, it does not explain much.

Competition

A popular science writer, Hazen, describes evolution in the following way:

> Charles Darwin proposed that evolution occurs because of the constant struggle for survival. Many more individuals of most species are born than can possibly survive. In the brutal competition for limited resources, individuals with advantageous traits are more favoured to survive long enough to pass those traits on to offspring. (1997, p.197)

This scary way of interpreting the evolutionary process, using phrases such as 'survival of the fittest', 'struggle', 'brutal competition' and so forth, is fairly typical. Such a view was already popular in Darwin's time, probably as a reaction to the idealisation and glorification of nature by the Romantic movement.[1] However, this outlook is biased. No doubt that struggle and competition exist, but cooperation and symbioses within a species and between species is at least equally important[2]. For example, in order to start creating multi-cell organisms, some single-cell organisms must give up their capacity to reproduce – which is a striking example of symbiotic cooperation leading to complexity, but is contrary to 'selfish gene' (or similar) interpretations. Using loaded adjectives such as 'brutal' even in connection to the predatory nature of certain species is misleading. Every organism must die, and the suffering of those individuals who are unfit or misfit would probably be longer and more brutal without predators.

More importantly, if competition is the only driving force (between species, as well as within a species), one would expect that super-bacteria, super-plants or super-animals would have developed well before the appearance of humans and have taken over the whole eco-system. Yet, a delicate balance in nature that allows development seems to be permanently preserved. In rare cases when a particular type of species starts to dominate to the extent that they prevent further evolution, they conspicuously get wiped out. Many researchers have argued, for example, that mammals and thus humans could not have evolved without the demise of the dinosaurs (presumably, this has not been the fate of humans, although they are now dominant, because evolution so far has continued within the species – a point taken on in the following chapters).

---

[1] His contemporary, poet Tennyson, famously characterised nature as 'red in tooth and claw'.

[2] After a long battle, the scientific community nowadays looks more favourably upon the proposition of Lynn Margulis that the cooperation between organisms, rather than competition, is the chief agent of natural selection. In a consolatory fashion, she said that 'Darwin's grand vision was not wrong, only incomplete'. The position here is that the same applies to some other tenets of Neo-Darwinism.

204

Gradualism

The Neo-Darwinian theory maintains that life has been subject to a process of gradual transformation that allowed it to move from simple forms to ever more complex ones in small steps. Early life consisted of tiny unicellular organisms living in water, and every other form, extant or extinct, is connected by an unbroken chain of intermediate species to these first ones. This is not exactly the picture that one would get from the available fossil evidence. If evolution had been gradational, there should be greater variations between fossil specimens reflecting every small step in the process. But, this does not seem to be the case. Although there are an abundance of fossils of fully formed species, there are few contenders for their transitional forms (hence the phrase 'missing link'). For example, there are no traces of the evolutionary ancestors of the trilobites in the rock layers beneath where the trilobites are found. It seems that trilobites, with their sophisticated optical systems, appear in the geological record relatively suddenly. These occurrences cannot be fully accounted for by the incompleteness of available data. Mounting paleontological evidence suggests that 'speciation' (the emergence of new species) is a rapid process. Species change in relatively swift bursts, without leisurely transition periods[1]. These episodes of fast speciation are separated by fairly long spans during which no significant alterations can be detected. In other words, species appear abruptly, often in entirely different forms, and remain substantially unchanged for millions of years – a condition of stasis at odds with Darwin's model of continuous change. Then, just as quickly they become extinct and are immediately followed by other very different species[2]. The fossil record demonstrates abundantly that each episode of extinction was followed by a period when new forms proliferated, filling the ecological niches emptied by the old. Not only individual species but entire genera make their appearance in relatively short time. One example is the so-called Cambrian explosion about half a billion years ago, the sudden emergence, in the span of a few million years, of a great variety of the bigger animals that now populate the earth. The rapid evolution of mammals between 60 and 65 million years ago is another instance of this recurrent phenomenon. It is significant that every new cycle is not made of species at the same level of complexity, but more advanced ones.

---

[1] Although it had its precursors, so-called punctuationism or punctuated equilibrium brought these facts to wider attention in the 1970s. It caused quite a stir, especially among dogmatic Neo-Darwinists, for fear that it could be used as a weapon against the theory of evolution as a whole.

[2] Of course, 'immediately' only in geological terms. For instance, Denton writes that 'the evolutionary pattern was one of millions of years of stasis interrupted by periods of no more than 100, 000 years of rapid and sudden change' (1998, p.297).

This does not refute the continuity of the evolutionary process and certainly does not imply that an external force directly interferes with it, as the creationists (or the proponents of 'Intelligent Design') would like to believe[1]. Slow, continuous change (within species) may be the norm during periods of environmental stability, while rapid speciation may occur during periods of environmental stress. When the milieu changes and the existing niches disappear, some species die out. Then the 'peripheral isolates' (species that live in relatively small numbers) invade the centres of dominance and take over as the new main species. Also there are some creative solutions. For example, a link between prokaryotes (cells without organelles) and eukaryotes (cells with organelles and other structures) has not been found. The difference between these single-cell species is striking, and yet there are no intermediate stages between them. There are many living samples of each, but none of the intermediate stages. One imaginative possibility, put forward by the biologist Margulis, is that eukaryotes could be the result of a symbiosis of two different prokaryote species.

However, even when the above hypotheses are taken into account, conventional Darwinian mechanisms do not seem sufficient to explain the stops and starts observed in the fossil record (why species appear so abruptly and why they persist so long without changing.). These punctuations are too radical to allow for Neo-Darwinian interpretation. The problem is not only to explain the sudden burst but also, as a science writer Richard Kerr puts it, 'what would maintain the equilibrium... keeping the new species from evolving in spite of environmental vagaries' (1995, p.1421-1422).

Intriguingly, growing evidence suggests that extinctions follow relatively regular periodic patterns[2]. The statistical chance of these patterns being a random occurrence is very small. Some of them may have been caused by physical factors (e.g. slight variations in the Earth's orbit over long periods, leading to a climate change). Nevertheless, it is conspicuous that new, and as a rule, more complex life always follows relatively soon after.

All the above makes it hardly plausible that new species could have arisen gradually by purely accidental transformation from one species into another.

---

[1] Punctuationism, strictly speaking, is not 'saltationism' (radical changes from one generation to the next or discontinuous appearance of new species), so it does not contradict the theory of evolution. It only adds weight to the argument that the traditional Darwinian mechanisms may not be the only factors.

[2] The figure of 2.5 million years seems significant in this respect. Paleobiologist Sepkoski also suggests 26 million years, but according to Muller and Rohde, a 62 million year pattern is even more striking.

The increase of complexity

It is difficult to explain why more and more complex organisms have steadily appeared throughout evolution if every life form is supposed to be a result of accidental changes in the genetic material. The second law of thermodynamics demands that in any closed system entropy increases. This means that energy tends to go towards equilibrium, disintegrating into simpler forms, rather than integrating into more complex ones. In other words, a system inevitably moves towards the state of maximum randomness and disorganisation. Life, of course, is not a closed system, so an increase in complexity does not violate the second law. Nevertheless, it seems strange that at every level there is a tendency in evolution to produce something new and more complex, going persistently against that law – from relatively simple and crude forms to complex and refined ones. Polanyi and Prosch comment:

> another unsolved problem arises from the continuous quantitative increase in DNA chains from those of bacteria to those of man – from about twenty million DNA alternatives to about twelve billion. DNA does not behave naturally. It moves from a lower energetic level to the higher, because it moves towards a higher complexity, which cannot be explained by DNA itself. There is no chemical model available to explain this enormous growth or the chemical explanation for this fundamental fact of the system, just as we have no chemical explanation for the historical origin of DNA or for its capacity to produce media that apparently anticipate the continued development of the embryo. (1975, p.167)

Materialists sometimes argue that all life could develop from a hypothetical first cell, as all new life develops from a single fertilised cell. However, a cell can develop into a complex organism only because all of the parts and instructions are in the original cell produced from conception. For large scale evolution, mutation *must* on average add information. It has been already demonstrated many times with detailed probabilistic analysis that this is extremely unlikely (most classic textbook cases of mutations cited in favour of neo-Darwinian evolution are, in fact, *losses* of information). So, it is incongruent to conclude that random mutations on their own can account for an increase of complexity.

Redundancy (two or more solutions for the same problem found in many species, such as the development of the vulva in the nematode) is a further challenge for the traditional view. Denton writes:

> ...the greater the degree of redundancy, the greater the need for simultaneous mutation to effect evolutionary change and the more difficult it is to believe that evolutionary change could have been engineered without intelligent direction. (1998, p.339)

Even if it is accepted that gradual incremental steps may in some cases accidentally lead to more complex structures, they could not do so in all. A comparison can be made with horse-drawn carts and motor cars. Carts and cars have some similarities (e.g. four wheels) and the same purpose, but cars did not gradually evolve from carts. Throughout centuries, carts had been steadily improved. However, in order to make a car, a leap that required the development and addition of several completely new components at the same time was needed. Even the simplest functional motor requires a few parts non-existent in the most advanced carts. And if just one of these components were missing, the motor would be nothing more but extra weight that the cart would be better off without. Similarly, the survival of a new species is dependent on all the necessary mechanisms (in at least a rudimentary form) being present to begin with. The problem is that obviously one gene mutation is not enough for more complex adaptation. But, if just two mutations are required at the same time to produce at least a slight advantage, the chance that this will happen accidentally decreases dramatically. One example from Dawkins' book *The Blind Watchmaker* may be a case in point (1986, p.97-99). Weakly electric fish use electric fields to navigate in muddy waters. However, this remarkable ability is of no use unless the body of the fish is absolutely rigid. To make up for this, the fish has developed one long fin, so that the rest of the body can remain still. Even with this fin, the movement of the fish is rather slow, but this is compensated for by its ability to detect electric fields in water. So, the navigation system is useless without the fin, and the fin is maladaptive without the navigation system. Their appearance had to be *synchronous*, but they require very different sets of genetic mutations (not to mention that these mechanisms must also be controlled by an appropriate nervous system and brain). Sometimes many simultaneous mutations are necessary, which makes chance, as their main cause, improbable. Considering that the vast majority of mutations are lethal anyway, it stretches belief that numerous beneficial mutations can occur at the same time accidentally.

This issue is even more striking in relation to macroevolution, the emergence of new (usually more complex) species from earlier ones, especially if it is taken into account that intermediary forms are often not found, and that no breeders have ever managed to produce one species from another. To quote Denton again:

> There are innumerable examples of complex organs and adaptations which are not led up to by any known or even, in some cases, conceivable series of feasible intermediates. In the case, for example, of the flight feather of a bird, the amniotic egg, the bacterial flagellum, the avian lung, no convincing explanation of how they could have evolved gradually has ever been provided. (1998, p.275)

Let us take one of these examples. No transitional fossil structure between scale and feather is known. This is not surprising, considering that a half-feather is likely to be a disadvantage rather than an advantage. A feather has a quite complicated structure that is light, and yet wind-resistant. This is possible because of the complex system of barbs and barbules. Barbules on one side of the barb are rigged, and on the other have hooks. It is hard to imagine that chance mutations could produce this precise cross-linking of the barbules to make a connecting lattice. Even if the chance mutation of a ridge/hook occurs in two of the barbules, it also needs to be translated to the rest of the structure. Moreover, if the lattice structure was not lubricated, the sliding joint made by the hooked and ridged barbules would soon fray, which means that the wings would be useless. Many others adaptations are necessary to have birds that can fly (forward-facing elbow joints, navigating tail, strong wing muscles, hollow bones etc.). Even if all of them have developed gradually, each step had to be synchronised and the new must be so great an advantage that it compensates for the losses (of fully functional forelimbs or strong bones). Moreover, not only does each modification have to have sufficient survival value, but the related genes also have to be dominant in order to pass it on to successive generations. Of course, once this transformation has occurred, natural selection will select the better wings from the less workable wings. Evolution clearly operates in part by Darwinian natural selection, but this process simply selects those transformations that have *already* occurred by different mechanisms.

The problem of complexity for undirected evolution resides not only in the remarkable number of components that are sometimes necessary, but also in the fact that life forms are such highly integrated systems that their components cannot be changed independently. Any functional change would require specific compensatory changes in the interacting subsystems. For instance, a change in a protein structure would necessitate many complex simultaneous changes throughout the molecule to preserve any biological function. Denton concludes that 'it is hard to envisage a reality less amenable to Darwinian change via a series of independent undirected mutations altering one component of the organism at a time' (*ibid.* p.342).

The above does not imply that complexity is irreducible, as proponents of Intelligent Design would like to present. For example, some components may have been adapted from existing structures that had a different faction, or more significantly, irreducibility may diminish on a molecular level. However, it still makes sense to challenge the claim that such complexities can be fully explained by the adaptive selection of purely accidental mutations.

Concluding Remarks

The above issues are not detrimental to evolution as such, nor do they necessarily lead to a conclusion that species were created as separate units by an external agency. For instance, the genomes of all organisms are clustered in a relatively small region of DNA sequence space forming a tree of related sequences that can all be inter-converted via a series of tiny incremental steps. So the sharp discontinuities between different organs and different types of organisms greatly diminish at the DNA level. What looks very different on the macro level, may not be so different on the DNA level:

> ...in DNA sequence space it is possible to move at least hypothetically from one adaptation (position) to another in DNA space via functionless or meaningless intermediate sequences. This is because a DNA sequence does not have to be functional to survive and be passed on through the generations. In fact, the greater part of all the DNA in nearly all the cells in higher organisms, although it is copied faithfully at each cell division, is never expressed... It is very easy to imagine how an evolving DNA sequence might be passed silently down through several generations before being expressed... [this] means that new sequences and hence new evolutionary innovations can be generated, at least hypothetically, via functionless intermediates. Thus, new organs and structures that cannot be reached via a series of functional morphological intermediates can still be reached by change in DNA sequence space. (Denton, 1998, p.278-279)

Some genetic changes, especially in higher organisms, have been largely a matter of the rearrangement of pre-existing genes rather than the emergence of new ones. Information specifying the future of evolutionary events may be stored in so-called junk DNA (non-protein-coding DNA). Many such sequences have been conserved over millions of years of evolution. This, however, does not explain the enormous increase of the DNA chain throughout evolution, and even if it is assumed that these dormant genes are the key, the questions remains why they are passed over to the next generations when they are not needed, and even more importantly, why they become active just when they are. To repeat, these objections do not invalidate the idea of evolution as an organising principle, only its reductionist interpretation. The above arguments are an attempt to show that mechanisms that Neo-Darwinists use to explain the evolutionary process are not sufficient, strongly indicating directed evolution:

> The sudden emergence of an entirely new type of organism, or of a functionally perfect novel organ system, would be almost impossible to account for except within some kind of directed evolutionary or teleological framework. (*ibid.*, p.296)

If this is the case, it is reasonable to consider what is the minimum that such a framework would require.

THEISTIC INTERPRETATIONS

The fact that the theory of evolution is incomplete does not mean that the older interpretations are necessarily right. The Old Testament account, for example, contains a number of incongruent and inconsistent statements that renders Creationist interpretations far less plausible than the theory of evolution. For instance, according to Genesis, fruit-bearing trees were created on the third 'day', while fish and other marine creatures were created two 'days' later. Whatever 'day' is supposed to mean, the fossil record shows clearly that fish pre-dated trees by hundreds of millions of years. The existence of redundant organs and other imperfections (e.g. the position of optic nerves in the human eye) is another reason why the creation of species by intelligent design is extremely implausible. An omnipotent designer should do better.

However, there have been many theologians (notably from the Jesuit breed) who have not interpreted the Bible literally and have even attempted to incorporate the theory of evolution within a religious framework. A prominent relatively recent example is Teilhard de Chardin, who took evolution as a central tenet of his theology[1]. His essentially Hegelian vision (see p.69-70), but extended beyond historical time, is far removed from conventional religious views with sometimes bizarre consequences. He argued in favour of the racial and cultural superiority of Europe, and even welcomed the atom bomb as a sign of humankind's triumph over nature. The other, more traditional position that can be traced back to St Augustine, emphasises God's transcendence, insisting that God only sets the starting parameters, after which nature follows the evolutionary path without any further interventions. It stems from the doctrine that the creation is perfect, so further interference is not necessary (such a view was taken to an extreme by deists in 18th century). This is also a challenge to the Biblical account that assumes the active involvement of God (from the story of Abraham to Jesus). In order to overcome these difficulties, philosopher Whitehead proposes a bipolar nature of God, one transcendent and one 'in the world', but the tension between these two poles appears to create more problems than it solves. Without delving into detailed analyses of these perspectives, one conclusion is inevitable. In order to incorporate the accepted facts in a meaningful way, the understanding of the creator and shis involvement has to undergo an evolutionary process too.

---

[1] In the East, a similar concept was espoused by Indian philosopher Sri Aurobindo.

THE SYNTHESIS PERSPECTIVE

The purpose of the above was to outline some problems with the current interpretation of evolution. However, just as the belief in chance being the main driving force is impossible to prove, an attempt to conclusively demonstrate that such a belief is incorrect is equally futile. Anything can happen by chance. Given an infinitely large eco-system and infinite time, everything is possible (although not necessary). But the eco-system of this planet is not infinite, and the time available, although huge, has not been infinite. So, the real challenge is, given these limitations, to provide a framework that is more plausible. It certainly makes sense to consider an interpretation that would give life and the evolutionary process a fair chance, rather than an astronomically small one.

In the mass of arguments and counter-arguments it is easily overlooked that Neo-Darwinism and Creationism have something in common. In both interpretations, life is essentially a passive material, moulded either by the all-powerful external agency or by 'blind' natural forces[1]. The evidence, however, suggests a different picture. Species not only adapt to, but also actively create the environment (the present composition of the Earth's atmosphere, for example, is to a large extent created by the activity of organisms). Life has played a key role in maintaining and modifying its environments, which made possible not only its continuation but also the appearance of new and more complex forms. Thus, the Synthesis perspective considers life an active participant in this process, and suggests two additional factors that influence evolution - the one on the micro level and the other on the macro level. The first is individual choice and the other one can be called evolutionary intent. So, the process of evolution is seen as the result of natural selection and mutations that are not completely random, but influenced by individual choices and an overall accumulative tendency of life to grow and develop. In other words, a creative act is moderated by environmental restrictions. In principle, this is not something that goes against the grain of the theory of evolution. Darwin himself confessed: 'I am convinced that Natural Selection has been the main but not exclusive means of modification' (1859, p.69).

---

[1] The Neo-Darwinian orthodoxy that adheres to the Newtonian mechanistic model does not permit any permeability between the internal (e.g. genes) and the external (the environment). In other words, phenotype (behaviour, experience and the other characteristics of an organism) cannot affect genotype (its genetic constitution). So, not only is life completely passive, but the environment has only a selective function. According to this view, 'blind' chance and 'blind' nature work in parallel (or in sequence) but they do not interact.

Choice

That agency plays a role in the evolutionary process should not come as a surprise if accepted that it is one of the fundamental properties of life (see p.68 and p.91). It seems that even very primitive organisms exhibit agency. Choice can be recognised in the way organisms react to stimuli - and they react (in subtle ways) differently, sometimes even contrary to their urges or to what is expected. The influence of choice has been already recognised by a number of evolutionists (see, for example, Hameroff, 1998). This does not need to be seen as a form of Lamarckism[1]. Choice does not need to trigger genetic mutations or other chemical alterations. By making certain choices, an organism changes and affects its environment and its own subsequent preferences, which can *indirectly* tip the balance in favour of some genes rather than others. Popper (who named this 'Organic evolution'), writes:

> Thus the activity, the preferences, the skill, and the idiosyncrasies of the individual animal may indirectly influence the selection pressures to which it is exposed, and with it, the outcome of natural selection. (1977, p.12)

This is compatible with Darwinism and is not acknowledged only because those who would like to see life in mechanical terms are not at ease with giving any credence to a factor that is so non-machine-like. As for Lamarckism, it has received a fresh breath of life recently. A new field of epigenetics (that studies what regulates genes, what turns them on and off) provides some support to the notion that choices we make can affect which genes will be activated in subsequent generations. A number of scientists are working on accumulating the evidence but the verdict is still open. Even if minimally proven right, the reliance on chance would be reduced further, but these ideas would have to overcome scientific inertia before being accepted. What is important, for the time being, is to recognise that choice does play a role in one way or another.

Nevertheless, although choice may explain some adaptations within species better than pure chance, it is not enough. To explain the more global aspects of the evolutionary process (e.g. an overall increase in complexity) another factor needs to be introduced.

---

[1] An interpretation of evolution that was very popular before Darwin, asserting that the striving of organisms is the major cause of changes. So (to use a typical example), giraffes have long necks because they were stretching their necks to reach leaves that were high up, which was gradually transmitted to subsequent generations. This description is worth including because it seems so common-sensical that even nowadays many people erroneously interpret Neo-Darwinism in a similar way (Neo-Darwinism does not allow any acquired characteristics to be directly transmitted to subsequent generations).

Evolutionary intent

Reductive materialism has its own reasons to reject the possibility that something else may be involved on the macro level besides pure chance. Polanyi observed that

> the action of the ordering principle underlying such a persistent creative trend is necessarily overlooked or denied by the theory of natural selection, since it cannot be accounted for in terms of accidental mutation plus natural selection. Its recognition would, indeed, reduce mutation and selection to their proper status of merely *releasing and sustaining the action of evolutionary principles* by which all major evolutionary achievements are defined. (1958, p.385)

However, too much selection, synchronisation, and amplification of the mutation rate take place to make credible the view that random mutations are the only source of the ever increasing complexity. A number of scholars who do not associate themselves with the creationist account or any religious credo take this view too. Laszlo, for instance, writes:

> One would need an almost blind faith in Darwinian theory to believe that chance alone could have produced in the line of birds all the modifications needed to make them high performing flying machines… it is hardly credible… that small random mutations and natural selection could have produced a dinosaur from an amoeba. (1993, p.98-99)

Evolution generally goes in the direction of more complex forms. Matter, on the other hand, is normally entropic, predisposed towards simplification, so it is unlikely that complex organisms would have developed if only physical and chemical processes were involved. This is not the only reason to reach a conclusion that evolution is not just a series of accidents. The uniformity of mutation rates may be another example:

> The curious equality of mutation rates and evolutionary substitution rates and the just as curious uniformity of protein evolution which have caused endless discussion over the past twenty years have not proved easy to reconcile with Darwinian explanations. And although in no sense can either of these two phenomena be claimed as evidence for design, they are suggestive of something more in the evolutionary process than purely random mutation. (Denton, 1998, p.383)

A further indication is also that evolution does not happen gradually as one would expect if Darwinism was completely right, but in leaps (rapid transformations) followed by long periods of relative equilibrium. This feature may point at something even more important. Namely, that the concerted intent of species, rather than the Intent, is responsible for evolutionary dynamics. If the Intent were directly involved, one would again expect a steady progress, there would have been no need for periods of stagnation. It is more likely, as already suggested, that the Intent is mainly involved in setting the boundary conditions by streamlining possibilities (in other words, enabling a fair chance), the rest is mostly left to life itself[1]:

> If neither natural selection nor any other sort of undirected evolutionary mechanism seem plausible, then could they conceivably have been the result of the activities of life itself operating via some as yet undefined type of inventiveness inherent in all life?... even if much of the overall order of organic nature was determined from the beginning, it is surely conceivable that the Creator... could have gifted organisms not only with the capacity for growth, reproduction, inheritance and variability, but also with a limited degree of genuine autonomous creativity so that the world of life might reflect and mirror in some small measure the creativity of God. (*ibid.*, p.364)

This implies that new species do not come from nowhere, there is no 'invisible hand' that creates them. The difference between the Creationist and this view can be compared to seeing the universal agency as an engineer or artist who makes a tree, or as a gardener who provides the right conditions for a tree to grow (and pruning it if and when necessary). A number of scientists have by now come to the conclusion that life must harbour some fundamental order-generated tendency:

> Already in mid [20th] century Hermann Weyl noted that because each of the molecules on which life is based consists of something like a million atoms, the number of possible atomic combinations is astronomical. On the other hand the number of combinations that could create viable genes is relatively limited. Thus the probability that such combinations would occur through random processes is negligible. A more likely solution, said Weyl, is that some sort of selective process has been taking place, probing different possibilities and gradually groping its way from simple to complex structures. (Laszlo, 1993, p.91-92)

Philosopher Henry Bergson argued for the existence of a unique vital impulse that is continually developing, implying that evolution was creative rather than mechanistic. He named this impulse *élan vital* (life force). Many traditions hold the same basic view. Hindus call the life force *prana*, Polynesians *mana*, Iroquois *orenda*, while in Islam it is called *baraka*. For the ancient Egyptians the world was permeated by *sa*, in China they use the term *Ch'I*. The notion of life force is discredited by its misuse in popular

---

[1] This is, however, not straightforward. For example, oxygen was a by-product of the metabolism of simple organisms that dominated the biosphere for a long while. When the oxygen production had enabled the development of more complex organisms, these simple ones vanished. It is hard to avoid the sense of a subtle background influence of the Intent in some instances (perhaps a demise of dinosaurs is also such an instance, but it will never be possible to prove it).

culture and dismissed by most scientists because it cannot be found. This should not be a problem in itself though; as already mentioned, gravitation cannot be directly found either. The effects of gravitation and other fields, however, can be easily measured, while the effects of evolutionary intent (that is a manifestation of life force) can be detected only over long periods. Nevertheless, the fact that evolution goes in the direction of increased complexity cannot be ignored, and this factor has potentially a greater explanatory power than blind chance or God the watchmaker. So, what is this life force? The suggestion here is that it is an intent of life to maximise existence and agency, which are the innate and irreducible drives embedded in every species.

Existence is manifested in a tendency to live, adapt and proliferate that can be called 'drive to survive' or 'survival intent' evident in all living organisms, but not in any inanimate objects. Biologists assume 'survival instinct' but do not explain it, because it has to be causally prior even to genes. Otherwise, why would genes 'want' to survive, maintain their complex dynamic structure as well as that of the system they belong to - the cell? Genes determine how organisms reproduce, but not why they reproduce in the first place. It is proposed that the energy intends to remain focused (which is a prerequisite of life). What helps in this respect, at least in the material world, are physical bodies. So, to realise itself, the non-material component forces the material one to fill in any gap that is available (like water that fills in any crack on its way), which is why there is such a huge variety of living organisms. As Denton puts it, 'the enormous diversity of the pattern of life on earth may not represent a full plenitude of all life forms, but it appears to approach closely this ideal.' (1998, p.383)

The agency, on the other hand, is not only manifested in the tendency (which does not need to be fully conscious) to exercise freedom or choice as suggested above, but also to increase it. Harman proposes that there is a 'sort of teleological "pull" in the evolutionary process, of evolution towards increased awareness, complexity, freedom – in short, of evolution *going somewhere* (not in a predetermined sense, but in the sense of preferred direction)' (1998, p.49). This pull that is the driving force behind the leaps in complexity could be called evolutionary intent. It leads to further differentiation and fragmentation into more complex units (with their own self, awareness and intent), enabling individualisation of energy. Non-material energy though, can be self-actualised only through matter, so there is a general trend to push matter in the direction of more complex and integrated structures, which results in biological evolution. This could explain the anti-entropic trend of organisms.

However, evolutionary intent is weak, and needs to accumulate before producing any result, which is why the process appears punctuated. This can be compared with generating a new idea. It may seem as if the idea has come suddenly, out of nowhere, but this is not the case. The person has probably been focusing on the problem for a while. This is the process of incubation, the accumulation of intent, which eventually enables the idea to break through. So, new ideas are neither the gifts of muses nor a random process. The appearance of new species may be similar[1]. Organisms can live for long periods in a relative equilibrium that can produce some adaptive changes within species, but does not spawn different and more complex ones. The much stronger material side is essentially inertive and resists the change. The build-up of intent (usually at the ecological peripheries) is necessary in order to overcome this resistance of the existing equilibrium. This is a very slow process considering how weak evolutionary intent is. Environmental conditions, of course, also need to be right. However, although natural disasters may in some cases facilitate a change, they are not necessary. When intent sufficiently accumulates, the matter gives in, and some species undergo a number of simultaneous mutations in a relatively short period of time.

It is possible that on the non-material level there are connections between the organisms within a species (the more primitive, the more connections) and some between different species. So, individual intents may add up to the collective intent of species and these intents, in turn, may add up to the 'global' intent, which (especially at the early stages of evolution) converges with the Intent, and can influence biological evolution. Denton indicates how this can be translated to the biological sphere:

> …the genomes of nearly all organisms contain so-called gene families, which consist of multiple identical copies of the same gene. Surprisingly, these copies are often identical not only within the genome of one individual but in the genomes of all the individuals in the species. A variety of genetic mechanisms have been identified which act to maintain the sequential *identity between all the copies of the same gene in any one species.* In the early eighties Cambridge geneticist Gabriel Dover suggested that the integrated effect of these various internal mechanisms is potentially capable of causing synchronous genetic changes in all the members of a population. He termed the effect 'molecular drive'. It is relatively easy to envisage how such processes could be utilized… to bring about cohesive directional mutational change during evolution. (1998, p.281)

---

[1] Comparable 'jumps' happen in the atomic world and also individual and social development. Relatively long periods of an accumulation of energy (an increase of pressure) lead suddenly to the leap of an electron, personal change in an individual, or a paradigm shift (in science, culture, or religion).

The direction

For ideological reasons Neo-Darwinism has to interpret evolution as directionless (directed evolution is incompatible with materialism). This, however, contradicts not only common sense but the facts too:

> The very great complexity of life, and especially its quite fantastic holistic nature, which seems to preclude any sort of evolutionary transformations via a succession of small independent changes, is perfectly compatible with the notion of directed evolution. (*ibid.,* p.383-384)

Natural selection, acting upon random mutations, could never produce such results. Denton collected data on every level of biological organisation that renders directionless evolution unlikely. He concludes:

> The evolutionary evidence is similar; it compounds. In isolation, the various pieces of evidence for direction, the speed of evolutionary change, the fantastic complexity of living things, the apparent gratuity of some of the ends achieved, are perhaps no more than suggestive, but taken together, the overall pattern points strongly to final causes... No other explanation makes as much sense of all the facts. (*ibid.,* p.384-385)

This, of course, does not mean that every biological blueprint is directed. Any particular form will depend on the available genetic material and environmental circumstances. There are many contingent adaptations (particularly noticeable in isolated environments). The evolutionary pull can be compared to the gravitational force that pulls river water in the same general direction. In conjunction with the environmental constrains a river-bed is created as a loose boundary that determines its general flow. Within this flow some variations can occur that may appear to have a different (even opposite) direction or stagnate. Similarly, many evolutionary lines are dead ends. Although there is a general trend towards complexity, some organisms get stuck in evolutionary terms, and sometimes even regress. Nevertheless, as with a river, an overall flow is maintained.

Broadly speaking, two dimensions (or directions) of biological evolution can be discerned: the horizontal (characterised by an increase in organisation, integration and diversity - expansion of life to unoccupied environmental niches) and the vertical (characterised by an increase in complexity, specialisation and dynamics). Both processes lead to a relative decrease in entropy. From this perspective, animals, for example, are a step further ahead than plants in the process of evolution:

> Animals are highly ordered systems that in contrast to most plants are largely synthesized from highly ordered (low-entropy) molecules. (Silver, 1998, p.352)

Ultimately, however, the aim of biological evolution can be linked to producing forms that would enable development of the non-material energy. This primarily means increasing and refining its main properties - awareness and intent, that are exercised through life experiences in the material world. So, the purpose of biological evolution can be defined as an enhancement of awareness and intent through developing more complex and independent biological forms. In other words, species become more aware and gain more control through the processes of evolution, fulfilling an overall tendency of life towards self-actualisation.

To avoid chaos though, this increase needs to be carried out in manageable steps, which is achieved through internal and environmental constraints. Thus, evolution can be seen as a result of the interaction between the material and non-material components of life, within the pre-set but dynamic boundaries that expand throughout the process. So, evolution starts with narrow awareness and intent that gradually develop, while the strength of biological and environmental determinism decreases. Greater awareness means that more energy can be affected by the self. The self is at the beginning a relatively passive observer and does not have a big impact, but through the process of evolution the individual selves become more pro-active and their influence grows. In other words, the role of intent becomes more prominent. It is reflected in a reduction of predictable, predetermined actions and behaviour.

To summarise, evolution enables individualisation and also the shaping and refining of energy, which is compatible with the overall aim of life. If evolution is characterised by the increase of complexity and organisation, and if the One is the source of the most complex and organised phenomena, the end result must be to become an equivalent, counterpart to the One.

This process is enabled mainly by a growth in complexity of the nervous system (more can be done with an advanced computer than with a simple one). Indeed, the awareness of higher organisms seems broader and more complex. Generally speaking, animal species are more aware than plants, and humans are more aware than animals. The self of an animal is capable of focusing (holding together) a relatively small range of qualitatively different pieces of information. Some of them may hear or smell better than humans, but they are not aware of much more besides these sensations, because their ability to organise and structure what they are aware of is limited. Thus, the consciousness that humans possess did not appear accidentally, but as a stage in the evolutionary process. There is a sound empirical basis for this assertion.

Humans

Some evolutionists agree that the appearance of humans could not be an accident:

> With all these examples of convergence it is difficult to avoid the conclusion that the evolution of a humanoid creature was very much on the cards since at least the time of the Cambrian explosion more than half a billion years ago, when all the major groups of animals we see today originated. (Morris, 2002, p.26)

This convergence of the evolutionary process is unlikely to be a random product of adaptation and is more compatible with directed evolution. All the distinct characteristics of humans (brain, tongue, standing upright) do not make sense if the Neo-Darwinian view is taken. They only have long term benefits (thinking, language and freeing hands to enable tool making) that could not be anticipated by purely biological evolution. It is worthwhile to look at these features in more detail.

The claim that human consciousness was developed as an adaptive mechanism does not seem valid considering that most (if not all) of it, in fact, did not have an immediate advantage. The human brain has unique capacities that cannot be rivalled by any other organ; because of the brain, humans are the only species on the Earth that can calculate, philosophise, produce art, contemplate God or the structure of an atom. Yet, none of these abilities were of any use when the human brain appeared (the brain did develop further, but not much, throughout human history). The first humans, as all other animals, could do well for what they needed to survive with a smaller and less sophisticated brain. In fact, it was a big disadvantage. The bigger head (to accommodate the bigger brain) made birth more difficult, which must have increased the mortality rate of mothers and newborns alike. The soft part of the skull, to accommodate growth of the brain after birth, made infants more vulnerable to injury. Heaviness of the head could only make balance harder, and disproportional consumption of the oxygen and glucose by the brain contributed to the species being less rather than more physically fit. Also, a big brain is accompanied by a slow physical development that enables learning, but leads to the off-spring being dependent on their parents for longer, which is another adaptive disadvantage. So, if adaptation to the environment was the only decisive factor, species with the human brain should have disappeared as soon as they appeared.

A similar argument can be applied to the development of the human tongue, which is quite different from a chimpanzee tongue. It has a thick muscle at the back which enables humans to speak (chimpanzees have a flat tongue). However, a bulky tongue makes swallowing more difficult and therefore those who have it less adapted. True, language appeared later to be a huge advantage, but what use could early humans have of their potential to speak, when no language yet existed? The argument that the thickness gradually developed in parallel with the development of a primitive language does not hold water. It is extremely unlikely that the several sets of unrelated but right mutations affecting the brain, speech apparatus, and skeleton would have happened within the same species accidentally. For example, to have the control over breathing that is necessary for complex speech, humans needed a wider vertebral canal behind the ribcage than their predecessors such as Homo-erectus had; also the larynx descended in the throat and by being lower, contributed to this ability. Such synchronised events would require directed evolution.

Standing up must have been an adaptive disadvantage in the early stages too. It made humans slower, they could not climb trees well, and injuring one leg would be fatal. Yet, it was necessary for the development of consciousness because it enabled the anatomical change of the thumb and the use of hands for tool making.

In 1927, biologist Julian Huxley (who was the first Director-General of UNESCO and a founder of the World Wildlife Fund[1]) wrote:

> Biology... has thus revealed man's place in nature. He is the highest form of life produced by the evolutionary process on this planet, the latest dominant type, and the only organism capable of further major advance or progress. Whether he knows it or not, whether he wishes it or not, he is now the main agency for the further evolution of the earth and its inhabitants. In other words, his destiny is to realise new possibilities for the whole terrestrial sector of the cosmic process, to be the instrument of further evolutionary progress on this planet. (in Edmunds, 1997, p.172)

A view like this may be unpopular nowadays for the fear of human *hubris*, but if the main point that it contains is not recognised, there is a real danger that the unique responsibility that humankind has will go unacknowledged too. This point is that evolution continues through the individual and group development of human beings. As biological species, individuals and societies can also regress, stagnate, as well as progress. However, due to the complexity of the brain and its unprecedented dynamic, humans have a potential to substantially develop even within a single life. This potential for personal development makes the process incomparably faster than biological evolution, and also allows huge variety even within the same species. The next chapter will address this subject.

---

[1] On the darker side, he is also associated with eugenics, although he quickly became its fervent critic, advocating that race is a cultural not a biological term.

Some possible questions

Why the animal kingdom appears to be so brutal?

Transitional physical bodies are not important in themselves, but what they are a vehicle for: the shaping and developing of energy and the passing on of genetic material so that the process can go on. Biological evolution is necessary for the evolution of the soul. Preserving the bio-environment, so that organisms can continue to develop, is more important than self-preservation. The more primitive organisms are, the more readily they perish after reproduction. This is because there is a very limited chance for progressing while attached to a relatively simple organic form.

If there is the evolutionary intent, why are there still so many simple organisms?

Biological life is interdependent, more complex organisms cannot survive without simple ones. This does not mean that evolution is deliberately stalled in some cases. There is a constant influx of crude non-material energy that needs primitive organisms.

What is the fundamental difference between animals and humans?

Both, animals and humans, have the self and soul. So, animals are aware and self-aware (e.g. they can be aware of their own pain), but their ability to construct reality, to integrate their experiences, is very limited. They are not able to conceptualise, so any mental structure relies chiefly on the consistency of immediate physical sensations. In this respect their experience resembles a dream-state (e.g. the past, the future or reality outside their vicinity is non-existent or fragmented at best). Also, they do not have 'I', a mental representation of themselves, so the inner and outer world are far less separated. As a consequence, they cannot distance themselves from, organise and reflect on their experiences, which means that it is unlikely that they can affect the content of their minds. Humans, on the other hand, can connect clusters of experience in much more elaborate ways because their brain size and structure is more complex (there are forms of connectivity among nerve cells not found in any animal). These connections lead to separating the internal and external further, which enables them to interpret, create and reflect upon the materials of awareness (giving rise to art, for example). However, as already mentioned (p.166), this 'barrier' makes humans less open to more direct experience and interactions, which does not seem uncommon in the animal kingdom (see, for example, Sheldrake, 2000).

INDIVIDUAL DEVELOPMENT

It is suggested that four factors influence individual development: nature (genes and the physical environment), nurture (the social environment), choice (exercising one's agency), and the 'shape' of the soul[1]. The first two factors have been examined thoroughly in psychology, while the other two have been largely ignored. However, the studies on identical twins, who have also shared the same environment, show that their traits correlate only to about 50%. Evidently, nature and nurture are insufficient. Out of those four factors nature and the 'shape' of the soul are the givens responsible for the character. A new born is not a blank slate - certain potentials can be already recognised in infancy. Innate character though, can acquire different forms and be modified throughout life, which makes one's personality. This is where the other two factors, nurture and personal choice, play a role. Turning to development itself, it is possible to distinguish two types: the quantitative and the qualitative.

QUANTITATIVE DEVELOPMENT

Quantitative development refers to developing capacities such as cognition, volition, affect, skills, etc. It is indicated by an increase in certain characteristics (some of which roughly correspond to the characteristics of biological evolution). The list of such characteristics is proposed below. This list may not be exhaustive and does not imply that all of them are necessary:

- Dynamism (e.g. interest, curiosity, a desire to learn)
- Complexity and differentiation (e.g. being able to recognise the composite elements of a whole; a capacity to grasp different viewpoints)
- Organisation and integration (e.g. an ability to connect and keep together various elements of a concept or operational segments of an activity)
- Perspective (e.g. considering long term plans, other people, global issues)
- Refinement (e.g. sensitivity to nuances, details or subtle points)
- Diversity and versatility (e.g. a variety of interests, knowledge or skills)
- Flexibility (e.g. an ability to incorporate or adapt to a change)
- Creativity (e.g. capacity to generate something new)
- Internal control (e.g. an ability to delay immediate gratification, self-discipline)
- Productivity (efficiency in utilising one's potentials and energy)

---

[1] This last one deserves special attention and will be discussed in the following chapter.

QUALITATIVE DEVELOPMENT

This type of development refers to progressive changes throughout the lifespan and involves the concept of developmental stages. Despite individual differences, it seems that some commonalities can be discerned in this respect. It was earlier proposed that the soul grows due to information, experience and intent (p 176). Thus, the three corresponding dimensions of development are suggested. They also correlate with the three dimensions of meaning (see p. 178). This is not surprising, since development is progressive and, therefore, intrinsically meaningful.

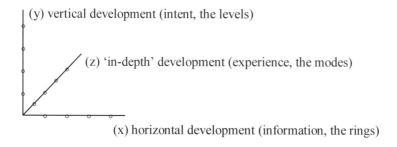

(y) vertical development (intent, the levels)

(z) 'in-depth' development (experience, the modes)

(x) horizontal development (information, the rings)

Each dimension has four points, representing the four stages: physical, conventional, personal and transcendent[1]. This is, of course, an idealised schema - each stage has sub-stages and there are huge variations within them. Also, they are not inevitable, the rate of change and the final stage reached differ widely from person to person.

It needs to be pointed out that the subsequent stages do not replace the previous ones, although they may modify them. Quantitative development (developing various capacities) within each stage can continue throughout one's life. This implies that a person on a further stage of development is not necessarily better or superior (as a third year student is not necessarily better than a second year student). Any aspect of a person can be well or poorly developed at any stage. In addition, although further stages may bring more freedom, there are also more chances to abuse it, so they require greater responsibility. Life is not easier at further stages. People face different challenges, that is all.

---

[1] These stages can be generally related to the domains distinguished in existentialism: *Umwelt, Mitwet, Eigenwelt* and *Überwelt* (Binswanger, 1946, Boss, 1963, Deurzen-Smith, 1984) and also to Wade's notetic model (1996): Reactive (1); Naïve and Egocentric (the transition between 1 and 2); Conformist (2); Achievement and Affiliative (between 2 and 3); Authentic (3); Transcendent and Unity (4).

Development of the rings

Horizontal development is concerned with information and knowledge that enable the formation of the rings (see page 162)[1].

The first ring starts taking shape possibly even before birth and consists of the two processes: synthesising the body image and the world image, and separating these two. The latter one derives from a discrepancy between the perceived continuity of one's body and discontinuity of external reality (e.g. people 'disappear' when they walk away) and a discrepancy between what can be directly controlled and what cannot. So, the infant starts perceiving the world as a whole, and at the same time, shimself separated from the world (which often causes anxiety). This differentiation happens gradually. At the beginning, the external is internalised, a child is in a unity with the world, but not fully conscious. As animals, infants do not know that the external world, as something outside their experiences, exists. Dreaming and reality are the same (in other words, everything is like a dream). This is why a newborn feels omnipotent; s/he is like a god in shis own world. Before the formation of the other rings there is only the present, the abilities of temporal (the past and the future) and non-temporal (abstract) thinking are not yet developed. The practical (kinaesthetic) learning mode, in conjunction with the environmental feedback, is dominant. Language is limited to simple signifiers representing single objects ('mama', 'doggy'). Usually, the first ring is formed around age two, but it can continue to change and grow throughout the life-span (in terms of quantitative development).

The second ring - the most important factor for its formation is the language acquisition. This ring is not based only on precepts but also concepts, which leads to further separation, expansion and greater freedom. Animals do not have this ring, so they cannot manipulate cognitive elements available to them. Conceptual thinking is a huge step in organising mental constructs (it allows, for instance, generalisation: the word 'chair' can refer to any imagined or perceived chair). The theoretical learning mode, in conjunction with social feedback, dominates. The term 'theoretical' is used in a broad sense that may include, for example, stories or myths since they do not have a direct practical value. This mode is mental and indirect (because it mainly comes through others). The second ring is normally formed by puberty although, as in the previous case, it can carry on developing even later.

---

[1] Although there are some differences, the first three stages of this development can be compared with Piaget's stages of cognitive development (preoperational thinking; concrete-operational thinking; formal-operational thinking), and also, all four, with Fowler's stages of faith: intuitive-projective (1); mythic-literal (between 1 and 2); synthetic-conventional (2); individuative-reflective (3); universalising (4).

The third ring typically starts forming around puberty or early adolescence. Usually at that time young people begin to seek the answer to the question 'Who am I?'. This is not to say that self-identity does not exist before adolescence. However, the various concepts of 'I' that have existed up until this point begin to coalesce into the kind of person one is and will become (Lloyed *at al*, 1990, p.723). The fluid personality of the child gives way to the firmer, more stable personality - ego. When ego is fully formed, one can 'separate the self cognitively from embeddedness in the social system' (Wade, 1996, p.135), which leads to greater independence. The methods that contribute to the formation of this ring are *reflection and self-reflection*: examining and often reorganising beliefs about the world and oneself. They are the result of an ability to separate, distance oneself from the world and the I (a past, present, future or imagined I). All the rings are formed through relations (in the case of the first ring to the physical world, and in case of the second to the social world or culture). A relation, however, also requires a distance (there can be no relation without some distance) - in this case from oneself. So, self-reflection derives, as it were, from the interaction between the person and shis 'I' that serves as a kind of mirror. Reflection and self-reflection enable not only objectifying and observing the elements of the mind, but also their deliberate restructuring, which increases choice. So, these processes contribute to the formation of the third ring by transforming the materials from the first two rings as well as by producing new ones. This is not to say that the third ring disposes of the previous ones, even if some of their elements may be abandoned. For example, the person at this stage may not believe in Santa Claus any more, but the idea of Santa Claus is still comprehensible to shim.

The fourth ring can start forming in late adolescence, which explains the tendency of that age group to discuss 'deep' issues. However, this process is in most cases quickly abandoned as impractical (usually reduced to conversations after a few glasses of wine and rarely considered seriously next morning). Such an attitude is to be expected, taking into account that, parallel to reflection at the third stage, the fourth ring relies on the intuitive learning mode and resonance recognition, so it lacks the relative solidity of the previous rings. It is mostly concerned with abstractions, processes and relations, and consists of general ideas, universal principles, or issues related to meaning. Everyday language is not always adequate to fully express and anchor these ideas. Moreover, this ring usually transcends divisions between various approaches and disciplines (i.e. science, philosophy and spirituality) and moves beyond ideological constrains. Not surprisingly, a person who operates from such a position is often seen as impractical or subversive of the existing structures. This may bring about a degree of social isolation, which is why it is difficult to sustain it.

Development of experience

The 'in depth' dimension involves the modes of experience[1].

The physical mode is a result of the interaction between the body and the physical environment. In other words, it is bound to the physical-ness of human existence. This mode starts possibly even in the pre-natal period and dominates early life. It can be associated with the range of physiological sensations, such as physical pain, hunger, thirst, sexual arousal, and those related to physical activity (vigour, tiredness etc.). The feeling of physical security (or its lack) can be included in this mode too.

The conventional mode derives mainly from a sense of belonging, being a part of a group or culture, and goes beyond physical experiences. It is especially prominent in ritualised situations such as religious ceremonies, weddings, or even sport events. However, this mode can also involve less situation-specific feelings, for instance fear and hatred (of those who are perceived to be different) or, on the other side of the spectrum, empathy, sympathy or care, especially for the members of one's group (e.g. one's family, culture, nationality or religion). Shame is also in this category - unlike guilt, shame is learned, socially induced.

The personal mode can be associated with personal depth (that may be triggered by external stimuli such as a book or music). It is possible to claim that every experience is personal. However, the distinctive characteristic of this mode is the element of absorption. For example, one may be in a crowd at a concert, and yet sink inside oneself – relating to the music, but excluding the crowd. Another example is a meaningful sexual experience. It involves a personal, unique relationship with the other, but it also excludes (at least momentarily) the rest of the world. 'Flow' (absorption in a usually solitary activity) can also be representative of such an experience. On the other side, so-called 'existential anxiety' (the consequence of recognising uncertainty as a life condition) is another typical feeling of this mode.

The transcendent mode transcends not only the physical boundaries but also the socially induced and ego boundaries, which is why an element of infinity may be present. One clarification is needed though. The transcendent mode is different from transpersonal experiences that can happen at any stage and

---

[1] This dimension has been largely neglected in psychology possibly because it is more fuzzy than the other ones. The closest parallel to its four modes are Maslow's motivational levels: physiological needs and safety (1); belongingness and love (2); esteem (the transition between 2 and 3); self-actualisation (3); and transcendence (only included in his model later) (4).

are usually interpreted within the framework of that stage (e.g. the experience of a unity with the nature[1]). Such experiences can be induced, for example, by psychotropic drugs, while the transcendent mode cannot. They happen sporadically, often accidentally, are short lived, and 'cannot be counted as a part of the modal repertoire' (Donaldson, 1992 p.235). The transcendent mode is more stable, and transpersonal experiences in this mode merge with other ones. To use Maslow's terminology, it is closer to a 'plateau experience' than 'peak experiences'. It may involve, for instance, transcending petty concerns, non-attachment, the sense of a larger perspective, and also the sense of connectedness, non-possessive love, or recognising beauty beyond personal inclinations, and it does not necessarily need to have a spiritual source[2]. So-called 'existential joy' that transcends existential anxiety (a characteristic of the previous mode) also belongs to this category (see Popovic, 2003). Its most important quality though, is starting to experience reality in terms of processes rather than discrete objects. Reality is perceived in a less segmented way: 'Spatial boundaries no longer appear stable but open and plastic, suggesting the permeability of permanent objects' (Wade, 1996, p.181). It is only natural that such a mode of experiencing leads to greater fluidity, decreased attachment to objects and, at the same time, the perception of an interrelatedness between them.

It should be emphasised that the above categories refer to the different modes of experiencing rather than the specific types of experience. The further modes are, in fact, inclusive in terms of the sources (or types) of experience. In other words, any event that can be experienced in early modes can also be experienced (albeit differently) in further ones, but certain experiences may be exclusive only to further modes. Eating may be an example. Food consumption can be a purely physical experience, when the focus is on the nutritional value, satisfying the need to eat; for the second mode a cultural embodiment is also important (e.g. a particular setting or type of food, the use of a knife and fork or chopsticks); the third would emphasise personal taste, and the fourth can perhaps best be described as mindful eating (after a form of meditation known in the West as 'mindfulness'). On the other hand, it is hard, for example, to derive any meaningful experience from reading Joyce's 'Ulysses' if in the first or second mode.

---

[1] Such a perceived unity is likely to be the result of a *temporary* expansion beyond the rings.

[2] Peak experiences too do not need to be linked to the spiritual. 'Transcendent ecstasy' can be triggered, for example, by intellectual activity, such as solving a mathematical problem (see Donaldson, 1992, p.305).

Development of intent

There are four levels to this type of development[1]. Potential freedom needs to be temporarily limited so, in a way, these levels have also a restraining role. Every further level first opposes the previous one and then, ideally, integrates it. So, development in this respect is not really a straightforward but dialectic process. A propensity for any level may exist in a latent form from the start, but they are expressed, in most cases, subsequently. This dimension has a special value because it relates to agency, and therefore it has the potential to directly affect other dimensions.

The physical level - this level starts from the moment the soul and body connect[2] and is manifested through the interaction of the body with the environment. In other words, one's own body is the reference point (what it can do and what it cannot). Physical determinism is dominant. An infant is driven by shis instincts and urges, of which the most important are the needs for body-preservation and physical development (that besides body growth also involves the utilisation of physical skills). Although rapid enlargement and activity of the neocortex can be detected, the senses and the so-called R-complex part of the brain (see p.155) are dominant. Considering that this level is to a great extent inertive, the challenge is to overcome indolence.

The conventional level - the physical level starts to be modified relatively early by significant others (i.e. parents) and culture; toilet training and acquisition of language are normally the first instances. This level is characterised by social determinism, known in psychology as *nurture*. One's reference point are cultural norms (that may be reinforced by socially induced feelings such as shame). Reaching this level is a gradual process that requires transcending the centrism of the previous one. The main motive on this level is social preservation, maintaining the sense of belonging and acceptance. Not surprisingly, emotions and the limbic system take a prominent role. As psychologist Turiel points out, 'social behaviour is, in the main, guided by emotions; reason is, at best, secondary' (1983, p.7). So, the major challenge of this level is to defeat ignorance.

---

[1] They can be related to Loevinger's Ego Development stages: pre-social & symbiotic, impulsive, self-protective (1); conformist, self-aware (2); conscientious, individualistic, autonomous (3); integrated (4); and Kohlberg's stages of moral development: pre-conventional (1); conventional (2); post-conventional (3); and universal - stage 6 and 7 in his system (4).

[2] When this happens exactly is difficult to say. The offset of awareness or agency needs to be determined, which is not easy. Almost certainly it is a pre-natal event, probably sometime between the first heart beat and the first kick (for a more detailed discussion on this issue see Wade, 1996, chapter 2).

The personal level - the move from the second to the third level normally starts around puberty and can be fully reached during adolescence (although this is not a rule). It is characterised by the development of will, self-affirmation, independence and autonomy[1]. This level involves separating oneself (first of all from significant others, i.e. parents) at least in behaviour and actions. Such a tendency facilitates forming links based on one's choice, so, personal relationships (friends, partners) are valued most. Typical motives are personal happiness and personal power. One's ego (self-image) and personal norms become the main reference point. Intellect and the neo-cortex start to dominate. The challenge is to defeat self-importance (or arrogance).

The transcendent level can be achieved (but does not have to) in the post-adolescent period. The motive is to find a meaning in one's life, to re-establish integration and unity, but this time fully-conscious. In other words, the person is in tune (synchronised) with the Intent, the purpose of life. This is not to say that spiritual awareness is necessary. A meaning in one's life can be congruent with the meaning of life without our acknowledging or even realising it. What is required though, is dedication and commitment, although of course, not every dedication indicates this level. It involves transcending the personal (without losing oneself) for the sake of something greater: others, a generally worthwhile idea or activity, or spiritual practice. In a way, through its legacy this level can transcend even death. The challenge is to defeat selfishness (being capable of genuinely selfless acts[2]), which requires a move beyond ego-boundaries. This is difficult, because it entails giving up ego-control. The reference point is universal norms mediated by post-verbal intuition rather than cognitive principles.

From what level one acts can be recognised in almost any situation that requires choice, even in the most mundane ones such as buying a pair of shoes: the determining factors, if acting from the first level, are to keep feet warm and clean, and prevent an injury; the driving force behind the second one is likely to be cultural norms; at the third level it is important that the shoes fit the personal image. An overall motive at the fourth level could be that shoes are meaningful, purposeful (not conspicuous or a distraction in any way, but comfortable and congruent with one's overall goals or activities). This, on the surface, does not differ much from the first level, but is based on a deliberate rather than instinctual choice, which implies greater awareness and freedom.

---

[1] Which should not be confused with the individuality of infants that is based on their character.

[2] Unselfish behaviour can also be a result of up-bringing, social conditioning.

Application

Several observations may be drawn from applying this model in practice. Firstly, it does not seem that an individual needs to be at the same stage in all these dimensions. In fact, people are often not (which creates difficulty for theories that do not recognise the different dimensions). To illustrate this point, the development can be represented with three figures where the first one refers to knowledge, the second to experience, and the third to intent. For example, fashion followers can be generally characterised in this way as 2, 1, 3[1]. Number (2) indicates that their concept of fashion is dictated by others or the media. This is applied to the physical experience (1) (as long as clothes are considered to be so). However, they are making a personal choice (they are not conditioned) to follow a particular trend (3). In comparison, those whose appearance is defined by their culture or a religious creed would be 2, 1, 2. On the other hand, 2, 1, 4 may refer, for instance, to the disciples of a yoga master. The first figure indicates that their knowledge depends on a teacher, the second that the focus is on the physical, the body, and the third that they are dedicated to transcendence. Those who practice reflectively would be 3, 1, 4, and those who abandon attachment to even their own way of doing yoga and follow intuition would be 4, 1, 4. A stage of development is, however, not stable and may fluctuate from situation to situation. Reaching a particular stage means that one's repertoire is expanded, not that the person remains always there. In fact, sometimes it is more appropriate to utilise or operate at earlier stages, in order to avoid a conflict with others or unnecessary complications (e.g. the 1st ring is normally most conducive to driving). Moreover, quantitative development plays an important role too. Any stage of any dimension can be well or poorly developed in this respect. Even a whole dimension (e.g. experience) may be neglected, which is different from being at its early stage. This all shows that although developmental models can be useful tools, any generalisations based on them (including the ones above) may not capture the complexity of real life.

One issue has not been addressed so far: the motivation for individual development. Of course, it is to some extent intrinsic (especially at the early stages) but this recedes over time. Many arrive at the point of asking themselves 'I am going to die any way, so why bother?' For this reason, it is important to consider what may happen after death and whether development may continue. This is the subject of the next chapter.

---

[1] The numbers represent stages: 1 - physical, 2 - conventional, 3 - personal, and 4 - transcendent.

AFTER DEATH

The Method

All four methods described in chapter five (phenomenological, inductive-deductive, transpersonal and reasoning) can contribute to this subject, but each of them is understandably somewhat limited, so combining them is essential in this case:

• Relevant materials from various traditions (the *Tibetan Book of Death* arguably still being the most authoritative one). Phenomenological method can help in separating the essence from its cultural embodiments. Discerning commonalities from different backgrounds may also be facilitative, although they could stem from cross-cultural fertilisation, rather than genuine similarities in experience[1].

• Research on Near Death Experiences (NDE). This source, however, can account only for the first stages of life after death and relies on untrained subjects (although some aspects of their reports can be verified).

• Transpersonal insights are essential, but they can be easily misinterpreted (e.g. they may relate to something else, rather than life after death).

• Reasoning is limited in its generating role, although some deductive inferences can be drawn to make an account complete. This method can also exclude elements that are inconsistent, incongruent with the available facts, and superfluous.

Death

Death has several purposes. It enables evolution, the emergence of more complex physical forms - without death the planet would soon be populated by primitive organisms and new ones would have no chance to appear. It is also an act of mercy on the biological level. The suffering of trapped, old, sick or injured animals would be indefinitely prolonged if there was no death. Death may also contribute to the individual development. Errors and mistakes of body and mind may accumulate during a life time to such an extent that is difficult to reverse them. Reincarnation (that will be discussed below) could offer a fresh start and still enable continuity, but reincarnation is impossible without death. Social development benefits from death too. If generations did not change, the societies would be far more conservative, solidified in their beliefs and practices.

---

[1] For instance, in Ancient Greece, Empedocles and Plato adopted the idea of reincarnation from the Pythagoreans, and Pythagoras himself had probably learned of it from his contacts with India.

Death is better considered a process rather than a point, and can be defined as the irreversible cessation of body functioning. However, this does not mean necessarily the end of life. Being an attribute of focused energy, life cannot cease to exist (as long as it remains focused), it can only be transformed. From this perspective, it is plausible that the soul continues its existence after death. Empirical support for the claim that an aspect of the human being remains alive after the body stops functioning is provided by research on NDEs (e.g. the work of professor Peter Fenwick in the UK). Because it is very difficult to locate the precise time of their occurrence, it is sometimes claimed that such experiences, in fact, happen before or after the period of brain inactivity, and therefore are a product of the brain. However, in several cases it was confirmed that they took place while the brain was not showing any activity. There are a number of other attempts to explain these experiences from the materialistic perspective, but none of them seem fully satisfactory[1].

A more contentious issue is what remains after death. Generally, there is a consensus that the body must return to its natural entropic state[2]. However, a dualistic perspective, that identifies the soul with the mind, entertains the possibility that the mind can be preserved in its entirety (including all the memories, for example). There are several objections to this view: firstly it is unlikely that the mind can be fully preserved, considering the extent to which it depends on the brain. Secondly, many materials of the mind are domain-specific so it would be pointless to preserve them when the environment changes (e.g. what would be the purpose of knowing traffic signs in non-material reality?). The Synthesis perspective takes a view that the mind gradually disintegrates, but the non-material component of an organism (the soul) remains. When the body ceases to produce oscillations that resonate with the soul, the soul separates from it. The aura also slowly breaks down. If the resonance is what connects the soul and the body, full separation may not occur even when the brain stops functioning, which is why people can 'return' after having an NDE.

---

[1] For their more detailed analyses see for example Blackmore, 2005b, and Wade, 1996, chapter 12.

[2] It is occasionally believed that even the body can be maintained in non-material reality but this is out of question. A body consists of atoms that are kept together by nuclear and electro-magnetic forces. If these forces do not apply, anything physical would be highly unstable - atoms would break up into energy, which would be the equivalent of a nuclear explosion. On the other hand, if that realm allows these forces, it could not be much different from material reality and should be susceptible to the effects of entropy (further deterioration). This point is brought up only to eliminate some unrealistic NDE claims.

The Intermediate Stage

NDEs can shed some light on that twilight zone between physical and non-physical life. There are several common elements of such experiences (largely independent of culture, age, education, or religious affiliation) that are worth considering.

• An OBE is, as a rule, a prelude to a NDE. Subjects report that they perceived the situation from a different point of view than where their bodies were, and were able to describe resuscitation procedures in detail (although they appeared unconscious and their eyes were shut). However, considering that an OBE can happen in other circumstances, these experiences do not say much about life after death, except adding to the argument that the body and mind cannot be identified.

• Going through a tunnel or other passage with a bright light at the end is also commonly reported. Researchers do not provide an explanation of what this 'tunnel' may be and whether it relates to something real (except misguided ones, such as that it is the memory of passing through the birth canal). One possibility is that the awareness shifts towards the other opening of the soul (towards non-material reality), but that would mean leaving the rings behind, which does not seem to fit well with the description of such experiences. Individuals sometimes tend to meet relatives and religious figures, which indicates a projection. Therefore, the rings must be involved, we do not lose our constructs immediately after death. A more plausible explanation could be that the soul goes through a tunnel that the rings themselves create. The purpose of it is to be able to maintain the rings in non-material reality. In other words, to minimise confusion and preserve one's own identity without the support of physical reality, dividing the two worlds is required. Such a separation is constructed as going through a tunnel or a corridor, and just as frequently, as crossing a river or a bridge.

• Subjects often report that their lives passed in front of their eyes. The freeing of the soul from the body may cause energy shifts, so suppressed experiences can resurface. They can trigger such a swift succession of images that they cannot be distorted (as they are in dreams) and, therefore, resemble real memories. It is sometimes claimed that the whole life is repeated, but this is likely to be a result of later interpretations.

• Acceptance of death and the sense of calm and purpose that can remain well after an experience and profoundly change the outlook on life of those who had them. These are non-interpretative phenomenological experiences that can be taken seriously. They make a difference between NDEs and pathological states that are sometimes invoked to explain NDEs. It is worth mentioning though, that even after an accident or serious illness that does not involve NDE people can have an enhanced sense of well-being and contentment. However, it is usually short lived and not accompanied by calm and acceptance or death as in the previous case.

Possible trajectories

There are three major beliefs (with many variations) about what happens after death: one is that nothing happens, the other is reincarnation, and the third is that the non-material aspect of the human being continues to exist in a different reality. Surprisingly, it seems that there is scope for a synthesis even here. Each of these interpretations are to some extent right, but they are burdened by ideological baggage that makes them seemingly incompatible. In other words, they are all epistemically valid, although the degree of their ontological status may differ. To draw a parallel, when swimmers reach the other end of a swimming pool, one can stay there and do nothing, the other can swim back, and the third can get out. However, the first one will eventually have to either swim back or get out, and the second one will eventually have to get out.

Several conclusions related to this subject can be drawn from the previous arguments. First of all, if the soul is non-material, it does not return or go to another world after death – the soul has never left that other world. What happens is that it loses the connection with and the support of the body. The soul can still remain a discrete unit of energy in non-material reality because it has a centre (the self) and also its unique 'shape' (the distribution of energy) that was re-formed during physical existence. This shape may be to some extent affected by the rings, but cannot be identified with them. It is more fluid and is sustained by an internal cohesive force, rather than structures acquired from the outside. The shape gives a character to the soul and does not disappear. The rings that are created through an interaction with the brain and the physical environment cannot be indefinitely sustained though, and slowly fade (the difficulty is not only to preserve their elements, but also their coherence). So, after death, constructs created during one's physical existence eventually disintegrate (which is to be expected, because they are not relevant any more). However, their effects, the imprints that they leave on a soul (the knowledge and experience content) are incorporated into its shape. In other words, the form is forgotten, but the essence remains. This may be compared to a computer disc that preserves a particular code, but not words and images. On the other hand, without the restrictions of the heavy brain, awareness has an opportunity to expand, and what happens after that is likely to depend on the stage of development achieved during material life. Several options are possible: the soul merges with a larger unit, reincarnates or, if the self is capable of keeping its energy together, remains aware and intentful in non-material reality. The following descriptions of these options are an interpretation that does not need to be taken onboard. What really matters is the notion that development can continue even after death.

• A soul is sometimes still connected to a larger energy unit (physical separation during material life does not mean necessarily that individual souls are fully separated in the non-material domain). In this case, the soul again becomes a part of the larger whole, within which it may still maintain a limited individuality or it can merge fully.

• If the body and bodily instincts were the main driving force during material existence the soul cannot, on its own, remain integrated after death (the first ring easily breaks when the soul loses the support of the senses and body to provide security and anchor it). Two reactions can be expected: panic, which leads to a rush attachment to any available new body or a (spontaneous or possibly assisted) enfolding of the soul, similar to a sleep without dreams, a state of rest and preservation until the next life begins. This means that the soul ceases to be aware of anything until a new life (which fits well with the materialists' view that nothing happens after death).

If the main force in life was social determination, the second ring can preserve the soul integrated for awhile. The experience is interpreted according to the cultural framework adopted during the lifetime. A person gives a recognisable shape to a new experience. Non-material energy takes familiar forms (relatives, angels, religious figures[1]). These constructs can persist for a while on the basis of inner 'monologue' or for even longer if a collective framework is created and supported by mutual interactions among participating souls. Nevertheless, those constructs do not have the same solidity and durability as in physical life (they create a state similar to a dream). Without the support of the brain and material world, sooner or later they also fade off. The second ring starts falling apart. The length of this process depends on how much the soul is attached to socially conditioned elements and whether they are reinforced by other souls. When this ring eventually disintegrates, awareness expands, but the soul that heavily relied on such constructs is unlikely to be able to adapt to the new, so the same happens as in the above case (i.e. reincarnation). On the other hand, if the person managed to transcend shimself within the conventional stage (through shis actions, for example), it may weaken the attachment and make possible to remain in non-material realm.

• If during physical life a person was predominantly on the third (ego) stage of development, shis soul is likely to be fully separated. An individual can temporarily create shis own environment, so personal expectations are fulfilled. The soul of a convinced materialist, for instance, can spontaneously enfold leading to 'hibernation' and supporting the belief that nothing

---

[1] Negative cultural descriptions such as devils or Hell are rare because they do not really correspond to anything in non-material reality. Also, the souls at this stage could not sufficiently develop the sense of personal responsibility that such ideas require in order to make sense out of them.

happens after death. More commonly, the soul can create the world of shis desires. Such an ego-created 'world' can be shared and supported by other souls that have similar affinities. However, this ego shell can consume much energy and be limiting. Furthermore, being transfixed with these identifications can become a trap. As long as the self is identified with ego, awareness is restricted (like awareness in a dream that is narrower than when awake). This is similar (although more intense) to being so involved in a computer game, fantasy or dream that one forgets the real world outside. The third stage, however, is notoriously unstable, so sooner or later the third ring also starts to break down. As in the previous instance, a soul at this point does not need to reincarnate any more if it is capable of opening enough and accepting the new, but this is far from easy. When reality is faced, the experience is still susceptible to personal interpretations and can look like Heaven or Hell. Heaven and Hell are in fact the same (an analogy can be drawn with, for example, London, that can be Heaven for one individual and Hell for another). It all depends to what extent the shape of the soul fits the new environment. Moral sense and an ability to give up personal importance play a significant role. For instance, people who, during their material existence, used physical strength or money to control others may feel lost because there are no bodies or money any more. In short, unless the person is able to transcend, reincarnation is again the most likely outcome.

• If the fourth stage of development was dominant (at least in one dimension) the self is likely to be able to preserve and control energy with expanded awareness. This is not to say that it is easy to maintain the soul coherent (as a separate unit) without the support of the rings, but transcendent stage is a good preparation in this respect. The fourth ring does not even need to contain elements about the non-material aspect of reality if a sufficient degree of non-attachment (to the constructs of the world and one's own ego) is involved. Thus, reincarnation is not needed any more, although it is traditionally believed that some souls may return to assist the collective development[1].

---

[1] This must be a hazardous undertaking because it is necessary to start from the beginning (such souls have to, of course, forget themselves first, and only in time remember or learn again).

Reincarnation

Reincarnation is, by far, the most frequent occurrence, which is why it deserves special attention. The pioneering work of Ian Stevenson and recently of other researchers can provide some fairly credible empirical evidence (as far as it can go) in this respect. From the Synthesis perspective, it makes sense that every soul goes through a series of lives. Reincarnation enables development of awareness and intent through experiences in the material world (although, of course, these experiences could also have negative effects). Thus, every physical life is an opportunity to increase awareness and control and to improve the 'shape' of the soul (so it is unlikely that a human soul would connect to an animal body, for example). The soul can stop reincarnating when a heavy and slow body is not necessary any more to keep it together - in other words, when a crude moulding is finished. Until the shape is optimal, until the self is able to maintain, expand and control energy without the help of the body, the soul goes from one life to another. When the first ring breaks apart, the other rings can maintain the energy coherent and separated from other souls, but only temporarily. Sooner or later, they break apart too, and the soul is, in most cases, again attracted by matter.

Previous lives are hard to remember because there is no connection – the associative chain is discontinued. As when we dream, not only do we not remember the awake state, but we usually don't remember previous dreams either. We are attached to the experience of the dream we are in, so if there is no link, there is no propensity to remember. How can one remember previous dreams, if s/he does not even know that s/he is dreaming? Even more importantly, those memories have lost their form and coherence (because the rings have broken down). Overall, this is an advantage, the previous memories could be confusing and not conducive to development (if you played draughts, and now you are learning how to play chess, better to forget draughts). Sometimes, however, especially in the cases of a sudden death and a rapid return, the rings do not dissolve completely, some 'pieces' may be still left attached to the soul after it connects to another body - which is why some people can recall a few fragments of their previous lives (but this is likely to be a less frequent occurrence than reported in popular literature). Snippets of memories can also be reconstructed by corresponding energy configurations and are normally accessed outside the present context (e.g. in sleep). Moreover, they are influenced by current experiences, so their interpretations may not be always correct.

Some possible questions

Why individual souls reincarnate?

It enables the continuity of individual development alongside the collective one, which accelerates the evolutionary process.

Can a collective soul also reincarnate?

Some collective souls of relatively primitive organisms can reincarnate (although they normally evolve). Complex organisms such as humans, as a rule, reincarnate individually, although there are some indications that they may be connected to something that would be an equivalent of a collective ring.

Is there such thing as karma?

It is plausible that the situation and the body a soul is reincarnated into depends to some extent on the shape of the soul, which in turn is influenced by the earlier experiences and conduct. However, this is a much more complex phenomenon than usually presented (that would require a book on its own). So, the fact that somebody is born in unfortunate circumstances cannot be taken as a sign that this person had done something bad in shis previous life. Such a linear interpretations are far too simplistic.

To what extent is the material life affected by prenatal experiences?

The soul can affect the person through pre-set intents and its shape, which is reflected in one's character. This is why (in addition to genes) even infants have character. Some intents can have a lasting effect on the shape of the soul and so can influence subsequent lives, although the person may not be aware of it or its source. However, other factors (physical and social determinants and choices we make) can override such effects.

When does the soul reincarnate?

The soul reincarnates when a new body is formed in material reality that can resonate with its configuration. This is a very complex process that depends on the genetic material, but also fluctuations in the social environment may be involved to some extent. The soul does not fully connect with the body immediately but gradually, step by step (which is determined by the development of the 'containers' – the body and mind). Thus, although an initial connection is normally established even before birth, new connections (with the same body) can be formed throughout one's life.

NON-MATERIAL REALITY

There is substantial data indicating that a soul can retain a larger perspective for a while *after* connecting to the body and even after the birth (see, for example, Wade, 1996, Chapter 2). Only gradually, it seems, does awareness become restricted by immediate experience, and the rest is forgotten. There may be several reasons why this forgetting happens: the sensations from material reality are stronger; the shock of birth breaks continuity; or the fluidity of these experiences makes it hard to retain them. Forgetting non-material existence is also beneficial. Such memories could intensify feelings of alienation and longing, and prevent focusing fully on this world. In contrast, when the rings start falling off after death, the self can become aware not only of non-material reality but also some experiences (although not necessarily their forms) from earlier lives that were incorporated into the soul. In any case, memories become a part of a wider perspective (like when one wakes up). Not everybody can adapt to the new environment, though. The difference between the imprints that expectations and beliefs left on the soul and reality as it is, can cause emotional reactions (e.g. fear or loss) that lead to reincarnation.

(Self)evaluation of the previous life is a persistent component of life after death accounts, but is often misunderstood. The soul seeks coherence (it is difficult to keep the energy together if there are internal conflicts), so this is more about coming to terms with the past experiences and choices, than evaluation. The sense of meaning is also enhanced. This does not lead to uniformity. Being aware that there is a purpose does not automatically mean interpreting it in the same way, or even accepting and working towards it. Also, there may be a plurality of views as to what is the best way to realise the purpose. Establishing contact with other souls makes sense, but meeting one's earthly relatives or religious figures are most likely projections (which does not rule out the possibility that they are projected onto something real). One's grandpa, for example, usually appears as one remembers him, not as an old sick person on his death bed or a man in his prime (which would be more likely if he could adopt an image of his choice). That non-material reality is populated by a conglomeration of gods and demi-gods from various cultures who just happen to be passing by is also unrealistic[1]. The conventional stage may still play some role, but its elements will certainly not take earthly forms.

---

[1] Regarding the visions of gods and demons *The Tibetan Book of the Dead* advises: 'Be not terrified. Be not awed. Recognize them to be the embodiment of thine own intellect'.

Certain differences between non-material and material realities can be discerned:

• Non-material life is very dissimilar in appearance, but not so much in experience. There are no bodies, cars, TV, money, pets, computers, phones, books, clothes, genders etc. (although all these can be constructed as mental projections). Yet, there is no reason why familiar feelings such as fear, joy, hate or love should not be present.

• Unrestricted experiences in non-material reality though, may have an additional quality of infinity. In fact, considering that the mind is affected by the soul, every experience potentially has this quality. It can be occasionally glimpsed even in the material world (as eloquently described in the first chapter of Colin Wilson's *Outsider*). But, because the rings have a tendency to close, this quality can be captured only for a moment. As soon as an experience becomes concrete, the element of infinity is lost (which often leads to disappointment). In the non-material world this does not need to be the case.

• Time is linked to entropy, so time cannot exist in the usual sense. Attributes like near and far, before and after may still be meaningful, but they do not belong to a space-time framework. This is similar to a dream, when a dreamer can recognise these categories, although s/he does not operate within the space-time continuum.

• Non-material reality is less solid, more fluid. This is not to say that it is experienced as such. Dreams too are felt as solid, although they are evidently not. However, this increased fluidity makes reality less stable. There is still permanency, but not of shapes or objects but the qualities of phenomena – similar to a river or sea or clouds that are lasting phenomena although they keep changing all the time.

• The perception depends more on an inner state. For instance, if two persons in the material world observe a dog, they see more or less the same object, although the meaning and feelings related to it can be very different. For one person, the dog may present a danger and frighten shim, while the other may feel love and friendship towards it. In non-material reality those two persons would even perceive such an energy unit in a somewhat different way. So, not only the meaning and feelings can differ, but the perception too, because it depends far more on an interaction between the subject and an object (a form is created, rather than given). This does not mean that non-material reality is completely subjective, but the perception is heavily influenced by the state of the perceiver. As a consequence, it is much more difficult to communicate, understand and maintain a shared reality. A lot of effort needs to be invested to stabilise the image of reality without the help of solid matter, so the compatibility of souls that perceive in a similar way must be highly valued.

Some possible questions

Can constructs be created in non-material reality?

In principle, there is no reason why energy cannot be constructed even without the help of the brain, body and language, although such constructs are likely to be different.

If knowledge is a construct, does that mean that it falls off after death, and therefore is only useful during physical life? What knowledge remains after death?

Forms that contribute to the structuring fall off (e.g. a particular language), but not the network that was established with the help of these forms (see p. 172). So, knowledge is not lost even if signifiers may be – only, it is not formulated in the same way as in physical life (it is not bound to specific end points and is also more fluid than when supported by the brain). Such knowledge is not a part of the rings that gradually break apart, but the energy configuration that corresponds to the rings and can be preserved after death. In other words, in the absence of synaptic connections, the implicit aspect of memories remain in the soul, although their specific form may be lost.

How is it that certain information can be preserved after death (at least temporarily), but some can be instantaneously lost following a brain-injury?

Temporary amnesia suggests that memories are not fully lost, otherwise they could not be retrieved. In some cases of brain injures a loss of memory may be even confused with an inability to communicate memories, but this cannot explain everything. A more complex way of looking at this issue is needed. Amnesiacs do not usually forget early memories, but only recent ones, which indicates that the rings are in the process of formation during the physical life, when the soul relies heavily on the brain. So, perhaps, only those memories that are not yet fully integrated are lost (like computer documents that are not saved). It is also possible that a brain injury actively prevents access to memory as long as there is a link between the soul and the brain (direct signals from the rings are weaker than those coming from the brain). Again, this can be compared with using computers. As long as a computer works well, a user relies on its 'memory'. Suppose, however, that the computer crashes and the user does not have a back-up. As long as s/he is attached to the computer, the effects of the malfunction apply. However, if s/he detaches from the machine, s/he may start to recreate what is lost from shis own more vague, less precise memory that nevertheless may bring about many pieces of information and their relations that can no longer be recovered from the computer.

Does the soul have an I? Is there an identity even after death?

In non-material reality a soul can still retain the rings for awhile, and therefore an I. A soul that loses its rings does not have a projected identity, but it has its unique 'shape'. This shape is, of course, less permanent and stable, but a soul in any case remains distinct because of its centre (the self) that provides a unique (first person) perspective.

Are all souls in non-material reality good?

There is no reason to believe so, considering that their development can still vary, that there is choice, and that there are different interpretations of what the purpose is and especially how to achieve it. Some interpretations are still necessary in the non-material realm, so even souls can be mistaken and delusional. The Intent may be beyond a dichotomy of 'good and evil', but souls are not.

Can non-material entities affect the physical world?

Considering that there are beings in non-material reality at different stages of development, the question of whether they can influence the material world cannot be avoided. In the end, all that folklore about spirits, saints, daemons, angels and so on, is perhaps not utterly groundless. What is certain is that they cannot move mountains (or even chairs - the physical world is stronger by far). Yet, there is no reason why they could not operate on the boundaries of natural laws or communicate certain meanings or ideas, providing that there are recipients able to pick up such subtle information. This should not be confused with talking to dead relatives or auto-projections when one's own wishful thinking or fears get externalised (e.g. seeing winged angels or hearing voices forcing the person to do something). Spiritualists (mainly in the 19th century, at the time when the radio and other transmission devices were invented) developed ingenious methods to prove that communication with the deceased is possible. However, even the credible ones are open to different interpretations, so they remain inconclusive. In any case, assuming that an interaction with non-material reality may happen, it should be an exceptional phenomenon for several reasons: it is difficult to penetrate through the barriers of the world structure (those who attempt to establish the contact must open up to an extraordinary extent). The ways of communicating in two realities are different and difficult to make compatible. Also, there is a lack of interest, souls that are able to permanently remain in non-material reality should be aware that heavy interference would go against the Intent. The possibility of some sublime influences (of which source we cannot be conclusive in order to preserve agency) is not excluded though. However, they can never override individual choice. So even if a 'message' is selected from the noise of the brain and interpreted correctly, it may still be ignored. In any case, such experiences are constructive only if necessary, so they must be rare. Any frequent occurrences or ongoing guidance would be, in fact, contrary to individual development, and therefore should be treated with scepticism.

Can souls die?

Unlike the body, the soul is not susceptible to entropy, so it cannot deteriorate or die in the common sense, 'naturally' (which would also be an enormous waste). However, souls are only potentially immortal. They can cease to exist as separate units if one of the two fundamental principles, static and dynamic, completely takes over (it is most likely though, that in this case their energy becomes a part of the greater whole). If the static principle becomes so strong as to prevent movement and the exchange of energy, it may lead to the 'extinguishing' of the soul. If the dynamic principle becomes so strong that the energy cannot remain focused any more, the soul disintegrates, dissolving the self. It is also worth mentioning that individual souls can be assimilated by other souls, which probably has a similar outcome.

Even if an individual soul manages to preserve itself as a whole, is it capable of surviving on its own in non-material reality or must it join other souls?

It does not have to. Souls have intrinsic needs for coherence and development. Whether these needs are satisfied through personal transformation, independent interaction, assimilation, or integration with other energy units may vary from case to case. This is not to say that others are not important. After all, to fulfil the purpose, the unity of souls must be eventually achieved. So, the subject of interaction with others (in material and non-material reality) may be worthwhile consideration.

THE INTERACTION WITH OTHERS

Besides the individual function, the mind also has a social function: it enables separation between souls, but also re-connection through an exchange of structured energy (no mind exists in isolation, but interacts with other minds). So, the others matter in every domain of material life, for both existence and agency:

1. In the *physical domain* others are important to maintain and perpetuate physical existence (cooperation, reproduction). Clearly, agency is dominant here, although others, of course, have a role regarding existence too (e.g. protection and help).

2. In the *public domain* others are important to create, maintain and confirm the image of the world and our own image through the process of socialisation. This is not to say that perception of reality is the product of a consensus. It does relate to something real, and cultural differences are not completely arbitrary variations. Shared reality is based on a similar range of sensory inputs and experiences, common language, etc. Existence dominates here, although agency also plays a role (e.g. creative expressions within the established paradigms through art, mythology, religion, literature etc.).

3. In the *personal domain* others are important to stimulate, to initiate energy shifts. A direct exchange of energy hardly ever occurs. Normally, energy first passes through the heavier filters, the body and mind. The rings act as shields, so others are rarely the cause of a shift, but they can be a trigger for the restructuring of existing energy (through our reactions). So, to what extent and what shift will happen, mainly depends on the person shimself, not on others (e.g. they do not upset us, upsetness is our chosen reaction that has become habituated). Obviously, agency dominates here again, although others may also serve as a mirror, to confirm one's existence.

4. Regarding the *transcendent domain* there is now mounting evidence supporting the commonly accepted wisdom that individuals and even whole groups can resonate, producing measurable effects at the time of heightened attention (see, for example, McTaggart, 2001, p.197-214)[1]. Expressions, such as 'being on the same wave-length' or 'feeling in tune' may be more than just metaphors. All this can have harmonising effects, linking the interaction in this domain to existence. However, in what way and to what extent agency can be affected is unclear. If there is any effect, it must be subtle so that freedom of choice can still be preserved.

---

[1] This should not be confused with a collective consciousness. That individual wave patterns may converge does not means that they create a new consciousness.

LOVE

There is one type of interaction that deserves special attention. The meaning of life cannot be just a theoretical concept, there must be an empirical equivalent at any level, including the level of human life. Otherwise, the suggested meaning is unlikely to be more than just a construct. It seems that such an equivalent does indeed exist. Love has an intrinsic sense of meaningfulness and infinity, which is why it is experienced as special.

Love is a very broad term regarding its typology and what it refers to (e.g. passionate love v. compassionate love; eros, philia, agape; caring love for children and elderly; not to mention some banal use of the term in everyday language, such as love for a particular type of food or activity). It would not be possible and necessary to address all these meanings here. The term is used in a much narrower sense, signifying a freely chosen intimate relationship between equal partners. It excludes infatuation (eros, passionate love), and agape (universal love or love of God) and is closest to philia or compassionate love (that should not be identified with friendship, to which it is sometimes inaccurately reduced).

If love is a reflection of the meaning of life, it is not surprising that the intimate relationships (which do not need to be restricted to only two people) is arguably the most complex phenomenon regarding human interactions. A good intimate relationship consists of an interplay between a tendency towards unity (which is also, on a larger scale, a prerequisite to the formation of the Other) and a tendency towards preserving separateness (enacting the separateness between the One and the Other). Although these two are intertwined, the former is what is prominent throughout the process of an intimate relationship (as well as through the process of achieving the final goal), while the latter acts as a corrective mechanism. So, the uniting will be taken as the dominant part, while the separateness can be considered (for the sake of simplicity) its 'shadow'.

Love has the same function in every domain: the bonding of the bodies in the physical domain; the socially constructed bonding (a ritualised unity such as marriage) in the public domain; the bonding of the egos (and the ensuing personal attachment) in the personal domain; and finally the bonding of the souls in the transcendent domain[1]. The last one goes beyond the body and mind, so it can indeed transcend illness (mental or physical), old age or death. Therefore, so-called eternal love is indeed possible (providing that those involved can survive in the after-death environment).

---

[1] The other side, separateness, is also present in every domain: unbridgeable separateness of the bodies in the physical domain, divisions of social roles in the public domain, preserving autonomy in the personal domain, and independent selves in the transcendent domain.

This is, however, not all. Love is also the road to fulfilling the purpose. If individual selves are to become the Other, the counterpart to the One, they will have to eventually merge too. The only appropriate way to achieve this is through the act of love. Love is the force that allows this process. However, not despite but precisely because of it, this ultimate act is also a most hazardous event, which is not only recognised in spiritual traditions, but its echo reaches common experiences too. Love is highly valued and desired, but it is often linked to death and a sense of annihilation. This is because the final merging requires a merging of the selves (rather than just souls), which is a highly delicate process. If, at the moment of merging, there is a shred of desire for control, fear, or inequality, the result could be a moment of panic that can lead to one soul assimilating or being assimilated by another rather than merging together. So, the risk is much greater than even the risk of physical death. If the person dies, there is always another chance. If the self is lost, there is no other chance. In a way, this is the only real death. Not surprisingly, such an act can cause extreme anxiety. Yet, the merging of selves is necessary. This is why individual development must include moral development (that can be best justified as a preparation for the act of love) and also affective development (the development of the un-constructed aspect). Equality between the partners (that, of course, permits differences) is also vital[1]. Inequality is not appealing in any case, because it takes away agency, but more importantly, it is dangerous. An unequal love can lead to assimilation rather than the merging of the selves. In fact, the unification does not have to be the result of love or mutual choice among equals; it can also be the consequence of forceful or accidental assimilation. However, not only does this annihilate another self, but also the energy acquired through assimilation (a set of information and experience) is a 'dead' energy, far less valuable than the active energy acquired through the merging of selves. So, a relationship that has a prospect of leading to assimilation rather than merging is unethical and far inferior.

Although the merging of souls can happen even in material reality, the merging of selves cannot, because the bodies always remain separated (therefore, perceptions, memories and experiences are also separate). This is good, considering that souls that identify with bodies are not yet ready for such an ultimate act. In fact, this final unification does not even happen at the early stages of non-material life but usually only at the later ones. Still, the journey of love leading to it starts here and is not restricted only to individuals. It may be hard to believe, but we are all already a part of this long voyage, which is the subject of the last chapter.

---

[1] So, loving God in terms of yearning to merge with God is pointless and likely to be rejected, as any lover usually instinctively rejects one whose love takes the form of inferiority. Therefore, love of God is best expressed through love of people.

SOCIAL DEVELOPMENT

Reducing social development to utilitarian purposes (e.g. maximising the chances of self-preservation or the transmission of genes) cannot account for the ubiquity of practices such as art, spirituality, philosophy and theoretical science (in its pre-application form). They play an important part in human life and yet largely do not contribute to, or at least are not primarily motivated by these ends. Human beings have an intrinsic urge to develop, and that urge is reflected in the development of human societies too.

The very term social development though, is abandoned nowadays in favour of social change because the former is associated with progress and there is a widespread opinion (in line with the dominant views at present, such as Neo-Darwinism) that there is no such thing as progress. The reasons for this, however, are not only ideological. There is a real difficulty to determine the criteria of progress (e.g. science taking over religion is progress for some, but not for others). What indicates progress from this perspective is a greater opportunity to increase overall awareness and freedom. Yet, even if this is accepted, there are other grounds to doubt progress: the destruction of fellow human beings and of the environment happened on an unprecedented scale during the 20th century. Fascism, Stalinism and the Khmer Rouge, the butcheries in Vietnam, the Balkans, or Rwanda, the damage to the ozone layer and the greenhouse effect are only some prominent examples. These distortions though, should not undermine a general positive trend. It was new freedom (accompanied with recklessness, arrogance and, to use Fromm's term, the *fear of freedom*) that arguably led to them. To make an analogy, although many engage in destructive and self-destructive activities in the period of adolescence, it is still recognised as a step of individual development. Indeed, the signs of maturation seem to be present in every aspect of life. Technology and science are self-evident. Developments in other areas of life may be less so, but they are still present; granted, not in every part of the world, but further than ever in some. Their indicators (relative to previous periods) are a greater egalitarianism, equality of genders and the protection of children; more widespread education and a decrease in superstition; greater freedom of speech and artistic expression; increased sophistication in spiritual awareness and philosophy (it is unlikely that Plato would pass a PhD exam these days with his writings). These achievements should not be undermined. They have been possible because knowledge, experience and constructive actions tend to accumulate. Of course, there are still many problems and serious mistakes are made, but they do not invalidate the whole idea of development. When society becomes more complex, it is expected to have more problems. Integral thinker Ken Wilber points out that, 'as society adds levels of depth, there are more things that can go wrong at every stage' (in Horgan, 2003, p.63). It is undeniable that regressive and destructive actions are far from being eradicated. However, in the past, some of them, including ownership of other human beings, killing for entertainment, torture of 'heretics', pillage and rape in wars, or subjugation of women were *institutionalised* throughout the world. Legitimised slavery, gladiator games, or the Inquisition are unthinkable nowadays more or less anywhere[1].

QUANTITATIVE DEVELOPMENT

Quantitative development may be a result of internal processes but also competition, cooperation or integration with other societies. An increase of the same characteristics that typify individual development in this sense can indicate social development too, although of course, different examples apply: dynamism (mobility, cultural exchange, internal social processes); complexity and differentiation (of knowledge and skills); organisation and integration (of various segments within society); the width of perspective (e.g. taking into account the effects on other societies or the environment); refinement (in art, philosophy, science or spirituality); diversity and versatility (e.g. multicultural coexistence and cooperation); flexibility (e.g. an ability to incorporate or adapt to changes); creativity (e.g. technological and other innovations); internal control (e.g. autonomy, self-governance); productivity (efficiency in utilising resources).

The demise of the native Americans can be an example of how these characteristics can affect the very survival of a society. One such characteristic is increased mobility. When the Europeans arrived in America, the indigenous societies were almost wiped out. Disease was a major factor. The Europeans did not die (at least not in such great numbers) because they were more mobile, so their immune system was more exposed and better adapted to various diseases. Another feature is integration. Upon their arrival, the Spanish were by far outnumbered, were not familiar with the terrain and could not rely on regular supplies. Yet, they managed to conquer the natives, largely because of infighting and disunity. One more characteristic is an increase in complexity (knowledge). In the above example, what also assisted the Spanish was superior war technology. This is not by any means a justification for the conquest and atrocities committed by the Europeans. It is rather an attempt to understand why it could happen on the first place.

---

[1] Some telling examples related to this point can be found in the chapter 'The moral *Zeitgeist*' (Dawkins, 2006, p.262-272).

QUALITATIVE DEVELOPMENT

It is proposed that societies develop through stages akin to those of individual development[1]. After all, any society consists of individuals (although, of course, it cannot be reduced to them). This view was popular in the past, but has been abandoned at present not so much because of empirical data (that are open to various interpretations), but mainly because of two concerns: determinism and inequality.

Determinism - until the 20th century the determinism of social development was a popular notion among both, idealists (e.g. Hegel) and materialists (e.g. Marx). In the 20th century, however, the idea that there is a particular trajectory was abandoned. The idealist concept was not acceptable for its teleological overtone (this issue has already been addressed, so it will not be discussed here). The other concern was that such a determinism is incompatible with human freedom. If global social processes were fully determined, this could mean that historical events and consequently individuals themselves are also determined, which does not leave much room for something that can be called free will. However, recognising that there is a particular trajectory of social development (at least up to a point, which will be clarified below) does not imply inevitability of any social event and can be compatible with self-determination. It only means that a society and humankind as a whole sooner or later, in one way or another, can reach a certain point or plateau (that is, if that society or humankind does not perish before). To make an analogy, the fact that every person (who lives long enough) goes through the stage of adolescence does not diminish shis freedom. So, as in quantum physics, a global pattern can be discerned but no single event can be claimed to be pre-determined. The Intent operates in accord with the principle of minimal interference. It only sets the boundaries to the process and is not concerned with immediate outcomes, so in a way, it is even beyond 'good and evil' as commonly understood. Siding with the good would be unproductive to developing agency - people would choose to be good because it pays off, which would reduce the whole process to conditioning. Improbable outcomes may occasionally occur, but only if something threatens the boundaries, and this is rare indeed. Therefore, events and individuals are not determined, but social processes and relations between them may be favourable to some events and individuals. In other words, they allow some potentials to be realised although, of course, in some cases circumstances may also play a role. For example, Napoleon (and

---

[1] This, of course, does not mean that individual and social development can be identified (tables have legs and animals have legs, but this is not to say that they are the same).

Kutuzov, the general who defeated Napoleon in Russia) became prominent not because they were creating history, but because the flow of history at that particular moment allowed them to surface. If they were not there (say, they died before the crucial events) somebody else would take their roles, which could affect particular happenings and their quality, but not the global dynamics. Individuals are important for history, they may speed up or slow down the process, and even change its direction on a local scale, but they are not irreplaceable. This also applies to societies. If one does not take a particular step, another will.

Inequality - there is a reasonable worry (if judging by the past) that the concept of stages could be used to legitimise the claim that some societies are superior. Such a claim is, however, groundless. To make again a parallel with students, a second year student is not a superior human being to a first year student. S/he may even be less intelligent or a worse scholar than the latter (which is not to say that using the term superior could be justified if s/he was not - there is more to being human than intelligence or studentship). The same applies to societies. A stage of development does not make them superior or inferior. In fact, more advanced societies are potentially more destructive, so a further stage only implies a greater responsibility. By the same token, being at an early stage of development does not imply being primitive. There are primitive individuals and groups at every stage, including the stage of transcendence (they can exhibit elitism, rigidity, dogmatism, exertion, lack of humour). Moreover, humankind may be better grounded if there are cultures at all stages (so attempting to force or coerce societies into change is a mistake). Those that have remained at one stage for a long time are likely to have acquired some wisdom that other societies lack. For example, the founder of multiple intelligences theory, Gardner, added spatial intelligence to the list after being impressed with the spatial orientation of some indigenous people.

The above concerns highlight possible dangers if the notion of stages is not correctly understood, but there is no need to 'throw the baby out with the bath water'. These issues are not intrinsically related to this concept, but are rather the consequence of its misinterpretation. To minimise this, a few further clarifications need to be made.

Although the stage a society is at and the average stage of the individuals in that society may coincide, these two cannot be equated. What matters is the dominant social pattern at that moment. Thus, the stage at which a particular group is can, perhaps, say something about the majority or else a powerful or influential minority, but nothing about an individual from that group, who can be at any stage. In fact, it is likely that within any reasonably large society there are individuals at all stages.

The stages of social development also cannot be associated with stable features, inherent to the group. Evidence clearly shows that such a link does not exist. Using biological (genetic) or geographical factors to determine a stage of development is nothing more than a crude attempt at reductionism. Those who try to connect race or nationality, for example, to development are most likely motivated by a need to simplify and generalise, which only reveals their own limited degree of development. Most people have a brain of sufficient capacity and other potentials to achieve any stage. If there are some minor chemical and structural differences between groups they may, arguably, affect the path of development, but not its stage. The stage depends on individuals and the society as a whole. Any group can progress, stagnate, and regress, even if the physical characteristics associated with a group do not. Of course, some circumstances and living conditions may not be favourable (e.g. not allowing any spare time for self-development), but this is a separate issue.

Stages may provide a platform, an opportunity for progress (that may happen or not), but progress should not, however, be identified with them. It seems that accumulative quantitative development plays a greater role in this respect. For example, while human sacrifices were common in the past throughout the world, nowadays they are extinct in all societies, at any stage.

The stages of social development are described below from a historical perspective (which is not to say that all societies nowadays are at the same stage). Each stage has its cross-cultural characteristics in every area of social life (religion, social and economic organisation, art, the interpretation of time, personality constructs etc.). The emphasis in the text will be on religion though, since it has less exceptions and is clearer in this respect than other areas (possibly because religion usually has a strong grip on society and affects other areas). It should be pointed out, however, that religions do not form, but provide a framework for the stages. They are taken as an example of social organisation that structures dominant processes. In any case, what follows is no more than an outline. Its only purpose is to illustrate a broad tendency, and is by no means an attempt to provide even a remotely comprehensive account of historical processes. It would be easy to find many aberrations and exceptions, but they should not cloud the view of an overall trend emerging from history.

The physical stage

This stage could also be called 'pre-historical' because there are no written records, and it was by far the longest period of human history (archaeologists are saying that the first modern humans appeared about 160 000 years ago). It consisted of 'hunter-gatherer' communities, usually organised in relatively small groups (tribes) with a low level of hierarchical differentiation. Such a society was in a relative unity with the environment, but instinctively rather than consciously (this state 'before the fall' was encapsulated in the story of Eden and other similar myths). The separation between the subject and the object only gradually occurred. Personality was not valued – a common use of masks indicates that an individual only represented something. Physical determinants (including the physical environment) and the first ring were dominant. The writer J. N. Sansonese notes that 'the more ancient the myth, the more often do parts of the human body play an explicit role in the myth' (1994, p.7).

In religion, elements of the physical world were worshiped: celestial objects (the Sun, Moon), the natural forces, as well as animals and plants that often had supernatural powers. In other words, nature was subjectivised. Deities were immanent (they became transcendent only later on). Rituals were based on the physical and instinctual (e.g. trance induced by rhythmic and repetitive sound and movement, or by the use of psychotropic drugs). The after-death life was inextricably fused with physical reality. Magic was a dominant way to control and learn about the world (through sorcerers or directly).

An abstract notion of time did not exist, significant events were used as a reference point instead. It is likely that art had a practical (magical) function. As any other stage, this one also had its dark side (e.g. body mutilation). However, its value should be recognised and respected. A lack of further rings can be facilitative to intuitive insights. Although there are no written records, the notions of the One, the Intent, reincarnation and the soul (atman) seem to be rooted, in a rudimentary form, in this period. Some societies have remained at this stage, either because their physical survival has been too demanding, or they have been isolated, or did not want to go further (e.g. because they have been well integrated with their environment). Nevertheless, they have contributed to many areas of modern life: education, medicine, art (music, painting), alternative life style (hippy communes), psychology (e.g. the effects of psychotropic plants), spirituality, anthropological understanding. This is not to say that this stage should be idealised. Even at present, there is a huge diversity between the groups within it (as a renowned anthropologist Margaret Mead made clear), of which some may be primitive and some may not.

The transition period between the physical and conventional stages[1]

Social development had already greatly escalated in this period. Its outset can be linked to the appearance of horticultural farming. Horticulture started as simple gardening, supplementary to hunting and gathering. It used relatively crude technology and was less efficient than agriculture. Nevertheless, this way of production had important social implications.

Establishing permanent settlements became possible. The villages were initially small, some no larger than the temporary ones of hunters and gatherers. However, because the soil would quickly get exhausted, new land had to be found, sometimes at the expense of neighbours, which in more populated regions greatly increased the chances of conflict. Large-scale warfare was not usual though, probably because there was no political or other unifying force that would amass a sufficient number of individuals for such endeavours. Horticulturalists had more material goods than most hunter-gatherers due to the greater stability of their settlements, with the implication that divisions, on the basis of wealth, started to emerge. However, this was a less physically demanding way of production than agriculture, so women were still able to work in the fields alongside men, with a consequence of greater equality between genders. Tracing one's ancestors through the mother's lineage has its root in such societies. Cults of goddesses rather than male dominated pantheons were widespread (this trend continued through the worship of Inanna in Sumer, and Ishtar in Assyria and Babylonia).

Nevertheless, in many respects the religion of horticultural people resembled that of the hunter-gatherers. Shamans, rites of passage, human sacrifices, animism (worship of plants or animals believed to be ancestral to clans or lineages) were common. In time, religions became more and more anthropomorphised though, deities were often represented in a half human, half animal form (this legacy can be found in as diverse civilisations as the Egyptian and Olmec). Among horticultural peoples with chiefdoms, the chief's remote ancestors, the founders of the lineage, became eventually the most important gods. More recent or less significant ancestors received a lesser status. The result was a hierarchy of gods moving religions in the direction of fully-fledged polytheism.

---

[1] 'Conventional stage' should not be identified with having a society or living in a group. Even animals live in groups and sometimes have a relatively complex social structure, but it does not mean that they are at this stage. Their social life is physically determined and is essentially the same from group to group, while the huge variations of human societies indicate that they are products of more than just adaptation to their environments. They transcend the strictly practical purpose of social organisation.

The conventional stage

Roughly speaking, this stage started around 6 000 B.C.E. with agricultural farming that allowed the establishment of relatively large settlements. All the old civilisations were founded in this period (Sumerian, Egyptian, Babylonian, Assyrian, and Ancient Indian, Chinese, Greek and Roman). Most importantly, writing appeared. Although it had mainly a practical purpose at the beginning, the value of writing for establishing and perpetuating social constructs can hardly be overestimated. Social determination, based on customs, conventions, duty (e.g. dharma in Hinduism), shame, reputation and glory, was dominant. Personality was externally defined (by the name, social position or heredity). The overriding psychological faculty was affect (e.g. fear of punishment), rather than instincts or thinking. A hierarchical differentiation within society was fully established (slave, caste and feudal systems)[1], as well as separation between groups ('us and them').

This stage was characterised by polytheistic religions that reflected the socio-political organisation (as practiced by early Hindus, the Ancient Greeks, Romans, and Vikings). Religion was based on cults and rituals, rather than ideas. These cults were elaborate conscious procedures, unlike the rites in the previous stage. Observance mattered more than belief. Mythology replaced magic. The separation between the two realities occurred, but the after-death world was inferior, a shadow of this reality. Fate and superstition regulated daily life (as evident from the Greek narratives, for example). Art had a predominantly social function - glorification of heroes, leaders, or victories. Time, in terms of the process, was perceived as cyclical (based on the seasons, vital for agriculture). The reference point was the past, rather then the future. Consequently, the ethos was essentially conservative: it valued the authority of ancestral custom. Innovation was regarded as dangerous and subversive: the Romans, for instance, were highly suspicious of movements that would challenge a tradition even if it was not their own (which is why they persecuted the early Christians). A lot of these attitudes still exist today: for example, many people who attend religious services are not interested in theology and dislike the idea of change. They find that the rituals provide them with a link with the past and give them a sense of security.

---

[1] This can easily be seen as a step backwards, but the previous stage should not be idealised (e.g. slaves that were exported to the Americas from Africa were captured mostly by other tribesmen). Also, however repugnant such a move may seem nowadays, it did bring some advantages at the time: it enabled social organisation on a larger scale, the undertaking of long term projects, and it created free time (at least for some) that could be devoted to activities that did not have an immediate practical purpose.

The transition period between the conventional and personal stages

Most documented history belongs to this period. Its beginning can be traced back to the 6th century B.C.E. (that philosopher Karl Jaspers called an 'axial age'). Karen Armstrong, who can be credited for providing a balanced, informative and yet accessible account of the history of monotheism, describes this period as follows:

> All the chief civilisations developed along parallel lines, even when there was no commercial contacts (as between China and the European area). There was a new prosperity that led to the rise of a merchant class. Power was shifting from king and priest, temple and palace, to the market place. The new wealth led to intellectual and cultural florescence and also to the development of the individual conscience.' (1993, p.36)

Within a very short time, all the major directions of human civilisation were laid (which can be compared, in its magnitude, to the Cambrian explosion in biological evolution). K'ung-Fu-tzu and Lao-tzu developed their teachings in China (known as Confucianism and Taoism, respectively). In India Siddhartha Gautama founded Buddhism, and Mahavira Jina, an early rebel against the caste system, Jainism. In the Middle East, Zoroaster created the first monotheistic religion (or, at least, it became prominent at that time). The greatest of the Hebrew prophets, Deutero-Isaiah appeared, and (while in Babylonian captivity) the Jews transcribed and compiled the Torah, the foundation of the Old Testament. The movement towards the belief in a single spiritual reality coincided with the search of Greek thinkers for a single principle to explain the material world. This was the start of classical philosophy (with the three Milesian 'natural philosophers', Thales, Anaximenes and Anaximander, and a little later Pythagoras). Although the evidence is sketchy, it seems that a 'paradigm shift' occurred at that time in central America too (the earliest Maya temple-pyramids were built then)[1].

Not all of them, however, chose the same direction. In fact, practically all the conceivable paths were attempted. For example, it looks like that the pre-Columbian civilisations of Latin America tried to skip the development all together and reach immediately for transcendence. This shift can be recognised in the fact that they had highly sophisticated art, architecture and astronomy - but not technology that remained on the stone-age level. They did not have metallurgy or use wheels (although they knew how to make them for toys, not transport). Physical existence was secondary and, not

---

[1] There is no data indicating that any significant developments happened in Sub-Saharan Africa at that time, even if several great cultures arose later on. It can be speculated that living in a highly hostile environment led to emphasis on quantitative development rather than a qualitative change (reflected, for example, in the achievements of the Bantu people in coping with disease, climate and topography).

surprisingly, (self)sacrifice became prominent. This had disastrous consequences when the content and meaning of such practices were lost and only a form (a ritual) remained, as later on with the Aztecs, leading to an obsession with sacrificing others on a massive scale. The other main directions can be linked to the dimensions of development (see p.223). Buddhism focused mainly on the experience and found a solution in going back into an undifferentiated state (similar to the state life came from). It is a truly rebellious doctrine denying the One and the universal purpose (although acknowledging other, lesser deities). Confucianism, at the same time, concentrated on the development of self-control, which led to emphasising stability and remaining where the society was at that point. The first Greek philosophers and Jewish scholars favoured thinking and discourse (developing the rings) which appeared to be the most conducive to this transition. This is not to say that other civilisations did not pay attention and contribute to the advancement of intellect (nor that the occidental cultures completely neglected experience and intent). Science and technology thrived in India and China too. The decimal numerical system and so-called Arabic numbers, commonly used nowadays, were Indian inventions (passed on by Arabs). The conceptualisation of zero, accepted in Europe only in the 15th century, is attributed to India too. The Chinese were using paper, gun powder (mostly for fireworks) and print much before Europeans. However, the West created relatively coherent frameworks (societal rings), which allowed the assimilation of invaders and integration of disparate groups, while the affinity towards discourse accelerated the process. In comparison, Buddhism, for instance, with its emphasis on experience and the inner world, managed to ascend to the status of an official doctrine and act as the means of social organisation only for a brief period (during the reign of king Asoka), and Hinduism took over again. Buddhism is nowadays practically wiped out in India and is the state religion in varied forms only in a few South East Asian countries and Tibet, after being heavily modified by the indigenous cultures. Confucianism produced a fortified culture (occasionally punctuated by invasions and rebellions), which contributed to stability but not to the evolving of the society. For example, although a Chinese fleet of 63 ships sailed as far as Africa in the 15th century, China remained relatively isolated (but tolerant, allowing foreigners to build their churches, temples and mosques).

For these reasons, in an attempt to summarise some general characteristics of the transition between the conventional and personal stage, the focus will be mainly on the occidental culture, spreading from the Middle East and Mediterranean Europe. This, by no means, implies its superiority (in fact, as the above indicates, some dimensions may have been better developed elsewhere). However, for better or worse, the occidental culture has been evidently the most influential. The Americas and Australia are practically its extensions. The political system in China is based on the ideology of a German philosopher, and the legacy of the British in India is ubiquitous from politics to sport.

In this period, that lasted almost until the 20th century, manufacturing and merchandise became the dominant economic forces. They encouraged innovation, exploration, discovery and interest in the new (which contributed to spreading the occidental culture to India, the Far East, and Americas). Time was seen as an arrow, so the future could be contemplated - not as a repetition, but something different (the book of Daniel being possibly the first written example).

Thinking became gradually a dominant faculty, which led to the development of philosophy. Philosophy in turn, enabled freedom from custom and convention. In the view of philosopher Martha Nussbaum, it promised to 'create a community of beings who can take charge of their own life story and their own thought' – a community, in other worlds, of autonomous individuals (Jenkins, 2002, p.17). Personality and with it personal responsibility (epitomised in equality before the law) emerged, and guilt took over from shame:

> The 'old commitment' in more stable, traditional cultures depended on maintaining a role in relationships, putting the good of the group above the good of the self, and avoiding punishment from the group for deviating from social expectations. The 'new commitment' depends more on the individual's decision-making about a given relationship... [it] is experienced more by the individual as coming from within and not from societal pressure. (Lund, 1991, p.213)

Consequently, the personal (inner, psychological life) became important. Sociologist Durkheim claims that individuality was not prized and the individual, in a certain sense, did not exist in traditional cultures; only with the emergence of modern societies and, more particularly, with the division of labour, did it become the focus of attention (in Giddens, 1991, p.75). In fact, the major changes in this period were usually initiated by an individual standing against society and social norms: Socrates is one of the first examples, but this trend continued with Jesus, Mohammad, Copernicus, Bruno, Luther, Nietzsche and Marx. What they all have in common is a move from action that is prescribed to action by choice. Such a trend also brought the scientific revolution in the seventeenth century and later on further orientation towards the personal, pluralism in values, and separation (this time between individuals – with the ensuing feeling of 'loneliness in the crowd').

This shift is reflected in art too. Greek dramas, for example, do not have personal conflicts (arguably, the only exception can be found in *Agamemnon* when Cassandra, a king's lover and slave, predicts that she will be killed if she enters the house, hesitates for a moment and turns back, but nevertheless enters out of duty). On the other hand, great dramas from the later periods are dominated by personal conflicts and dilemmas (e.g. Shakespeare's *Hamlet* or Ibsen's *A Doll's House*). Epics are another example. For Milton (in comparison to Homer) true epic action occurs in the mind (where, when and how we make decisions). Joyce takes it to an extreme in *Ulysses* – rejecting any structure – it is an epic about events of the human psyche, not external events.

In religion, the whole period is marked by the gradual prevalence of monotheism over polytheism, which was an essential step towards the third stage. Armstrong writes:

> The personal god has helped monotheists to value the sacred and inalienable rights of the individual and to cultivate an appreciation of human personality. (1993, p.242)

It is suggestive that even in strictly polytheistic societies many individuals whose own development superseded the conventional one reached this point. For instance, in Ancient Greece, a number of great thinkers and artists including Socrates, Plato and Aristotle had monotheistic tendencies. Xenophane, for example, wrote:

> *One god, alone among gods and alone among men, is the greatest,*
> *Neither in body does he nor in mind resemble the mortals.*
> *Always in one place he abides: he never is moving;*
> *Nor is it fitting for him to change now hereto, now thereto.*
> *Effortless he moves the world by thought and intention.*
> *All of him is sight; all is knowing; and all is hearing.*

Monotheism is not only about reducing the number of gods, it is a qualitative shift. Religious belief gradually replaced religious observance, deity became transcendent rather than immanent. Mythology is banished in favour of theology. God became more and more distant and less interfering (which is to be expected with the increase of independence). The after death reality was split in two (Heaven and Hell) to accommodate choice and personal responsibility and, of course, to maintain social control. Significantly, it was not any more a mere shadow of the material world, but became an aim, something to look forward to, so the future became important.

This transition period is, however, a relatively slow process that has many steps, which can be illustrated by the development of monotheism through various religions.

Zoroastrianism is arguably the first major monotheistic religion. Many of its elements: a battle between good and evil, beneficent angels, immortality of the soul, a saviour born of a virgin, Heaven and Hell, and the final judgement, were later incorporated into other ones (the Jews were exposed to Zoroastrianism during their exile in Babylonia). Its essentially dualistic nature (Good and Evil) and the emphasis of its ethics on human free will contributed to the shift from the prescribed order of the 2nd stage and to the development of individuality. Good thoughts and conduct mattered rather than sacrifice. Some other characteristics of the third stage were germinated too: choice, personal responsibility and equality (including, up to a point, the equality of women). However, understandably, the conventional stage was still very strong. Not surprisingly, Zoroastrianism had many polytheistic elements, even another creator responsible for evil in the world, and a host of other deities and semi-deities (six of which were especially prominent).

Judaism had a profound effect on social development in that part of the world. It 'provided for the first time a moral reference point which would help people to rebel against their rulers on the grounds of individual conscience' (Brazier, 2001, p.30). Displacement of the Jewish tribes contributed to the sense of further psychological separation from the divine world (the purpose). The Hebrew *kaddosh* means otherness, a radical separation. Seraphim (high ranking angels) were crying 'Yahweh is other! Other! Other!'. This facilitated a turn towards the personal, the internal, which is a necessary step of individualisation. The deed became more important than the creed, and that led to valuing debate and freedom of thought. However, although monotheism won, the previous stage was still prevalent which, combined with the social circumstances, lead to a limited individualisation within the nation (a phenomenon that has re-occurred throughout history, as in 19th century Europe). Israelites were very reluctant to give up the cult of other gods. In fact, it is difficult to situate The Old Testament within a purely monotheistic framework. Although there is only one creator, Heaven is inhabited by a number of supernatural beings (angels and archangels who are helping an omnipotent God, Satan who is making a wager with the all knowing God, etc.). The very idea of the covenant 'only made sense in a polytheistic setting. The Israelites did not believe that Yahweh, the God of Sinai, was the *only* God, but promised, in their covenant, that they would ignore all the other deities and worship him alone. It is very difficult to find a single monotheistic statement in the whole of the Pentateuch. Even the Ten Commandments delivered on Mount Sinai take the existence of other gods for granted...' (Armstrong, 1993, p.31).

Early Christianity is another decisive move towards the personal stage[1]. Christianity made the person the centre of the religious life in a way that was unique in the history of religion: it took the personalism inherent in Judaism to an extreme. Religion is no longer identified with a particular group of people or nation. It becomes a question of personal choice. The essential message of Christianity is that 'God shows Himself in the freedom of individual human action... Without the freedom, and the historical development of the human to which it gives rise, there would be no God' (McMullin, 1987, p.78). An individual became the image of God. The internalisation of sin (that replaced sacrifice) led to taking the inner world of self-reflection seriously. Personal psychology became important. Augustine (and later on Bonaventure and others) urged introspection, descending into the depths of oneself as a way of discovering God.

Of course, the conventional stage was still powerful in early Christianity, reflected in various polytheistic tendencies. Everybody assumed that there were many otherworldly beings. St Paul, for example, referred to Thrones, Dominations, Sovereignties and Powers. These invisible forces were believed to be the ancient gods that were intermediaries between humans and the One. Gnostics also believed in an array of supernatural entities. In Eastern Europe, polytheistic elements were incorporated in the form of saints that are worshiped even nowadays. However, the most important of such elements was tritheism: the belief that there are three emanations of God: Father, Son and Spirit. In the Orthodox church, where the previous stage was more prominent, the idea of the trinity was central. It has never been as important in the West as it has remained for the Eastern church. The Greeks always started with the three hypostases, while the West began with the notion of God's unity and then considered the three entities within that unity. When Western Europe moved further towards individualism, this issue caused the first schism. Individualism was also reflected in the Catholic church by an elaborate hierarchy, with one person at the top (i.e. a pope). In any society the priesthood had a prominent role, but never before was so much power concentrated in the hands of one man, who was in most cases even above kings.

However, even in the West, in periods of crises and later in the time of decline, polytheistic elements would resurface, indicating a retreat to the conventional stage. Armstrong writes that 'soldier saints like St George, St Mercury and St Demetrious figured more than God in first crusaders' piety and, in practice, differed little from pagan deities' (1993, p.229). During the

---

[1] Although nominally polytheistic, the Roman Empire, within which Christianity developed, contributed to this shift. Somewhat paradoxically, the winning of individualistic values against collectivistic ones was signalled by Caesar's abolition of the Roman republic (the reason: his personal worth).

14th and 15th centuries, people in Europe were more and more making other human beings the centre of their spiritual life. The medieval cult of Mary and of the saints increased alongside the devotion to Jesus the man. Even nowadays in some catholic societies (e.g. in Ireland or South America) saints or the cult of Mary are dominant.

Islam. Monotheism was adopted in the Arabic world as a unifying force: 'Muhammad knew that monotheism was inimical to tribalism: a single deity who was the focus of all worship would integrate society as well as the individual' (*ibid.*, p.175). However, Islam became more than that: another integral step towards the third stage. Several factors contributed to this.

The Koran was written in Arabic, therefore directly accessible to all literate people. There was no priesthood, sanctified intermediaries. Religion became more about the personal relationship with God and personal responsibility. While Christians at that time attempted to wipe out free-thinkers and non-conformists (as in the case of the Cathars), in the Islamic world they were not persecuted. Rationality, which is a characteristic of the third stage, became more prominent. Muslim scholars in the Middle Ages had a decisive role in moving from Platonic intuitionism to Aristotelian rationalism, which greatly contributed to the development of the Western world and the rise of science. They used paper and printing, and introduced algebra and Arabic numbers (that originated in India). In the 9th and 10th centuries, more scientific discoveries were achieved in the Abbasid empire than in any previous period. Islam was, at that time, a step forward in social organisation too, which is reflected, for example, in a greater egalitarianism and equality of genders (the right to inheritance and divorce). This all goes parallel with the trend of increasing the distance between God and humans: 'In the Koran, al-Lah… is more impersonal than YHWH [Jehovah]. He lacks the pathos and passion of the biblical God' (*ibid.*, p.167).

Yet, even Islam, from the start, was not immune to polytheistic influences (as exemplified by the so-called 'Satanic verses'). The decline in Muslim society (due to numerous invasions and a geographical shift of trade routes and economic power) inevitably led to a retreat to the conventional stage, and as a consequence, the re-surfacing of polytheistic elements. Muhammad and the members of his family gained the status of deities and even imams 'were revered as avatars of the divine, each one has been "proof" of god's presence on earth and, in some mysterious sense, made the divine incarnate in a human being' (*ibid.*, p.190).

Protestantism was another step towards the personal stage. Until the 4th century Christianity was still very much about society. After Augustine, it became more about the individual (saving shis own soul) who was still passive though. With the Reformation the person became active (had a *duty* to be active) in shaping shis destiny. This was also accompanied by strengthening monotheism. Protestant reformers (and Catholic too) insisted on turning away from saints and angels and focusing on God alone.

In 16th century Europe Luther's translation of the Bible into German and call for education for all resulted in the democratisation of religion and a heightened sense of individualism. Shortly after, Calvin managed to transform society on a small scale (in Geneva), so people started to believe that they could make a difference in this world. Calvinist pre-determinism of salvation may seem on first sight to remove choice but, in fact, it furthered individualisation – social control became harder without the belief that one's thoughts and behaviour will affect the outcome. By the end of the 16th century Christianity was fragmented into many groups, so religion became more than ever a question of choice. Moreover, 'instead of expressing their faith in external, collective ways, the people of Europe were beginning to explore the more interior consequences of religion' (*ibid.*, p.318). The cornerstone of modern philosophy, Descartes, urged to turn inside, self-reflection being the only reliable method to cognise reality. Isolation and autonomy that sprang from the Cartesian method were to become the central characteristic of the Western mentality.

When introducing what is now known as *Pascal's wager*, Pascal 'was the first modern' (*ibid.*, p.343), conceding that a belief in God was the matter of personal choice. In the 17th and 18th centuries Deism emerged as an attempt to reconcile religion with reason. Nothing was left except an impersonal God, who does not interfere with human affairs and could be discovered only by one's own efforts. This was only one step away from discarding God all together, which was yet to come. New self-reliance would soon lead many people to reject the whole idea of God who reduces them to the state of a dependant. All of that prepared the ground for a radical break with the past and a turn towards the future. While traditional societies resisted innovation and change, a new feeling that people are in charge of their own affairs provided a fertile ground for the development of technology on an unprecedented scale.

This is not to say that reformed religion did not leave its mark. Even when an image of God was discarded, its ethos could be expressed in a secular way. The idea that people make their own destinies was perfectly aligned with the emergence of a new economic system, capitalism, that glorified work and favoured competition over cooperation.

The personal stage

Although it very much depends on the geographical location, it can be said that this stage started, in earnest, roughly in the mid 19th century. At that time, the idea of progress became dominant: the previous stages were looking for guidance in the past, while this one made a deliberate break with the past and institutionalised change. Science and technology became the leading economic forces. It is a mistaken belief, though, that science brought the demise of the old religion. After all, most scientists (including Newton, who is considered the originator of the mechanistic view of the world) were spiritual or religious. Quite the opposite, according to physicist and theologian Stanley Jaki (1970), *mechanistic* science arose in Europe as an outgrowth of the development of religious outlook, where God was becoming steadily more and more removed from the material world.

This stage is fully realised in secular societies dominated by materialist ideologies. Materialism can be considered a form of religion too (true, it does not have a deity, but some other religions, such as Buddhism, also do not have a deity). 'The death of God' really means the death of an old form of religion, and the rise of a new one. What makes atheism a religion is that as other religions, it is based on a set of arbitrary beliefs, and is an attempt to conform reality and experience to this set of beliefs (the existence of non-material reality, for instance, is rejected *a priori*). Materialism should not be identified with humanism that has always existed (in parallel with religious attitudes). The difference is that a humanist may accept that non-material reality exists, but is not concerned with it. The focus of shis attention is this world (s/he may be dedicated, for example, to improving the living conditions of the poor). A materialist, on the other hand, as a starting premise, adheres to an ideological framework that rejects the possibility that non-material reality may exist. Although the roots of this new religion can be traced to the renaissance and enlightenment (and even earlier), it really took hold in the 19th century. Philosopher Nietzsche (among others) can be seen as its prophet. As already mentioned, Zoroaster started the shift towards the personal stage. Appropriately, Nietzsche used his character to herald the last step in this process, and chose to write in a form more suitable for religious rather than philosophical books. He was aware that he was endorsing a new religion that disposed of the image of God. Socrates and Jesus were fighting the establishment and died at the hands of the establishment, while Nietzsche, consistent with this stage and his philosophy, created his own demise (syphilis and madness).

Materialism replaced a transcendental being with self-transcendence, an attempt to overcome human nature (*Übermensch*) by focusing on the *ego*, or the third ring. Observance is replaced with self-observance. The cult of personality replaced other cults. Confession was replaced by psychotherapy.

As personal responsibility is internalised (no punishment and reward), nothing happens after death. Freud, one of the main contributors to this shift, encapsulates in his theory the conflict between a socially determined I (superego) and a physically determined I (id) that need to be negotiated through individuality (ego). It is not difficult to see this schema as the struggle for dominance of an aspect of personality that is an expression of the third stage with the aspects linked to the second and first stages. This, however, did not bring freedom as hoped, but replaced the old forms of conditioning with ego conditioning – in a way, people became slaves to their own wants. As the father of public relations and a relative of Freud, Edward Bernays realised, sublimation of the 'primitive drives' (aggression and sex) and other tenets of Freudian theory could be used to manipulate the masses, for commercial and political ends.

As other ideologies, materialism also ends in its opposite[1]. A doctrine that had begun with the aim to humanise the individual, led to dehumanising the world. In a way, materialism reaches the opposite side of the spectrum. While at the beginning the external world was subjectivised, the subjective here became objectified (in some cases, rejecting even consciousness itself). In its extreme, human beings and other life forms are considered to be sophisticated machines, objects. This can be explained by fear of uncertainty and fluidity, and an attempt to find security in the solid matter. However, it created a contradiction, because at the time when personal freedom and personal responsibility were valued more than ever, the existence of subjects (and subjectivity as something unique) were denied.

The disastrous consequences of attempts to tailor destiny according to human-created ideologies (disregarding universal guidelines) became apparent in the 20th century with Fascism and Stalinism. Such an obsession with power has happened before and could happen at any time (the magnitude of destruction is the result of technological advances). The difference is that these ones were the result of a relatively new belief that society can be engineered in accord with utopian images of the future. The reason why so many people were susceptible to such ideologies is that freedom and separation also brought a sense of isolation and anxiety. Similarly, adolescents who need to reach a certain level of autonomy and independence in order to become responsible adults, 'abandon' and even rebel against their parents, only to conform and identify themselves with their peer group. Whole societies, especially at times of economic downfall, are also susceptible to experiencing this 'fear of freedom'.

---

[1] Christianity had started with an ideal of love and ended up as one of the most aggressive religions, Islam had started with an egalitarian model, but in time has created highly unequal societies.

All these extremes, however, generally failed and only slowed down, but did not stop the steady march of individual freedom. It can be hardly a coincidence, for example, that nonconformity in such different fields as mathematics and music, was reached around the same time, in the mid 20th century. Other areas of life were developing in the same direction. After the World War II, parliamentary democracy, in which individuals have a greater role, became more and more the dominant political system. Personal aims and achievements were valued. Philosophy was not concerned any more with producing grand systems but with the individual, while art had the function of personal expression (even art that commented on social events). Unlike the conventional stage that imposed uniformity, the third stage individual morality was based on non-intrusion (not hurting others). Spirituality, that was growing more and more separate from religion, also became highly personalised, as exemplified in the New Age movements.

The major problem with this stage appeared to be instability. Its logical consequence is ending itself, which found its expression in post-modernism. Not only religion, but philosophy, science and art, as they were known before, came to en end. Post-modernism cleared the table, but it is an unsustainable position:

> Without an organizing centre, post-modern man is lost, wandering in a wilderness of confusing plurality. But, paradoxically, being bereft of set moral landmarks, he is in a unique position to undertake a new journey. (Keen, 1991, p.110-111)

This resembles an improvisation in jazz (which is not only an expression of a musician's skills, but also shis individual freedom) that seeks a resolution at the end in a more stable tone or aria. The third stage also seeks a resolution in a more stable society, which renders a transition period unlikely (or very brief)[1]. Thus, the fourth stage will be addressed next.

---

[1] A further comparison with musical tones can be made. Between the tones G, A and H there are semitones (Gis and Ais). But between H and C there is no semi-tone. The third stage can be paralleled to the tone H.

The transcendent stage

No society has yet reached this point, but it is possible to extrapolate what such a society would look like on the basis of individuals and groups that, although operating within a different stage, have moved in this direction, and also on the basis of the corresponding characteristics of individual development.

The main feature of such a society is a turn towards the universal. There is a similarity, in this respect, with the first stage (because of their proximity to the Intent), but this time it is a conscious, deliberate act. For example, personality ('I') is considered only a form of the self (the equivalent of a mask at the first stage). Individuality is preserved, but it operates within a larger framework that is not imposed, but recognised (the synthesis between freedom and necessity). Rather than the nuclear family, the basic social unit is a community that does not rely on blood relations (or even physical proximity), but on shared experiences, goals and interests. Nationalism and other forms of social segregation lose their significance. This also applies to knowledge – the segregation of various disciplines and approaches (e.g. science and spirituality) is transcended. In the 'axial age' the Greek philosophers, Buddha and K'ung-Fu-tzu heralded the three dimensions of development (the rings, experience, and intent) and their corresponding methods (reasoning, non-attachment, and commitment). The importance of all of them is finally recognised. This makes such a society less constructed and more permeable and fluid. Religions, including atheism and other ideologies such as Marxism, are not needed (the New Jerusalem does not have churches). They are replaced by spirituality (that may be secular, humanistic) and the awareness of the relation between the individual and the universal. So, although the universal is acknowledged, it is also recognised that such a relation may differ between groups and also between individuals. This means accepting cultural differences, but also a common core: trans-cultural underlying humanity. The image of God (as a social construct) is transcended, without denying the possibility of a universal agency.

An economic system is not based on the exploitation of, but working with the environment and others. Cooperation is balanced with competition on all levels. Art in such a society has a transcendent function (expressing the timeless, catching glimpses of infinity). While the temporal locus of the first stage is the present, of the second the past, and of the third the future, at this stage they are integrated. The social process is seen as a spiral (see below), which is, in fact, a combination of point time (characterising the first stage), cyclical time (the second stage) and arrow of time (the third stage).

TRAJECTORY

In dialectic terms social development can be described first as the move away from the universal and then back towards the universal. The thesis (an unconscious unity) would correspond to the first stage; the antithesis (separation – the process of individualisation and independence) would include the move from the 1st via the 2nd, and reaching its peak at the 3rd stage; the synthesis (a conscious re-alignment with the universal) is represented by the 4th stage, which is also potentially the beginning of a new period.

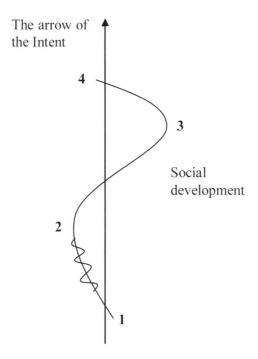

This graph is only a simplified two-dimensional representation. The curve should be imagined as a spiral around the central axis (the length of its segments do not correspond to physical time, but to an amount of change, 'eventfulness'). In fact, a coil around the spiral (as it is drawn between 1 and 2) would present the process even more precisely. The shape of this coil and the speed are the result of human freedom. Nevertheless, to move along the curve, the two basic principles (static and dynamic) need to be in relative balance. If the process is too slow, the society can diminish (or be taken over). Too fast a move can lead to disintegration, chaos. The two principles are manifested as conservative and progressive forces that usually alternate. The points at which it is possible to change direction are the moments of supreme responsibility, everything else is inertia.

The curve reflects a well known symbol from ancient times, depicted with two intertwined serpents around god's staff, called the *caduceus* (still used nowadays as a medical emblem). It is, perhaps, not a coincidence that this symbol resembles the double helix of DNA. In esoteric tradition, the two serpents of the caduceus represent the process of evolution[1], 'spirit descending into matter and rising again enlightened into spirit' (Watson, 1991, p.307). The serpent has traditionally symbolised knowledge, enlightenment and wisdom (the Western association with evil is relatively recent and  atypical). From this perspective, the myth of the serpent inviting Adam and Eve to eat of the tree of knowledge, can be interpreted as the start of a new phase of the evolutionary process, 'a liberation from unconscious limitations and the dawn of self-consciousness' (*ibid*).

For the sake of simplification, the social development diagram has only one curve, while the caduceus has two (one black and one white), which is more accurate. Both, the coil around the spiral and the spiral itself, have their counterparts that can be called the shadows. The shadow is a corrective mechanism, and not in itself something negative. As the symbol shows, what is dominant at one point becomes a shadow at the next and vice versa. This is similar to parliamentary politics: the opposition is a shadow, but has an important role to keep the government in check. At a certain point, the opposition may become the government, and the governing party opposition. The shadow is necessary, because human beings have a tendency to push the boundaries, as a demonstration of their freedom and control over various faculties. This can be recognised at every stage: physical self-mutilations are wide-spread at the first stage. Various forms of emotional mutilation (public humiliations, ritualised superstitions, chauvinism) are frequent on the second. A fascination with the morbid side of the mind is well documented in the third stage (as exemplified by artists such as Dostoyevsky, Shelley or Poe, and later by some approaches in psychotherapy). The fourth stage is also not immune from these extremes: fanaticism in following certain techniques or doctrines, severe deprivations, radical detachment, or attempts to annihilate the self, are a few examples. These and many other excesses can be kept in check by opposing forces that moderate the dominant trend.

---

[1] Caduceus has a greater number of bends because it presumably personifies the whole of evolution, while the above diagram refers only to human social development.

The Futures

One of the purposes of the above brief historical account is to show that human freedom increases throughout this process and consequently does its influence on social development. In the past, physical and social determinants have had a much greater role, therefore the social processes were highly conditioned. However, this trend has been steadily decreasing, to be overtaken by choice. At present we are at the crucial point of the lowest determinism. Human beings are for the first time in a situation where they are able to create their own destiny, which greatly increases responsibility. Although this point was already reached some time ago (roughly around the 1960's) the final choice after which the inertia takes over has not yet been made. This means that the future is truly unpredictable. It is postulated that there are four possible directions[1].

Down: falling back into anachronic social structures, run by a religious or ideological oligarchy. It would be a step backwards that would postpone the real choice for some time, but not indefinitely[2].

Right: moving away from the Intent, which would end in a technocratic autocracy (a nightmarish world, often depicted in futuristic stories and films). This option is likely to eventually lead to destruction, possibly through an environmental disaster or a global war. So, the suffering and efforts of myriad life forms that contributed to our evolution and social development would be in vain. This would be a tragedy of unimaginable proportions, but it is not impossible.

Up: continuing in the same direction would lead to meaningless, apathetic reality, in which entropy would be constantly increasing, ending eventually in chaos and anarchy. This one is unlikely to destroy the world completely, simply because the means of destruction would malfunction too. However, it would result in a slow decline. To reverse this trend, a new conceptual framework (a new start) would be required.

Left: recognising and aligning the individual and social intentions and actions with the universal (discovering, or in the case of humanism, creating a common purpose).

---

[1] Their names are created as a convenience, and do not have any value or ideological connotation.

[2] Some find returning even further, to a pre-industrial, child-like state, as a way to get rid of consumerist society, attractive. But children are, in fact, easily mesmerised with multi-coloured superstores, junk-food outlets and expensive but worthless toys. Similarly, adults from traditional pre-industrial societies seem to be even more fascinated by flashy cars, golden rings and watches, and other consumer products.

270

These choices are shown in the following diagram:

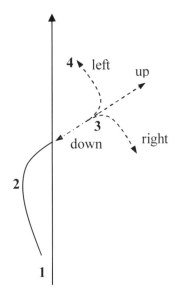

It is impossible to predict which of them will prevail. What is certain is that they are all already germinated. The rise of religious fundamentalism, for example, in some parts of the Middle East and the USA indicates the down direction. Extreme materialism that started in the Reagan – Thatcher era, but is now slowly taking roots in newly developed countries, points towards the right; the post-modern secularism (in the liberal parts of the USA, most of continental Europe, Australia etc.) represents the tendency towards the up direction. Some movements, atheistic and theistic, show signs of the shift towards the left. These are a few examples: an increasing number of individuals and organisations (e.g. some NGOs or environmental agencies) dedicated to raise awareness and tackle global issues in politics; the growth of the so-called third sector (charities, 'social enterprises') that are driven by contribution to community rather than profit in the business world; certain aspects of globalisation such as the internet that provides free and decentralised information and a vast knowledge base (regrettably not yet widely available); non-theistic spirituality based on the idea of self-generated systems (popularised, for example, by Laszlo or the Gaia movement); the emergence and fast spreading of grass-root spirituality (not aligned to any specific religious doctrine)[1]. Although this last choice may not prevail, it is the most interesting one, so considering its possibilities may be worthwhile.

---

[1] For further details, see Forman, 2004

It is proposed that the options on this route may be grouped into three broad categories. This diagram represents the possible trajectories:

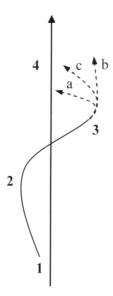

a) *Intuitionism* (emphasising experience and often seen as an expression of the feminine principle) is likely to lead to a sharp turn towards the Intent. Its consequence could be approaching the Intent from a somewhat wrong angle, like a boat that tries to enter a river perpendicular to its flow, which would run the risk of being thrown back.

b) *Rationalism* (emphasising reason and usually identified with the masculine principle) is positioned in between the left and up direction and could lead to approaching the Intent very slowly or even moving in parallel to the Intent (because it is likely to be dominated by a non-theistic fourth stage). This direction could solve many practical problems (creating a society akin to a 'Star-trek' type utopia), but the meaning would remain more or less elusive, and the search would continue indefinitely.

c) *The synthesis* of the feminine and masculine principles[1] would facilitate an approach to the Intent from the correct angle and aligning with it. The question may be asked what would happen in such a case. Metaphorically speaking, a bridge will be created, and human beings will not be alone any more.

---

[1] They are of course not identified with genders. Every person (female or male) has the capacity for both principles, although there may be a preference (or bias) for one of them.

AFTERWARD

This book is based on a method that may provide a more coherent interpretation than the existing ones, but it cannot offer certainty. There are some intrinsic limitations that allow any text to approach the truth only asymptotically. These limitations can be grouped into four categories:

a) The limits of the subject (an author) refer to a finite mental capacity, time and information available to an individual (so some details may be missed or mistaken).

b) The limits of the medium (a language) refer to the fact that no existing language is fully adequate to express the multi-dimensional nature of reality.

c) The limits of the object (facts) refer to the imperfection of the factual knowledge. For example, not taking into account presently accepted facts that may turn out to be mistaken in the future would end up in the current incompleteness, but taking them into account would lead to a future incongruence (when they are corrected).

d) The limits of the background. Any text is created at a particular time, in a particular place and within a particular mentality. Therefore, it is inevitably affected, at least to some extent, by its locality, which may not fully resonate with a different time, space, or mentality.

This does not mean that the epistemological value of the materials can be relativised (in a post-modern fashion). To what extent they approximate the truth should be judged on the basis of to what extent they comply with the criteria described in the first part. It is unlikely that new ways of knowledge acquisition will be discovered, and any reduction to one or some of them cannot be superior to their synthesis (the problem with the existing ideological frameworks, including the materialistic ones, is not so much in what they are saying, but in what they are denying). The above limitations, however, do indicate that no interpretation can be perfect and universal. Moreover, if any interpretation is allowed to solidify and turn into an ideology, it becomes reactionary. Therefore the Synthesis should be taken as a dynamic process that can continue to be refined. There will always be some space for further improvements, the only conditions being that the stated criteria are followed or their change is justified. Therefore, this should not be considered the end, but the beginning.

BIBLIOGRAPHY

Armstrong, K. (1993) *A History of God,* London: Vintage.

Ash, D. (1995) *The New Science of the Spirit,* London: The College of Psychic Studies.

Baars, B. J., Newman, J. and Taylor, J. G. (1998) 'Neuronal Mechanisms of Consciousness: A Relational Global Workspace Framework' in Hameroff, S. R., Kaszniak, A. W. and Scott, A. C. (eds.) *Towards a Science of Consciousness II*, Cambridge, MA: The MIT Press.

Becker, R. O. and Selden, G. (1985) *The Body Electric,* New York: William Morrow.

Beloff, J. (1994) 'Mind and Machines: A Radical Dualist Perspective' *Journal of Consciousness Studies,* Vol. 1, No. 1.

Bem, D. J. and Honorton, C. (1994) 'Does psi exist? Replicable evidence for an anomalous process of information transfer' *Psychological Bulletin,* Vol. 115, No.1.

Binswanger, L. (1946) 'The existential analysis school of thought' in May, R., Angel, E. and Ellenberger, H. F. (eds.) *Existence*, New York: Basic Books, 1958.

Blackmore, S. (2005a) 'Out of body experiences' in Henry, J. (ed.) *Parapsychology*, London and New York: Rutledge.

Blackmore, S. (2005b) 'Near death experiences' in Henry, J. (ed.) *Parapsychology*, London and New York: Rutledge.

Block, N. (1998) 'How Not to Find the Neural Correlate of Consciousness' in Hameroff, S. R., Kaszniak, A. W. and Scott, A. C. (eds.) *Towards a Science of Consciousness II*, Cambridge, MA: The MIT Press.

Bogen, J. (1998) 'Locating the Subjectivity Pump: The Thalamic Intralaminar Nuclei' in Hameroff, S. R., Kaszniak, A. W. and Scott, A. C. (eds.) *Towards a Science of Consciousness II*, Cambridge, MA: The MIT Press.

Boss, M. (1963) *Psychoanalysis and Daseinsanalysis,* New York: Basic Books.

Brazier, C. (2001) *The No-nonsense Guide to World History,* Oxford: NI publications.

Butler, L. T. and Berry, D.C. (2001) 'Implicit memory: intention and awareness revisited' *Trends in Cognitive Sciences,* Vol. 5, No. 5.

Capra, F. (2000) *The Tao of Physics,* Boston: Shambhala.

Chalmers, A. F. (1980) *What is this thing called science?* Milton Keynes: Open University Press.

Chalmers, D. (1995) 'Facing up to the Problem of Consciousness' *Journal of Consciousness Studies*, Vol. 2, No. 3.

Chandler, K. (1995) 'Descartes, Flanagan and Moody' *Journal of Consciousness Studies*, Vol. 2, No. 4.

Churchland, P. S. (1998) 'Brainshy: Nonneural Theories of Conscious Experience' in Hameroff, S. R., Kaszniak, A. W. and Scott, A. C. (eds.) *Towards a Science of Consciousness II*, London, Cambridge, MA: A Bradford Book, The MIT Press.

Collins, H. and Pinch, T. (1993) *The Golem,* Cambridge: Cambridge University Press.

Crick, F. and Koch, C. (1990) 'Towards a neurobiological theory of consciousness' *Seminars in the Neurosciences*, Vol. 2.

Csikszentmihalyi, M. (1992) *Flow*, London [...]: Rider.

Dana, C. L. (1921) 'The anatomic seat of the emotions: a discussion of the James-Lange theory' *Archives of Neurology and Psychiatry,* Vol. 6.

Daniels, M. (2005) *Shadow, Self, Spirit,* Exeter: Imprint-Academic.

Darwin, C. (1859) *Origin of Species by Means of Natural Selection*, Harmondsworth: Penguin, 1985.

Davies, P. (1982) *The Accidental Universe,* Cambridge: Cambridge University Press.

Davies, P. (1992) *The Mind of God,* London: Penguin Books, 1993.

Davis, P. (2007) *The Goldilocks Enigma,* London: Penguin Books.

Dawkins, R. (1986) *The Blind Watchmaker,* Harlow: Longman Scientific & Technical.

Dawkins, R. (2006) *The God Delusion,* London [...]: Bantam Press.

Denton, M. (1998) *Nature's Destiny*, New York [...]: The Free Press

Deurzen-Smith, E. van (1988) *Existential Counselling in Practice*, London: Sage.

Donaldson, M. *(*1992*) Human Minds*, London: Penguin.

Edmunds, L. F. (1997) *Quest for Meaning,* New York: Continuum.

Einstein, A. (1949) *The World As I See It,* New York: Philosophical Library.

Fontana, D. (2003) 'Some objections to Darwinism' *Transpersonal Psychology Review,* Vol. 7, No 1.

Forman, R. (2004) *Grassroots Spirituality,* Exeter: Imprint Academic.

Gibson, J. J. (1980) *The Ecological Approach to Visual Perception,* Cambridge MA: MIT Press.

Giddens, A. (1991) *Modernity and Self-Identity,* Cambridge: Polity Press.

Gilling, D. and Brightwell, R. (1982) *The Human Brain*, London: Orbis Publishing.

Giulio, T. (2004) 'An information integration theory of consciousness' *BMC Neuroscience* Vol. 5, Article no. 42

Gould, S. (1988) 'Ladders and Cones: Constraining Evolution by Canonical Icons' in Silvers, R. (ed.) *Hidden Histories of Science*, London: Granta books.

Gregory, R. (ed.) (1987) *The Oxford Companion to the Mind,* Oxford, New York: OUP.

Güzeldere, G. (1995a) 'Consciousness: What it is, How to Study it, What to Learn from its History' *Journal of Consciousness Studies,* Vol. 2, No. 1.

Güzeldere, G. (1995b) 'Problems of Consciousness: A Perspective on Contemporary Issues, Current Debates' *Journal of Consciousness Studies,* Vol. 2, No. 2.

Hameroff, S. R. (1994) 'Quantum Coherence in Microtubules: a Neural Basis for Emergent Consciousness?' *Journal of Consciousness Studies,* Vol. 1, No. 1.

Hameroff, S.R. (1998) 'Did Consciousness Cause the Cambrian Evolutionary Explosion?' in Hameroff, S. R., Kaszniak, A. W. and Scott, A. C. (eds.) *Towards a Science of Consciousness II,* Cambridge, MA: The MIT Press.

Hanfling, O. (1980) *Body and Mind,* Milton Keynes: The Open University Press.

Harman, W. (1998) *Global Mind Change,* Sausalito: IONS.

Harth, E. (1993) *The Creative Loop,* Reading MA: Addison-Wesley.

Hawking, S. (1988) *A Brief History of Time,* Toronto [...]: Bantam Books.

Hay, D. (1990) *Religious Experience Today,* London: Mowbray.

Hazen, R. M. (1997) Why *aren't Black Holes Black?* Doubleday: Anchor Books.

Heisenberg, W. (1952) *Philosophic Problems of Nuclear Science,* New York: Fawcett.

Heisenberg, W. (1958) *Physics and Philosophy,* New York: Harper & Row.

Hobson, J. A., and McCarley, R. W. (1977) 'The Brain as a Dream State Generator: An Activation-synthesis Hypothesis of the Dream Process' *American Journal of Psychiatry,* Issue 134.

Hodgson, D. (1994) 'Neuroscience and Folk Psychology' *Journal of Consciousness Studies,* Vol. 1, No. 2.

Hohmann, G. W. (1966) 'Some effects of spinal cord lesions on experienced emotional feelings' *Psychophysiology,* Vol. 3.

Home, D. and Robinson, A. (1995) 'Einstein and Tagore: Man, Nature and Mysticism' *Journal of Consciousness Studies,* Vol. 2, No. 2.

Honderich, T. (1995) *The Oxford Companion To Philosophy,* Oxford: Oxford University Press.

Horgan, J. (1996) *The End of Science,* London: Little, Brown and Company.

Horgan, J. (2003) *Rational Mysticism,* Boston, New York: Houghton Mifflin Company.

Hoyle, F. (1983) *The Intelligent Universe,* New York: W. W. Norton.

Jaki, S. (1970) *The Relevance of Physics,* Chicago: University of Chicago Press.

Jenkins, F. (2002) 'Therapies of Desire and Aesthetics of Existence: On Foucault's Relevance for Philosophical Counselling' *Practical Philosophy*, Vol.4, No.3.

John, E. R. (1972) 'Switchboard versus Statistical theories of Learning and Memory' *Science*, Vol. 177, No. 4052.

Jung, C. G. and Pauli, W. (1955) *Interpretation of Nature and the Psyche,* New York: Bollingen.

Keen, S. (1991) *Fire in the Belly,* Toronto [...]: Bantam Books.

Kerr, R. A. (1995) 'Did Darwin Get it Right?' *Science*, No. 267.

Koch, C. (1992) 'What is Consciousness?' (interview) *Discover*, Vol. 13, No. 11.

Köhler, W. (1925) *The Mentality of Apes,* London: Rutledge & Kegan Paul.

Laszlo E. (1993) *The Creative Cosmos*, Edinburgh: Floris Books.

Lem, S. (1981) 'Non Serviam' in Hofstadter, D. and Dennett, D. (eds.) *The Mind's I,* London: Penguin Books.

Lewontin, R. (1997) 'Billions and Billions of Demons', *The New York Review,* 09 January.

Libet, B. (1994) 'A Testable Field Theory of Mind-Brain Interaction' *Journal of Consciousness Studies*, Vol. 1, No. 1.

Libet, B. (2004) *Mind Time,* Cambridge MA, London: Harvard University Press.

Llinas, R. and Ribary, U. (1993) 'Coherent 40-Hz Oscillation Characterizes Dream State in Humans' *Proceedings of National Academy of Science USA,* No. 90.

Lloyed, P., Mayes, A., Manstead, A. S .R., Meudell, P. R. and Wagner, H. L. (1990) *Introduction to Psychology*, London: Fontana Press.

Lockwood, M. (1998) 'The Enigma of Sentience' in Hameroff, S. R., Kaszniak, A. W. and Scott, A. C. (eds.) *Towards a Science of Consciousness II*, London, Cambridge, MA: A Bradford Book, The MIT Press.

Lund, M. (1991) 'Commitment old and new: social pressure and individual choice in making relationships last' in Hinde, R. A. and Groebel, J. (eds.) *Cooperation and Prosocial Behaviour,* Cambridge: Cambridge University Press.

Macnamara, J. (1972) 'Cognitive basis of language learning in infants' *Psychological Review,* No. 79.

Madell, G. (1981) *The Identity of the Self*, Edinburgh: Edinburgh University Press.

Marris, P. (1982) 'Attachment and Society' in Parkes, C. M. and Stevenson-Hinde, J. (eds.) *The Place of Attachment in Human Behaviour,* London: Tavistock Publications.

McGinn, C. (1995) 'Consciousness and Space' *Journal of Consciousness Studies*, Vol. 2, No. 3.

McMullin, E. (1987) 'The Impact of the Theory of Evolution on Western Religious Thought' in Singh, T. D. and Gomatam, R. (eds.) *Synthesis of Science, and Religion* San Francisco, Bombay: The Bhaktivedanta Institute.

McTaggart, L. (2001) *The Field,* London: HarperCollins.

Morowitz, H. J. (1981) 'Rediscovering the Mind' in Hofstadter, D. and Dennett, D. (eds.) *The Mind's I,* London: Penguin Books.

Morris, S. (2002) 'We were meant to be...' *New Scientist,* Vol. 176, Issue 2369.

Nagel, T. (1981) 'What Is It Like to Be a Bat?' in Hofstadter, D. and Dennett, D. (eds.) *The Mind's I,* London: Penguin Books

Nunn, C. (1996) *Awareness,* London, New York: Rutledge.

Nunn, C. M. H., Terrace, B., Blott, B. H. (1994) 'Collapse of a Quantum Field may Affect Brain Function' *Journal of Consciousness Studies,* Vol. 1, No. 1.

Overman, D. (1997) *A Case Against Accident and Self-Organisation*, New York: Rowman & Littlefield.

Patton, M. Q. (1990) *Qualitative Evaluation and Research Methods*, Newbury Park, CA: Sage.

Penfield, W. & Perot, P. (1963) 'The brain's record of auditory and visual experience' *Brain,* No. 86.

Penfield, W. (1975) *The Mystery of Mind,* Princeton, N.Y.: Princeton University Press.

Podvoll, E. M. (1990) *Seduction of Madness*, London: Century.

Polanyi, M. (1958) *Personal Knowledge,* London: Rutledge & Kegan Paul.

Polanyi, M. (1969) *Knowing and Being*, London: Rutledge & Kegan Paul.

Polanyi, M. and Prosch, H. (1975) *Meaning*, Chicago: The University of Chicago Press.

Popovic, N. (2003) 'Existential Anxiety and Existential Joy' *Practical Philosophy*, Vol. 5, No. 2.

Popper, K. R. and Eccles, J. C. (1977) *The Self and Its Brain*, London: Rutledge, 2000.

Puccetti, R. & Dykes, R. W. (1978) 'Sensory cortex and the mind-brain problem' *The Behavioral and Brain Sciences*, Vol. 3.

Rock, I. (1975) *An Introduction to Perception,* New York: Macmillan.

Rosenfield, I. (1992) *Strange, Familiar and Forgotten,* London: Picador.

Schilder, P. (1935) *The Image and Appearance of the Human Body*, London: Kegan, Paul, Trench, Trubner & Co.

Schlitz, M. and May, E. (1998) 'Parapsychology: Fact or Fiction? Replicable evidence for Unusual Consciousness Effects' in Hameroff, S. R., Kaszniak, A. W. and Scott, A. C. (eds.) *Towards a Science of Consciousness II,* Cambridge, MA: The MIT Press.

Schrödinger, E. (1958) *Mind and Matter,* Cambridge: Cambridge University Press.

Scott, A. (1994) 'J. C. Eccles, How the SELF Controls its BRAIN' *Journal of Consciousness Studies,* Vol. 1, No. 1.

Scott, A. C. (1998) 'Reductionism Revisited' in Hameroff, S. R., Kaszniak, A. W. and Scott, A. C. (eds.) *Towards a Science of Consciousness II,* Cambridge, MA: The MIT Press.

Scott, Alwyn (1995) *Stairway to the Mind,* New York: Copernicus.

Seager, W. (1995) 'Consciousness, Information and Panpsychism' *Journal of Consciousness Studies,* Vol. 2, No. 3.

Searle, J. R. (1992) *The Rediscovery of the Mind,.* Cambridge: MIT Press.

Sutherland, K. (1994) 'Consciousness – its place in contemporary science' *Journal of Consciousness Studies,* Vol. 1, No. 2.

Sherrington, C. S. (1940) *Man on his nature,* London: Penguin Books.

Silver, B. L. (1998) *The Ascent of Science,* New York: Oxford University Press.

Smart, J. J. (1963) 'Materialism' *The Journal of Philosophy,* No. 60.

Solomon, R. C. (1988) *Continental Philosophy since 1750: The Rise and Fall of the Self,* Oxford: Oxford University Press.

Sperry, R. (1981) 'Changing Priorities' *Annual Review of Neuroscience,* Vol. 4.

Srivastava, J. (1987) 'Spirituality: the link between science and religion' in Singh, T. D. and Gomatam, R. (eds) *Synthesis of Science and Religion,* San Francisco, Bombay: The Bhaktivedanta Institute.

Sheldrake, R. (2000) *Dogs That Know When Their Owners Are Coming Home,* London: Arrow Books.

Sunsonese, J. N. (1994) *The Body of Myth: Mythology, Shamanic Trance, and the Sacred Geography of the Body,* Rochester, VT: Inner Traditions International.

Swinburne, R. (1991) *The Existence of God,* Oxford: Clarendon Press.

Tart, C. (2005) 'Toward the objective exploration of non-ordinary reality' in *Transpersonal Psychology Review,* Special issue, Winter 2005.

Teichman, J. (1974) *The Mind and the Soul,* New York: Humanities Press.

Thomson, M. (1997) *Philosophy of Religion,* London: Hodder Headline Plc.

Toffler, A. (1970) *Future Shock,* London: Pan Books.

Treisman, A. (1986) 'Features and objects in visual processing', *Scientific American,* No. 254.

Turiel, E. (1983) *The Development of Social Knowledge,* Cambridge University Press.

Velmans, M. (1995) 'The relation of Consciousness to the material world' *Journal of Consciousness Studies,* Vol. 2, No. 3.

Wade, J. (1996) *Changes of Mind,* New York: State University of New York Press.

Watson, D. (1991) *A Dictionary of Mind and Spirit,* London: Optima, 1993.

Weizenbaum, J. (1987) 'The Computer as Idol' in Singh, T. D. and Gomatam, R. (eds.) *Synthesis of Science and Religion*, San Francisco, Bombay: The Bhaktivedanta Institute.

Wickers, D. (1972) 'Characteristics of word encoding', in Melton, A. and Martin, E. (eds.) *Coding Processes in Human Memory,* Washington, DC: Winston & Sons.

Zajonc, R. B. (1960) 'Balance, Congruity and Dissonance' in Jahoda, M. and Warren, N. (eds.) *Attitudes,* London: Penguin, 1966.

Zechmeister, E. B. and Nyberg, S. E. (1982) *Human Memory: an Introduction to Research and Theory*, Monterely, Calif.: Brooks/Cole.

Zeldin, T. (1998) *An Intimate History of Humanity,* London: Vintage.

SUBJECT INDEX

NAME INDEX

For further information and forum please visit:
www.thesynthesis.info

Correspondence:
book@thesynthesis.info